ROYAL FOLLIES

A CHRONICLE OF ROYAL MISBEHAVIOR

ROYAL FOLLIES

A CHRONICLE OF ROYAL MISBEHAVIOR

David Randall

 Sterling Publishing Co., Inc.   New York

Published in 1988 by
Sterling Publishing Co., Inc.
Two Park Avenue
New York, New York 10016

ISBN 0-8069-6734-X

First published in 1987 in Great Britain
Published by arrangement with W. H. Allen & Co. Plc, London
This edition available in the United States, Canada and
Australia only

Printed in U.S.A.

For my Mum and Dad,
whose behaviour has done so much to
foster my interest in the old and the unusual.

Introduction

Of all the lessons that history can teach, none is written in bolder letters than this simple rule: few kings earn their crowns and fewer still deserve them.

Indeed, it would be strange if it were otherwise. In the royalist state the genetic accident is king and he (or she) inherits as great a scope for mischief as any human institution has to offer. The people take whom the fates have given them, put a crown on his head, seat him on a throne and, in effect, tell him this: 'No matter how feeble-minded, dissolute or otherwise unsuitable you may be, we would like you to rule us. In return, we will give you virtually unlimited power, money and privilege. You can make laws, make war or, if the mood takes you, just make whoopee. We will obey everything you say, however absurd, and all your jokes will be funny. You will have palaces, fine clothes, beautiful women and as much food as you can eat. Regardless of how disreputable you may be, we will bow and scrape when we greet you and do the same when we depart. To your face we will never cease praising you. Furthermore, everywhere you go, people will cheer you and some will even think you a god.'

If that, then, was the theory, it is small wonder that in practice so many sovereigns should have had their heads turned. This book is largely about such cases: the mad, the bad; the rude, the lewd; the needy, the seedy and the greedy. No species of misrule is omitted, from the kings and queens who calculated their own advantage with the lives and liberties of their subjects, right down to those for whom monarchy was the apprenticeship that fitted them for a straitjacket. The exceptional few who have avoided such excesses are also included, as are any other remarkable royalties. Here, too, lurking around the edges of the book, hoping to catch the eye, are the sycophants and servants – those whose nodding heads and ready agreement have bolstered many a majestic ego.

However, what you will not find here are many entries for present members of the British royal family. There are two reasons for this and the first is that royalty's capacity for folly and indiscretion diminishes as its power subsides. Ours is a constitutional monarchy, hemmed in by restraint. Its function is largely decorative and, except on its outer fringes, it must behave itself, which it does. Secondly, the truth about royal personages only emerges when they are dead and even then, perhaps not for many years. The rumours of Princess Diana's fiery temperament or the tales of Prince Charles' dabblings in ethereal matters, for instance, will probably remain speculation until at least the middle decades of the next century. For what it is worth this author, for one, strongly suspects that both yarns contain less fact than fancy.

In the meantime, what passes for information about them and the rest of their family consists principally of what they themselves choose to make known or what the tabloid press cares to make up. The content of this book may be many things but it is not publicity material for royalty, nor is it invented – at least, not by me. The sources I have used are listed at the back and two books in particular deserve an honourable mention in this despatch. They are John Lord's *The Maharajahs* and Noel Barber's book on the Turkish sultans, *Lords of The Golden Horn*, both of which are unrivalled in their fields and essential reading for those interested in the dirty linen of history.

Finally, I must thank my wife Pamela for her considerable assistance and helpful suggestions. Literary criticism is not an exact science but her ill-stifled yawns during the reading of many a rough draft were always an unfailing indication that it was time to uncap the rewrite pen. However, her finest achievement was ensuring that a corner of our chaotic home always remained available for scholarship and contemplation. Her success in keeping Guy, Paul, Simon and Tommy at bay will, I am sure, become recognised in time as a major landmark in the treatment and rehabilitation of infantile offenders.

ROYAL
FOLLIES

A

'Whatever folly kings commit, the people suffer.'

HORACE.

Abdul Aziz (1830–1876). Sultan of the Ottoman Empire and a versatile degenerate. He managed to combine extravagance, gluttony, dissipation, bouts of madness and cruelty in a reign that lasted less than 15 years.

Its tone was immediately apparent to his court when, within hours of ascending Turkey's throne, he ordered an eight-foot bed and, to fill it entertainingly, increased his harem to an active strength of 900. These ladies were, however, a mere fraction of the number of minions hired to minister to his outlandish needs. His staff included 400 musicians, 400 grooms, 200 men to care for the contents of his private zoo and no fewer than 5,000 house servants. Among these was one man whose sole purpose in life was to replace the royal backgammon board after use and another factotum whose onerous task was to sit around waiting for Abdul's fingernails to grow long enough for him to spring forward with his scissors and cut them. With the purchase of such essentials as a ruby and emerald-studded gold dinner service and enough mother-of-pearl to line the walls of one of his palaces, the Sultan's housekeeping bill was soon topping £2 million a year.

This figure, of course, took no account of the pocket money that he allowed himself. Much of this was blown on such practical purchases as the dozens of grand pianos he once bought so that his servants could try and lug them about wherever he went and serenade him. Needless to say, they couldn't. Then there were the iron ships, acquired in a moment of rash enthusiasm, but left to rust in port for the want of any sailors who knew how to operate them. He also bought shiny new locomotives, which were all very fine and serviceable, except for the fact that his country had no rails to run them on. Not to be outdone, his Queen Mother did her bit to empty the royal coffers by playing Lady Bountiful. Every day she would buy 50 dresses of Brusa silk and distribute most of them to slaves. She described this as 'spreading happiness around me'.

Abdul's happiness required more complicated arrangements. If he became bored with lying on a divan having his jaded tastes pandered to by the duty concubine, he had two alternative pastimes. The first was playing soldiers; not with toys but with real live infantrymen. As night fell, these troops would be marched down to the palace cellars and ordered to engage in mortal combat as the gloating Sultan watched through a grating from above. These war-games often lasted all night and Abdul always made sure that he was on hand to see the wounded being assisted from the catacombs at first light.

The other great passion of this unpleasant man was to chase chickens around his palace. At a given signal, several squawking birds would be released and the royal staff would look on in amazement as their infallible ruler, known in all official literature as 'Emperor and Conqueror of the Earth, Overlord of Emperors for All Time' and 'He Who Invests Monarchs With Their Crowns', pursued them round pillars, through doorways and down corridors until he caught one. Then, as the captured hen fluttered frantically in the royal grasp, Abdul would giggle maniacally and hang the Ottoman Empire's most prestigious award for gallantry around its scrawny neck. If a hen so honoured ever appeared at any subsequent romp without its medal in place, then the servant responsible was dismissed.

His obsession with chickens was not confined to their potential as playmates. He was also a prodigious consumer of their eggs and his habit of eating a dozen fried ones at a single sitting contributed significantly to his vast bulk of 17 stone. At other times, he lived for days on nothing but hard-boiled eggs served up in black crepe, although this habit was prompted more by his periodic fears that his usual diet was being tampered with than by any love of the horrid things. He also developed an occasional phobia about fire. He would then refuse to go to bed until he had been assured that his room had been cleared of all wooden objects, and insist on his night-light being put in a bucket of water.

As he grew older, Abdul's strange fixations multiplied. Sometimes he would take a dislike to black ink and angrily reject any papers brought to him unless they had been copied out in a more acceptable red hue. On another occasion he was so outraged when he discovered that a bureaucrat had the same name as himself that he demanded every government official called Aziz change his name to something else. He also ordered all Turkish schoolbooks to be comprehensively rewritten to exclude any mention of Turkish defeats, the French Revolution or the Christian religion. Yet though he might censor history, there was a limit to Abdul's ability to suppress word of his own excesses, especially when three-quarters of Europe was up in arms at the atrocities of his bully-boys in the Balkans. Not long after a particularly unpleasant incident in Bulgaria and a spectacular famine in his own lands, Abdul was deposed by reformists and, five days later, did the honourable thing for the first time in his life and slashed his wrists.

Adahoozou I (16th Century). King of Dahomey in West Africa who made novel use of his more disposable subjects by having the walls of his capital city lined with their heads. Moreover, he was not too fussy about how the materials for this unique pebble-dashing were obtained. When the builders of Colmina's walls reported that there were not quite enough heads to finish the project, the King replied, 'Get more or I'll use yours.' Another 127 heads were quickly found.

Adelaide (1792–1849). Queen of England, wife of William IV and a rare British example of generous royal alms-giving. She was said to spend one-third of her large income on private and public charity and even maintained in her household an almoner whose duty it was to investigate all applications for royal benevolence. Her one instance of meanness, for some unaccountable reason, concerned pins. She could not bear even a single one being lost and if a maid of honour dropped a pin then the search continued, for hours if necessary, until it was found. Any pin that was taken from her pincushion had to be put back in exactly the same position as before and a constant theme of her conversation, much to the weariness of her attendants, was the whereabouts of the world's lost pins.

Agha Mohammed Khan (d. 1797). Shah of Iran and a great stickler for protocol. When 20,000 citizens of Kerman refused to bow down to him, he had their eyes put out. Few mourned his subsequent assassination.

Ahmed III (1673–1736). Sultan of the Ottoman Empire whose costly passion for tulips brought his treasury to the verge of bankruptcy. Every year he had tens of thousands of bulbs imported for the gardens of the Seraglio, or inner palace, and in time he had over 1,200 different varieties of the plant growing there.

The finest specimens were chosen for display at the extravagant and gaudy Tulip Fete that he held each April. Miles of custom-made shelving would be erected in the Seraglio gardens and this would be filled with vases of prize tulips, alternating with glass globes containing coloured water and lamps of stained glass. Ahmed was so particular about the details of the fetes that he even forbade guests to dress in colours that did not harmonise with his lurid exhibits – a problem not eased by the presence of dozens of cages of canaries hanging from each tree. The cost of these farcical jamborees imposed such a relentless strain on national resources that Ahmed was deposed in 1730.

Aiyaruk (14th Century). Mongolian Princess and medieval sportswoman. She had many admirers and her method for sorting out which of them would make a suitable mate was simple: each was challenged to two rounds of wrestling with her. Just to add a little interest to the action, she always insisted on a side bet of 100 horses. By the age of 30 she was believed to have won herself a stable of over 10,000 horses.

Albert Victor, Duke of Clarence (1864–1892). Son of Edward VII, heir presumptive and sometime Jack the Ripper suspect. He was also, if well-informed Victorian gossip was anything to go by, a homosexual half-wit who could not even be trusted to cross the road without succumbing to temptation. This atrocious reputation has persisted and it is now a firm part of the British royal family's tribal memory that Prince Albert Victor's premature death from pneumonia at the age of 28 saved the throne from a potentially disastrous occupation. Even today, many a royalist shudders at the thought of what would have happened if it had been King Albert the First, rather than his brother George V, opening Parliament and addressing the nation at Christmastime.

It would be nice to expose this view as a travesty of the truth and reveal the prince to be a well-balanced closet intellectual whose name has been mercilessly blackened down the years. But while he was certainly not the congenital numskull that he is invariably made out to be, Albert Victor was, even by the standards of the British royal family, decidedly unpromising material. To begin with, there was his appearance. With his full lips, heavily-lidded eyes and long, languid face, he looked like the 'after' picture in the pamphlets that warned against self-abuse. Eddy, as his family called him, also had a high-rise neck and arms that looked as if they had been artificially extended – features which he accentuated by the cut of his jackets and shirts. Observing this, his father (who was ever ready with a wounding remark aimed at those who could not answer back) gave him the nickname of 'collars and cuffs'. The upshot, especially when his gangling frame was encased in a Norfolk jacket, was that Eddy managed to look both effeminate and clottish at one and the same time.

As far as his sexual leanings were concerned, this impression seems to have been entirely correct. Not only did he visit the male brothel in Cleveland Street, London which was later the centre of a scandal that nearly embroiled him, but he was also a member of the notorious Hundred Guineas Club whose habitués were obliged to assume a female persona. Eddy, showing a surprising turn of wit, always signed himself in as 'Victoria'.

Mercifully, his grandmother never found out, which was something of a wonder since speculation about Eddy's proclivities was a much-aired topic in the London of the 1880s and 1890s. When he was at Cambridge, for instance, *Punch* published a cartoon of Eddy on a balcony, underneath which were pictured two swooning nancy boys. One is saying, 'Isn't it beautiful?' and the other replies, 'Too beautiful to look at.' The implication was obvious, as was that contained in an article which later appeared in *Truth* magazine. The piece consisted of an imaginary interview with Eddy about his tour of the East. It was constructed in crudely metred verse and included a reference to Eddy's alleged dalliance with a laundryman in India:

'You asked me what impressed me most
Whilst Hindustan I travelled o'er?
My answer is a certain man
I came across at Shuttadore.'

At which, no doubt, the drawing-rooms of Victorian England echoed to the collapse of stout and snickering parties.

That Eddy looked like an idiot, and often behaved like one, there is no doubt. However, what is open to speculation is whether he actually was one. The case for the prosecution is mainly in the hands of his tutors, of whom he was frequently the despair, and their scathing reports portrayed him as little more than the Sandringham village idiot. The Rev John Neale Dalton, for instance, wrote that Eddy 'fails not in one or two subjects but in all', referred to 'the abnormally dormant condition of his mind' and said that he had 'virtually no powers of concentration at all' and 'sits listless and vacant'. Just to rub it in, J.K. Stephen, the man charged with cramming the royal pupil for Cambridge, wrote that 'he hardly knows the meaning of the words "to read" '.

Against this damning evidence, the defence of Eddy's brainpower can produce several exhibits. First there is the psychiatric record of tutor Stephen, who was far from balanced and later went hopelessly mad, then there are the handicaps under which we now know Eddy struggled. He suffered from a mild form of epilepsy and also a hearing deficiency and because his mother was also subject to the latter affliction, she was never told and so Eddy's partial deafness went untreated. His biographer Michael Harrison also insists that when he entered the 10th Hussars he was far from a disaster as an officer and that his letters home were as good and chatty as the parents of any 20-year-old have a right to expect. A verdict of 'somewhat backward but not actually pea-brained' seems in order.

Whatever his intellectual shortcomings, they were magnified by his lack of energy and initiative. Eddy was always easily led and it was this, plus his curiosity and over-affectionate nature, as much as any innate deviancy, which made him experiment with homosexuality and, by all accounts, several other things besides. These scrapes seemed to come his way whether he was at home or abroad and so, as he passed his mid-twenties, the matter of marrying him off became one of urgency. He could not be trusted to choose his own bride, for when left to his own devices he formed crushing passions for women judged to be quite unsuitable – Lady Sybil St Clair Erskine (who, despite her name, was thought to be far too common) and Princess Hélène of France (who was a Roman Catholic).

With his parents' desire for speed rapidly turning to near-panic, the Princess May of Teck was chosen as his bride and future consort. Eddy decided that he was in love with her and, in due course, proposed. Naturally she knew nothing of the prince's murkier escapades and so when he died suddenly of pneumonia a few weeks later, he was, in her eyes, an affectionate innocent cut down before his prime. She went on to marry his brother, the future George V, and his family was left to lament him in their own individual ways. His father, for example, who knew more of Eddy's capacity for indiscretion than any other, wrote to the Archbishop of Canterbury, 'Our beloved son is happier now than if he were exposed to the miseries and temptations of this world.'

Thus, Eddy became fixed in popular memory as that strange, gangling figure peering out of fading photographs – the king who, mercifully for all, never was. So he remained until, in 1970, he briefly became something altogether more sinister – a fully documented Jack the Ripper suspect. The image of Eddy as a rather simple trainee roué was replaced by that of the psychopathic Duke of Clarence, revenging himself on whoredom for a dose of the clap, or some such nonsense. Unfortunately for the *Sunday Times* and one or two individuals who promoted this unlikely thesis, a more thorough study of the said documents and the contemporary court circulars revealed that Eddy was neither the suspect referred to, nor could he possibly have been present at the scene of several of the crimes. A variety of authorities have demolished the 'Eddy as Ripper' theory, all of them making the obvious point that besides lacking the opportunity, he also lacked the cunning, strength and, frankly, the energy. Limp of wrist and dull of brain he may have been, but Prince Albert Victor, heir presumptive and grandson of Queen Victoria, was far from being the stuff of which homicidal maniacs are made.

Albrecht I (b. 1905). The rightful King of England, if supporters of the Stuart claim to the throne are to be believed. Unfortunately for them, he lives the life of a country gentleman in Bavaria and has no intention of giving that up to press his by now rather tenuous claim to Elizabeth II's crown. This sizable obstacle to a restoration of the Stuart succession is, however, unlikely to deflect Britain's handful of Jacobites from their dreams. They are a persistent lot and even as late as the 1920s they were still demonstrating their allegiance to the cause by putting stamps bearing the head of George V upside down on envelopes. George somehow survived.

This, and several other futile gestures like it, was fully two and a half centuries after the original kerfuffle when James II legged it to France, leaving the Great Seal at the bottom of the Thames and his crown in the hands of William and Mary. Thereafter, supporters of the House of Stuart have peered mournfully out to sea through the mists and spoken wistfully of the King Over The Water, Old Pretenders, Young Pretenders and fainter and fainter lines of other pretenders. While the rest of Britain was ruled by its Georges, Victorias and Edwards, these were the kings and queens to whom Jacobites have owed their true loyalty:

1685–1701	James II
1701–1766	James III (the Old Pretender)
1766–1788	Charles III (the Young Pretender)
1788–1807	Henry IX (Cardinal and Bishop of Frascati)
1807–1819	Charles IV (alias King Charles Emmanuel IV of Sardinia)
1819–1824	Victor I (alias King Victor Emmanuel I of Sardinia – a dreadful old reactionary, whose subjects had to obtain their monarch's permission if they so much as wanted to read a newspaper)
1824–1840	Mary II (daughter of above)
1840–1875	Francis I (Duke Francis V of Modena and son of above)
1875–1919	Mary III (niece of above)
1919–1955	Rupert I (Crown Prince of Bavaria, son of above and commander of the 6th German Army in the First World War. Both he and his wife were strongly anti-Hitler and were persecuted by the Nazis)
1955–	Albrecht I (son of above and twice married. His son, the Stuart Prince of Wales, is Prince Francis, born in 1933)

Alexander III (1845–1894). Emperor of Russia, brother-in-law of Edward VII and royal buffoon. He was the kind of man who thought that apple-pie beds were the last word in sophisticated humour and farts the funniest thing that he had ever heard. Fortunately his royal relatives were as easily amused as he was and his escapades with syringes of water, coins stuck to the floor and imitation edibles consistently reduced them to helpless mirth. One of his better efforts was the prank he played on particularly po-faced and precious-looking dames at state receptions. As they curtsied before him, their Emperor would squeeze a rubber bladder hidden in his coat, thereby producing a loud and embarrassing noise at the vital moment.

Alexander was also a giant of a man with the strength to match, and typically he developed one or two little party pieces to show off his brawn. He would break horseshoes in half and, when staying with his in-laws, would have the horses removed from the royal carriage, take their place between the shafts and pull the King and Queen of Denmark around the courtyard. Oh, how this couple must have laughed; but not, one suspects (for they were very poor), when Alexander displayed his muscles by bending one of the Danish royal family's few pieces of silver plate. Nevertheless, his brute strength did have its uses and once, when his train crashed after an explosive attempt on his life, he held up the fractured roof of the compartment while his wife and children escaped.

Alexandra (19th Century). Bavarian Princess whose life was complicated by her firm conviction that she had once swallowed a grand piano made of glass. The only excuse for this extraordinary delusion is that madness ran in her family like water down a steep hill.

Alexandra (1844–1925). Queen of England, long-suffering wife of Edward VII and, in her spare moments, a friend and comforter of the famous Elephant Man.

She first met this great untouchable of Victorian England in May 1887. His real name was Joseph Merrick and he suffered from a progressive disease which so contorted and obscured his features that it looked for all the world as if he wore his brain on the outside, rather than the inside, of his skull. By the mid-1880s he was so sickeningly deformed that even the unscrupulous showmen who had used him as a sideshow freak had no further use for him. He was disowned, shunned and mocked and about the only people who could bring themselves to look at him were a surgeon and his staff at the London Hospital, where Merrick was by then resident. So when Alexandra came to open a new wing at the hospital in 1887, she was warned that Merrick was one inmate she might care to avoid. After all, some people had been known to be physically sick at the very sight of him.

Yet despite being somewhat theatrical in her emotions, Alexandra had a genuine concern for the sick and she insisted on seeing him. She was ushered into his room and, far from being revolted at his appearance, stayed chatting with him for some time – something few of her subjects would have had the stomach to do. A few days later she gave him a signed photograph of herself and Merrick was touched to the point of tears. Thereafter, she sent him a special Christmas card each year, made sure his hospital diet was regularly supplemented by game from her husband's estate and, according to hospital legend, paid him several unheralded visits.

Her befriending of Merrick was but the most striking example of her lifelong interest in the care of the sick – an enthusiasm reflected in the nursing service and hundreds of hospitals and wards up and down the country that still bear her name. Towards the end of her life she even became something of a medical pioneer herself when, at her husband's coronation in 1902, the by now chronically deaf Queen wore the world's first ever instrument to amplify sound electronically.

Alfonso VI (1643–1683). King of Portugal and public nuisance. Before his belated confinement to a place of safety, he would roam the streets of Lisbon with a set of ruffianly companions, assaulting passers-by, firing into the coaches of the nobles and routing religious processions at the point of a sword. Only the most hardened of his capital's common prostitutes were sorry to see him eventually secured behind locked doors.

Alfonso XII (1857–1885). Saintly and compassionate King of Spain who seemed to be the victim of a most dogged curse. The origin of these misfortunes appeared to be an opal ring. On his wedding day Alfonso presented the ring to his wife Mercedes. She died shortly afterwards. Before her funeral was held, the King gave it to his sister Maria. A few days later she was dead. Still suspecting nothing, despite opal's long association with unpleasant happenings, he gave the ring to his sister-in-law, Princess Christina. She died within three months.

Even Alfonso began to suspect something now and, lest any more female members of his family be struck down, he decided to wear the ring himself. Sure enough, he was dead within the year – at the age of 28. The Queen Regent was now taking no chances. She attached the offending object to a gold chain and suspended it from the neck of a statue of the Virgin in Madrid.

Alfonso XIII (1886–1941). King of Spain, he was reputed to have the evil eye. Both his sons died in car crashes but the principal evidence for this startling claim is based on a particularly eventful official visit that Alfonso paid to Italy in 1923. Even now, over 60 years later, some families are only just recovering from the trail of carnage that Alfonso left in his wake.

The misfortunes began even before this unhappy monarch stepped ashore, when several sailors in the flotilla sent to greet him were washed overboard and drowned. This was rapidly followed by an explosion in one of the accompanying submarines. Then, the very moment that Alfonso set foot on Italian soil, an ancient cannon fired in his honour blew up, obliterating all its crew. To emphasise the dangers of even the most fleeting contact with Alfonso, a naval officer with whom he had shaken hands collapsed and died shortly afterwards. By now the disastrous turn of events was taking on an air of inevitability and no one was in the least surprised when, on his tour of Lake Gleno, a dam burst, killing 50 people and making 500 homeless. Mussolini, never one content to let the women and children have first pick of the lifeboats, was so intimidated by Alfonso's reputation that he refused to meet him and conducted all negotiations through an intermediary.

As if this apparent curse was not burden enough for one man, Alfonso was also tone deaf. This meant that he was, among other things, incapable of recognising his own national anthem and so, to avoid embarrassment, a man was hired to accompany Alfonso to all state functions and nudge him when the band struck up.

Prince Alfred (1844–1900). Duke of Edinburgh and second son of Queen Victoria, he supplemented his income of £25,000 per annum by professionally introducing various snobs and social climbers to his royal relatives. His services did not come cheap. In Paris, for example, the going rate for his brother, the Prince of Wales, was 5 louis for a presentation and 50 for a luncheon.

Alfred (1874–1899). Prince of Edinburgh, grandson of Queen Victoria and the subject of one of the most successful cover-ups in British royal history.

According to contemporary reports, this heir to the dukedom of Saxe-Coburg-Gotha was taken poorly at the time of his parents' silver wedding celebrations and, within a month, had died from tuberculosis. Various royal biographers steadfastly maintained this version of events and if mention was made of him at all in family writings, it consisted of the obliquest of references. His sister Marie, for instance, wrote in her memoirs, 'His death . . . was a staggering blow. We were all so healthy, so strong, illness was an unknown thing in our family.' Yet what perhaps even Marie did not know was that Alfred was no more a consumptive than she was. What killed him was not tuberculosis but a set of circumstances regarded as so shameful that it was hushed up and kept secret for the next 80 years.

As regards his early life, there is no dispute. He was born in 1874 in Buckingham Palace, the eldest child of the Duke and Duchess of Edinburgh. Since he was due in time to succeed to the little duchy of Coburg, his parents had him educated in Germany by a martinet of a tutor, known to the family by the sinister nickname of 'Dr X'. As Alfred approached manhood he enlisted in the 1st Regiment of the Prussian Guards and it is at this point that most accounts draw a veil over his life. His sister Marie makes a tantalisingly unexplained reference to him in her book, saying he 'later became secretive, led a double life and made a mess of things.' She provides no details, however, and it was not until the publication of a little-known book in 1984 that the truth came out. The book was a biography of Alfred's father written by John Van der Kiste and Bee Jordaan and it makes plain that the death of the young grandson of Queen Victoria had more to do with women than TB.

It seems that soon after joining the army Alfred began to go astray, drinking wildly and falling under the spell of several of the doxies who hung around the barracks. Then, at the age of 23, he married an Irishwoman called Mabel Fitzgerald in Potsdam. She was a commoner and so the union was illegal under the 1772 Royal Marriages Act. Not surprisingly, Alfred's parents refused to recognise Mabel as their daughter-in-law. The Duchess was apparently especially scathing and the ensuing disputes made Alfred, a sensitive person at the best of times, acutely depressed. As the recriminations wore on, his condition was hardly improved by the onset of the venereal disease that he had contracted some years before.

The crunch came after a particularly violent row with his mother. Alfred took his pistol and shot himself. The suicide bid failed – for the time being – but left him seriously wounded. Thus, while his family gathered to celebrate his parents' silver wedding anniversary at Schloss Friedenstein in Gotha in 1899, Alfred lay in a bedroom on the lower floor, ostensibly suffering from his 'illness'. His mother was not only angry but fearful that the truth about this living skeleton in the family cupboard might be discovered. Despite the objections of the doctors, who said that if Alfred was moved he would not survive the week, the Duchess ordered him to be sent away. He was taken to Meran in the Tyrol and within a fortnight he was dead.

The grief of his parents knew virtually no bounds. At the funeral, his usually undemonstrative mother sank to her knees, sobbed uncontrollably and crossed herself repeatedly. His father never really recovered from the shock, thereafter drinking even more heavily than before. He blamed his wife for the tragedy and, according to some authorities, made sure that he never spent another night under the same roof as her. Neither of them, however, were so devastated that they neglected to hush up the matter. The obituaries published at the time said that Alfred had succumbed to consumption and this fiction, along with total silence on the subject of his marriage to Mabel Fitzgerald, was stoutly maintained down the years. Until Van der Kiste and Jordaan published their findings in 1984, the only known mention of Alfred's suicide was a glancing reference in the 1924 memoirs of Lady Paget. Such long-standing discretion has surely made the curious death of Prince Alfred of Edinburgh one of the best-kept royal secrets of the last 100 years.

Princess Alice of Battenburg (1885–1969). Wife of Prince Andrew of Greece, mother of Prince Philip and religious eccentric. This great grand-daughter of Queen Victoria had always been rather pious but her sudden exile from Greece, the onset of deafness and an increasingly cold marriage turned her spiritual enthusiasm into crankiness. The final straw for her husband (who was no paragon himself) came when Alice announced her intention of renouncing all material possessions and marrying Christ.

Several centuries before, such an ambition in a princess would have been taken as a sign of saintliness. The twentieth century, however, regarded her plans as certain evidence that Alice had gone dangerously on the blink. So while Andrew sloped off to Monte Carlo and his mistress, Holy Alice was bundled off to a series of nursing homes in Switzerland and Bavaria to be treated for a mental breakdown. By the late Thirties she had regained sufficient composure to be liberated and she went to live in a small house in the centre of Athens with an equally devout female for company. In 1949 she founded the Christian Sisterhood of Martha and Mary and for the next two decades she lived a reclusive life of godly contemplation.

Just a few years before she died, Alice came to lodge with her son at Buckingham Palace. She was rarely – if ever – seen in public and few of the subjects and tourists who daily mustered at the palace gates would have been aware that inside, walking the corridors in the grey, flowing robes of her sisterhood, was the Queen of England's bizarre mother-in-law.

Maharajah Jai Singh of Alwar (1882–1937). Indian Prince, English knight, honorary colonel in the British Army and weirdo. His sinister practices and autocratic ways made him, for a time, the most notorious of all the maharajahs. Yet the British seemed prepared to tolerate the allegations made against him; until, that is, the day when he was cruel to his polo pony and then, citing his 'gross misrule', they had him summarily deposed. The incident in question had occurred on the gracious lawns of Mount Abu, the local headquarters of the Indian Army. After losing a particularly vital chukka, Jai Singh was so overwhelmed with rage at his pony's feeble performance that instead of simply kicking it or sending it to its stable without any hay, he doused it in petrol and set light to the poor animal.

This unsporting behaviour, however, was nothing compared to some of the things that this feline-looking potentate was supposed to get up to. Many a prim colonial lip must have smacked at the tale of how he took babies from the women of his state and used them as tiger bait (always with the assurance to the mother that he had never missed the tiger – yet). There was much of the apocryphal in this and other yarns but it was certain that he loathed all dogs, killing on sight any specimen that crossed his path, and undeniable that his house guests were treated to some sickeningly cruel displays. One such, a favourite entertainment for those dining on his palace verandah, was to tether a goat to a table on the lawns and sit back and watch as a trained leopard came and killed it.

Indeed, he was apt to regard his dusty and hilly state as little more than a personal game park and for years he opposed the building of a road from Delhi through Alwar on the grounds that it would interfere with his tigers. His resistance was certainly not due to a dislike of motor cars, which he collected avidly. He favoured Hispano-Suizas – the Ferraris of his day – and his models were always finished in blue and purchased in threes. When he tired of them he had them driven out into the hills around his palace and ceremonially buried. Even at several thousand pounds a time they were no great loss to a man who could afford to dress in costly brocades and emerald necklaces. If he ran short of cash he could always raise the state taxes – an option he was never slow to exercise.

On some occasions there could be a curious kind of logic to his antics, such as the time he summoned a renowned astrologer to trek all the way from Bombay and then had him flung into a dungeon as soon as the man reached his palace. A few days later the bewildered seer was released with the explanation that it was a pretty poor kind of clairvoyant who could not foresee his own wretched fate. Yet as time went on, Jai Singh increasingly became a prisoner of his own fevered imaginings. He even grew convinced that he was the reincarnation of the god Rama and employed an expert to calculate the precise dimensions of that deity's head-dress so that he could have a copy made for himself.

In 1933 he was exiled to Paris, where he ended his days four years later. Yet even in death he could make a stir, and few funeral processions have been the bizarre equal of the one that Jai Singh instructed to be carried out. His body was borne back to India in the usual manner but then met on the borders of his old state by his favourite car, a 1924 custom-built, gold-plated Lanchester. This vehicle was a magnificent hybrid – a limousine in front and a British coronation coach behind, complete with gold carriage lamps, golden crowns on its doors and accommodation for two footmen in the rear. As the engine was turned over, Jai Singh's body was dressed in one of his finest satin suits, seated bolt upright in the back of his car, a pair of sunglasses was fixed on his nose and then, at a suitably dignified pace, this absurd cortege drove through the streets of his old capital towards the Maharajah's final resting place.

Andronicus I (1118–1185). Byzantine Emperor and a key figure in the farcical disintegration of his dynasty. The rot had set in many years previously but after the accession of Andronicus the pace picked up handsomely and from then on it was every man for himself.

The action got under way in 1183 when Andronicus had the 14-year-old Alexius II strangled with a bowstring. After two years of tyranny he himself was deposed and executed with commendable attention to detail by Isaac II. The method involved, at various times and in various combinations: starvation, chains, boiling water, a moth-eaten camel, hand-lopping, beard-pulling, teeth-breaking, blinding, hanging and stabbing. Isaac managed to hang onto his throne for ten uncertain years before he in turn was deposed, blinded and imprisoned by his brother Alexius III.

Was this the man to restore stability? No. In 1203 the Crusaders rolled up at the gates of Constantinople and Alexius III did a flit with the contents of the treasury. His nephew Alexius IV took over and brought his blinded, ex-emperor father Isaac back from gaol as co-ruler. They somehow managed to repel all assassins, usurpers and ambitious relatives for five whole months, until January 1204 when Alexius V hove into view. He took one look at Alexius IV, strangled him and was about to do the same to Isaac when the old man selfishly dropped down dead of fright. By now the local population were tired of asking who their emperor was when they woke up in the mornings and put a stop to all this nonsense by executing Alexius V for regicide. After that, it was rather difficult to persuade any man of substance that the Byzantine imperial crown was worth the trouble.

Anna (1693–1740). Empress of Russia, she devised some remarkably novel punishments for those courtiers whom she believed had stepped out of line. Once, when three nobles committed some minor misdemeanour, she decreed that they should all live as hens for a week. No detail was spared. Three large baskets were each stuffed with straw, hollowed out into a nest and filled with a dozen new-laid eggs. The baskets were then placed in the centre of one of the palace's main reception rooms and the miscreants, suitably decked out in feathery costumes, were led in and ordered, on pain of death, to sit on the nest and squawk away for seven days.

Her most outlandish idea, however, was reserved for one Prince Michael Alexsyevitch Golitsin, who had been careless enough to marry a Catholic lady while on his travels abroad. This match was not to Anna's liking and, to show her displeasure, she stripped him of his title and made the 40-year-old aristocrat her court buffoon. This, for poor Golitsin, was the good news. Worse, much worse, was to follow. When his Italian wife died in 1740 the Empress showed she had far from finished with him by arranging perhaps the most humiliating wedding and honeymoon there has ever been.

First of all, Anna commanded him to take as his bride a servant called Anna Buzheninova who was reputed at court to be the ugliest girl in all Russia. When he saw her face, which apparently resembled that of a Pekinese dog with a skin problem, he knew the courtiers had not been exaggerating. With this unfortunate creature at his side, Golitsin then had to endure the unusual nuptials that Anna had prepared. To describe this occasion as a tasteless and chaotic send-up would be wrong. It was less dignified than that. At the head of the procession were the prize items from Anna's collection of deformed and freakish human beings – the halt, the lame and the wretchedly malformed. Then, in carriages pulled by pigs, goats and dogs, came a company of the worst drunkards and reprobates in St Petersburg, to be followed in mock pomp by representatives from Russia's component states in lurid versions of their national dress. Finally, surrounded by yah-booing courtiers, came the far-from-happy couple ensconced in a cage which was strapped to the back of an aged elephant.

After a slapstick ceremony and riotous wedding breakfast

held in the huge riding school, the entire circus-like procession wound its moaning and cackling way towards the extraordinary honeymoon venue beside the deeply-frozen River Neva. This was, it should be recalled, all taking place in the depths of the winter of 1740, an exceptionally severe one, even by Russian standards, and this opportunity for something spectacularly malicious had not been lost on the Empress Anna. There, on the banks of the icily petrified river, and for the benefit of the newlyweds, she had ordered to be built a palace made entirely of ice.

It was, without doubt, a most outrageous structure, fully 80 ft long, 32 ft high, 23 ft deep and every part of it made from meticulously measured blocks of ice. The rooms consisted of a vestibule, ballroom and a bedroom, which came complete with four-poster, mattress, quilt and two pillows – all carved from ice. In the grounds were ice statues and ice trees, in whose branches perched birds sculpted from ice and painted in their natural colours. There were even half a dozen ice cannon which, after a little coaxing, actually managed to fire. The only part of this small, frozen estate not constructed of ice was the stout wooden fence which had been placed around the grounds to keep out the inquisitive populace.

To anyone who gazed upon it, the ice palace must have been a wondrous sight. To anyone, that is, except Golitsin and his blushing bride; for they knew that it was here that they had been ordered to spend their wedding night. Now, to the accompaniment of the drunken jeers of their guests, they were escorted into the ornate refrigerator and publicly and forcibly bedded down for the night on the glacial divan. Just in case they had any rash thoughts of escaping, guards were posted by the sealed ice doors.

Miraculously, they survived their sub-Arctic honeymoon and Anna duly lost interest in the couple whom she had so grotesquely brought together. Instead, she reverted to her former interests of shooting (she even kept loaded guns by the windows of her palaces so she could take pot shots at passing birds) and maintaining the gaudy display of her court (she decreed, for example, that only bright colours were to be worn in her presence). Then, at the age of 47, this most unlovable woman died. Golitsin had a special reason for marking the day of her death, for not only was it about nine months after his unforgettable night in the ice palace but it was also the day when his ugly little wife presented him with twin baby boys. Contemporary reports firmly insist that they – and their sons – lived long and happily ever after.

Anne (1665–1714). Queen of England whose great bulk and incapacitation caused the coronation ritual to be revised. Before her, the spurs of St George used to be buckled onto the legs of a new monarch but Anne's legs were so inflated with gout that the spurs would not go round them. She had instead to be content with a ceremonial touching. Her legs, whose bow shape has been so faithfully copied by furniture designers, also had to bear the weight of a body swollen by 18 pregnancies. By the time of her accession, this load had become intolerable, so Anne was conveyed to her crowning at Westminster Abbey in a sedan chair. This was left at the great west door and she managed, with some assistance, to hobble to the altar.

Anne has good cause to be judged England's most medically distressed monarch. Apart from her weight problem, she suffered from pseudocyesis or hysterical pregnancies – a particularly cruel condition for a woman who had not one grown child to show for her 18 confinements. Only five children were born alive and only one, the Duke of Gloucester, survived infancy – and he died aged 11. Troubled sight from birth meant that she had an almost perpetual squint, her face was pitted because of a childhood bout of smallpox, she was a martyr to chronic rheumatism, gout plagued her without ceasing and she also developed an allergy to the scent of roses. Despite these bodily trials, she will always be remembered fondly by a grateful nation as the foundress of the Royal Ascot race meeting.

Margrave of Ansbach (18th Century). A German princeling and a truly formidable parent. He tried to instil valour into his son by housing a family of bears in the lad's apartments. The experiment, alas, was a failure and had to be abandoned when one of the growling pets made off with a servant.

Duc d'Antin (17th Century). Louis XIV's supervisor of buildings at Versailles and the most sickening toady to royalty. He was so eager to ingratiate himself with his master that he placed pieces of wood under the statues in the grounds of the palace so that the King would notice that they were awry and d'Antin would then have the chance to praise his perceptiveness.

Archie Armstrong (1590–1672). The penultimate official court jester of England, he was ceremonially stripped of his robes of office by Charles I in 1637 for persistently insulting the Archbishop of Canterbury. Despite this misfortune, he had sufficiently enriched himself during his days at court to enjoy a comfortable retirement on his Cumbrian estates. He was succeeded as jester by Muckle John.

Augustus (1670–1733). King of Saxony, sometime ruler of Poland and an extrovert strongman. If a state occasion showed any signs of lapsing into the humdrum, he would immediately liven things up a bit by performing one of his feats of strength, such as wrestling with bears or straightening horseshoes with his bare hands. These little tricks always seemed to earn a gratifying reception but his Polish subjects preferred another of his party pieces. This was when he would pick up a young state trumpeter in each brawny hand and hold them out at arm's length for five minutes while they played a fanfare.

However, not all his muscular feats were performed in public. Some of his finest moments must have taken place in the bedroom, for he fathered no fewer than 354 bastards, an astonishing total only made possible by an almost numberless succession of obliging lady friends. Some authorities, when discussing the quantity of his mistresses, give the extraordinarily precise figure of 356 which, unless it is a fiction, suggests that he either employed an official scorer or kept his own meticulous records. This latter explanation is certainly open to doubt because one inamorata at least, a Countess Orzelska, was his daughter by a previous liaison. Considering this hectic and complicated love-life, it is a remarkable testimony to his strength that he managed to keep going until the age of 63.

Augustus II (1696–1763). King of Saxony and a dedicated fop. Not only did he own such a vast collection of clothes that his wardrobe filled two halls of the palace but for each of his suits – and there were thousands of them – there was a matching watch, snuffbox, sword and cane. Every outfit was painted in detail in a book and this 'dandy's encyclopedia' was presented to him each morning so that he could select his apparel for the day. To complete his chosen ensemble, he had the pick of over 1,500 wigs – a total which prompted Frederick the Great to remark, 'So many perukes for a man who has no head.'

> *'All I say is, kings is kings and you got to make allowances.'*
>
> MARK TWAIN, The Adventures of Huckleberry Finn.

B

Babur (1483–1530). Descendant of Genghis Khan, founder of the Mogul Empire and an optimistic imbiber. He planned to renounce all alcohol when he reached the age of 40 and so felt at liberty to indulge freely in the meantime. To ensure a plentiful supply of his favourite tipple, he ordered a pond 20 foot square to be cut out of solid rock and then filled with his best wine. Sadly, by the time the wine lake was completed he had reached his deadline for abstinence and so the pond had to be flooded with lemonade instead.

Prince Jung Badahur (19th Century). Prime Minister to the Maharajah of Nepal, he was so rich and so desperate for a nocturnal companion that in 1850 he paid London's leading prostitute, Laura Bell, £250,000 for one night's pleasure. Unfortunately, it is not recorded whether he felt that he had obtained value for money. Laura, who presumably was well satisfied, later got religion, married the Bishop of Norwich's nephew and became, if you will pardon the expression, a lay preacher. All, however, did not end happily and her husband was finally forced to publish in the London newspapers an announcement that he would no longer be responsible for his wife's debts.

Maharajah Khande Rao, Gaekwad of Baroda (b. 1856). Indian Prince and pigeon-fancier extraordinaire. He was the proud owner of the world's largest collection of these birds, eventually acquiring some 60,000 of them in all colours, shapes and sizes. Yet he was easily bored and found in time that the hobby had its limits as a source of pulse-racing excitement. So, in an attempt to revive his flagging interest, he decided to bring a little pomp and ceremony to the breeding process. He selected the finest cock and hen, had the two pigeons solemnly married by his priests and celebrated their nuptials by organising a vast wedding breakfast, complete with slap-up meal and fireworks. Sadly, the happy event was somewhat marred when a palace cat ate the bridegroom before he even had a chance to consummate the union. In an effort to forget this tragedy, the Maharajah then sought solace in another part of his aviary and threw himself into preparations for his next big production – a pitched battle between 500 nightingales.

The impracticality of such schemes was never likely to be drawn to his attention, for his courtiers were as big a bunch of sycophants as any ruler could wish to meet. Such was the extent of their boot-licking that when the Maharajah yawned, all present would click their fingers to discourage flies and if he did anything as accomplished as a fart or a belch then they would immediately burst into riotous applause. Since royal wind-breaking was regarded as nothing less than a state occasion, it was hardly surprising that there should be no check on his strange and sudden enthusiasms, few of which ever seemed to work out quite as intended.

One of his most notable failures was when he thought it would be nice to have a guru about the place. He finally found just what he was looking for: a suitably ethereal-looking holy man who was discovered sitting on a dunghill by the roadside. He had the man shipped back to his palace, surrounded him with monks and other religious characters and sat back and waited for the pearls of wisdom to fall from the sacred lips. Regrettably he waited in vain, for the man had been meditating on top of a dunghill for so long that he was past all human communication. However he was addressed, whatever stimulation he was given, he just sat staring blankly into space. Not even the firing of a pistol by his ear could draw any response. The Maharajah, of course, just shrugged his shoulders and passed on to his next ill-starred fad.

Baromaraja II (d. 1448). The accidental King of ancient Siam. His father, King Intr'araja, had died in 1424 and it was decided that the old ruler's two elder sons should contest the succession by fighting a duel to the death on the backs of their elephants. It must have seemed like a good idea at the time but when it came to the grand tournament, the two princes charged, each knocked the other off his elephant simultaneously, both were killed and the spectating Baromaraja was left, by this curious process of elimination, as the new King.

Basil II Bulgaroctones (958–1025). Byzantine Emperor and successful general; yet his behaviour in victory lacked a certain magnanimity. After defeating the Bulgarians at Ochrida in 1014, he ordered the blinding of all 15,000 of his prisoners 'as an example'. The only concession he would make was that every 100th man would be allowed to keep the sight of one eye so that he could lead his comrades back home. Not surprisingly, the Bulgarian Khan dropped down dead with shock on hearing the news.

Henry Beauchamp (15th Century). Duke of Warwick and the first, last and only King of the Isle of Wight. He was given this title in 1446 by Henry VI, who in addition to crowning the new monarch himself, also created him King of Guernsey and Jersey.

Bertoldo (6th Century). Fool to Alboin, King of the Lombards. Monumentally ugly he may have been, with his eyebrows like pig's bristles, carroty red hair and unhygienic complexion, but at the uncouth court of his master, Bertoldo definitely possessed what passed for star quality. He did not trade in belly laughs or slapstick, blue jokes or puns; instead his speciality was solving riddles. In the sixth century, if you wanted sophistication in your show, then you had to book Bertoldo.

One conundrum that provoked almost incessant debate among Alboin's courtiers was the knotty problem: is daylight whiter than milk? Bertoldo thought it was and when challenged by his doubting King to prove his case, he accepted. That night he entered the royal bedchamber, closed the blinds, placed a pail of milk in the middle of the room and crept out. A few hours later, while it was still dark, the unsuspecting Albion rose, walked a few sleepy paces, collided with the bucket and overturned it. When he called for light he was answered by Bertoldo that if milk had been clearer than daylight, he would have seen the former without the latter. It was proof also of one of history's great lessons: that the average jester is brighter than the average king.

Bokassa I (b. 1921). Self-styled, self-proclaimed and self-crowned Emperor of the Central African Empire. His monstrously lavish coronation in December 1977 was intended to establish him as an imposing presence on the African stage but all it really established was Bokassa's crazed vanity. His crown alone cost over £3 million and the total cost of the celebrations neared £18 million – fully a quarter of the annual income for this, one of the world's poorest nations. While his subjects slaved in diamond mines or coffee plantations to earn a mere £16.50p a year, Bokassa saw fit to spend the equivalent of a year's development aid from France on this gaudy and useless display. To him it was a day of glory but to the rest of the world it was, with its glass coaches, sumptuous robes and gem-encrusted baubles, nothing less than the definitive satire on the trappings of royalty.

Jean Badel Bokassa had seized power in this former French colony from his brother-in-law in 1965. He governed by personal whim, typified by his action on Mother's Day 1971 when he released all women prisoners but ordered the execution of all men convicted of assaults on women. By 1972 he had declared himself Life President and was increasingly resembling the very model of the two-bit despot. Across his chest, for example, he wore 48 medals, two of which were legitimate (won with the French army in Vietnam) but the rest were nearly all bogus, one being nothing more than the metal badge of a Swiss ski resort. That he should visit such places was no longer a surprise. His people may have been classified by the United Nations as one of the 25 poorest nations in the world but Bokassa owned five castles and eight other properties in France, a mansion on the Riviera and a villa in Switzerland, as well as palaces all over his own country and a fleet of fabulous limousines.

To be the one man who stood proud in his land was not, however, enough for Bokassa. He wanted more and so, in 1976, he renamed the Central African Republic an Empire, declared himself Emperor and began preparations for his coronation. For a man who had already planted a statue of himself at every one of the crossroads in the capital of Bangui, it was never likely to be a low-key affair. But no one, not even his most toadying adviser, could have imagined quite how gross the spectacle would prove to be.

The ceremony was modelled on Napoleon's crowning in 1804 and this absurdly inappropriate style for equatorial Africa kept French craftsmen profitably employed for months before the day itself. In a workshop near Nice was constructed an eight-ton gilded carriage in the shape of a golden eagle and other coaches in glass and gilt; Guiselin of Paris worked on his robes, the cloak and train of which was fully 39 foot long, encrusted with 785,000 pearls, 1,220,000 crystal beads and cost nearly £80,000; Paris couturiers prepared him 10 Napoleonic uniforms, made 5,000 others for his army and ran up his consort's gold lamé gown which was studded with three-quarters of a million pearls; French jewellers set 2,000 diamonds in his £3 million crown and made his six-foot long bejewelled sceptre; metalworkers toiled away at his two-ton Imperial throne, a striking affair which incorporated a gilded eagle with a 15-foot wingspan. Then, of course, there were the other little details for his coronation – the 2,000 yards of scarlet tapestry to drape Bangui Cathedral, 12 triumphal arches, an eight-foot-high iced cake and 35 dappled grey horses brought from a Normandy stud farm at £2,350 each to pull this whole nonsensical cavalcade from the palace to the crowning.

On 4 December 1977, every beggar was swept from the capital and the procession wound its way down a route patrolled by women soldiers of the Imperial Guard dressed in their black rubber boots, black shirts and red tunics. The coronation itself took place in a sports stadium and in the absence of the Pope, who had declined Bokassa's invitation to crown him, the Emperor did the job himself. Then, as his attendants sweltered in temperatures in excess of 100 degrees, the procession went to the palace for the banquet. On their way they passed by a grave-yard filled with the bodies of children unfortunate enough to be born in a country where one in five infants die before their first birthday. Not that one would have guessed that statistic from the spread that awaited the 5,000 guests. With caviare, antelope, foie gras, crayfish, Mouton Lafite Rothschild at £70 a bottle, 150 tons of other wines and 24,000 bottles of champagne, the banquet weighed in at £200 a head. By the time it was all over, the coronation was estimated to have cost £18 million and some put the figure at nearer £20 million.

After such an appalling occasion, it was never likely that Bokassa would settle down to rule benignly and well. Nor did he. Soon there were reports that he was taking a rake-off from his country's industries, feeding his opponents to the crocodiles, maintaining a harem of young girls and ruling with corrupt brutality. He banned the foreign press from the country but still the accounts leaked out and in September 1979, while he was visiting Libya, Bokassa was deposed amid allegations that he had personally killed some of the 100 schoolchildren massacred in a prison six months before. In no time at all the new government had prepared an indictment against him which included mass murder, embezzlement and even cannibalism. Despite his wails of innocence from exile, Bokassa was sentenced to death in his absence.

By 1985 his life was a far cry from the superficial splendours of his coronation. His money virtually all gone and most of his relations and hangers-on having scattered, the unemployed

Emperor was living with a shrunken retinue in a tumble-down chateau outside Paris. The telephone had been cut off and, although the water supply had recently been restored, there was no electricity. He was literally down to his last wife and most of his 54 children had gone too. Three were in care after they had been caught shoplifting for food and, in January 1985, the 64-year-old Bokassa applied for six more of them to be farmed out. What he would not have given then for just one of the 2,000 diamonds in his old crown?

Then, at the end of 1986, he suddenly and secretly left France and returned to his former capital. No one knows why. He may have found the life of continued penury no longer bearable or he may even have grown sufficiently deluded in exile to imagine that he would be welcomed like a hero and swept back to power on a wave of popular enthusiasm. He wasn't. As he stepped from the aircraft there was no bunting, no flag-waving throng of followers and no garlands. Instead, the reception committee consisted of Lt-Col Claude Mansion and an elite corps of the Presidential Guard. Bokassa was under arrest.

At his trial he faced 14 charges ranging from embezzlement and murder to cannibalism. There would have been more had the *Code Napoleon*, under which the republic conducted its legal matters, not dictated that he could only face those charges levelled against him immediately after his hurried dethronement of some eight years before. Yet, despite this, the wiliness of the two lawyers hired to defend him and the gaps in the prosecution case, there seemed little chance that he could avoid conviction on at least some of the counts. As the trial wore on through the summer of 1987, the most likely outcome seemed a sentence of death, to be followed in due course by a reprieve and exile – this time for good.

Boleslaus II (1039–1081). A very reluctant King of Poland. He was elected against his will in 1076 and was still protesting that he did not want the wretched job when it came to his coronation. Courtiers had to thrust the sceptre into his hands, more or less frogmarch him up to the throne and, even when seated, he could not suppress one final wail of regret. 'I had rather tug at the oar,' he moaned, 'than occupy such a place.' This heart-rending fragment of history had caused some scholars to identify Boleslaus as the king at the centre of the following story.

Once upon a time in the Middle Ages, a royal hunting party left the King of Poland's castle for a day in the field. There was much hearty whooping and hollering, for the Poles were fanatical hunters who boasted they could track a beetle through a haystack and never lose it. All the more surprising then that they should return in rather less buoyant mood some hours later with the disturbing news that they had lost not only their quarry but also the King.

For the next few days the courtiers searched every place they could think of. They covered everywhere so thoroughly that some of them even began to wonder if the King actually wanted to be found. Then came their answer; for there, in the market-place of the capital, was their King, disguised as a porter, hiring out the use of his shoulders for a few pence a day. The court was thrown into immediate confusion. Some nobles refused to believe that this ragged figure was their King; while others, recalling his distaste for his royal duties, were appalled that one so exalted should demean himself in this way. They begged him to return to his vacant throne. The King, however, had not gone AWOL on the hunting field just to have a few days slumming it. He meant to stay where he was and, drawing himself up to his full height, he addressed the assembly with these words:

'Upon my honour, gentlemen, the load which I quitted is far heavier than the one you see me carry here; the weightiest is but a straw when compared to that world under which I laboured. I have slept more in four nights than I have in all my reign. I begin to live and be a king of myself. Elect whom you choose. For me, who am so well, it were madness to return to court.' So saying, the ex-sovereign subsided once more into the role of a porter and disappeared through the astonished crowd to his humble lodgings.

That, at any rate, is the legend. More prosaic minds have it that Boleslaus was, in fact, exiled after executing one bishop too many. Yet the romantically inclined will prefer to believe that there was once on the throne of Poland a man too well-balanced to want anything to do with the cares and vanities of kingship.

Anne Boleyn (1507–1536). Briefly the Queen of England and formerly mistress of Henry VIII, she was not quite the demure and perfectly formed beauty normally portrayed on stage and screen. She was, in fact, a small-scale genetic calamity, having a large and unsightly birthmark on her neck, an extra nipple on her chest and six fingers on her left hand. Besides this, her table manners were deplorable. If she was enjoying her food but had already eaten her fill, she would make room for another helping by deliberately vomiting. The only nicety observed was that a noblewoman would hold up a sheet so that Anne could jettison her meal with visual, if not aural, privacy. Small wonder that her husband had her executed.

Don Alfonso de Borbon y Borbon (1866–1934). Great-grandson of Charles III of Spain and the proud but often confused owner of no fewer than 89 Christian names – several of which were lengthened by hyphenation.

Boris (1895–1943). Czar of Bulgaria and railway fanatic. Such was his interest in trains that it could not be satisfied merely by studying them or collecting their numbers – Boris would insist on driving them as well. He particularly enjoyed taking the controls of the Orient Express, either with the permission of the company who ran this magnificent service or, if necessary, without. It is, however, doubtful if the well-heeled passengers felt the same sense of giddy pleasure as did Boris. He may always have dressed for the footplate in an immaculately tailored boiler suit but he was not a cautious driver and his taste for rattling along at a great lick was a constant threat to the train's expensive fixtures and fittings.

Regrettably, the dangers of riding the rails with the Czar of

Bulgaria were not confined to mere derailment. Once, when trying to make up for lost time on a stretch leading to Sofia, he was so desperate to build up a good head of steam that he seriously misjudged the furnace's capacity for coal. The draught blew back the flames and his poor fireman was burnt to death. Eventually, that splendid organisation, the Compagnie Internationale des Wagon-Lits et des Grands Express Européens, who owned the Orient Express, became so alarmed at the prospect of Boris entering the cab that they firmly asked him not to do so and threatened with dismissal any driver who allowed the royal enthusiast onto his footplate. Naturally it made no difference. Boris would sit in his private carriage until the train crossed the border into Bulgaria then order the train to stop, change into his natty overalls, alight, climb into the cab and take the controls, once, apparently, at gunpoint. No one, he maintained, could stop him driving a train in his own kingdom.

The only complication in this respect was his brother, Crown Prince Cyril, who was an equally ardent railway maniac. At times this rivalry was a positive embarrassment. When Edward VIII paid a visit in 1936, his departure was delayed somewhat by Boris and Cyril arguing over whose turn it was to drive the royal train back to the capital. Yet for all these shenanigans with railways, Boris – who bore a startling resemblance to Clement Attlee – was a cultured man. He spoke six languages, was a knowledgeable botanist and an excellent mechanic. Indeed, he once said, 'I have no fear of losing the throne through revolution because I could always get a job in the United States as an engineer or college professor.' Alas, he never had the chance to find out if this was so, dying in mysterious circumstances in 1943 after flying back from a Berlin meeting with Hitler.

Alice Botiller (15th Century). Nurse to Henry VI, England's youngest monarch. He became king at the age of only 269 days and Alice was naturally concerned that her inevitable scolding and disciplining of the infant sovereign should not be a cause of reprisals when he grew up. So she asked for and obtained an indemnity which permitted her 'to chasten us from time to time as the case shall require, so that you shall not be molested, hurt or injured from this cause in future time.'

John Brown (1826–1883). Queen Victoria's minder and probably the most outspoken royal servant in history. He bullied and bossed his royal mistress, addressing her as 'woman' and virtually running her life, regarded her relations as little more than bothersome pests and treated her ministers with a contempt that he made no effort to conceal. As a result, Victoria adored him, while her family loathed the very sight of him and society thought him a jumped-up rustic who presumed far too much. In the country at large there were even rumours of a secret marriage between him and his queen and it was widely believed that he exerted some kind of sinister hold on her.

Even if he had wielded some strange influence over her, he would never have needed to use it. From the moment Brown came into close contact with her in 1861, to his death more than 20 years later, she believed him to be the fount of all common sense and trusted his judgement implicitly. To her, he was the true successor to Albert as the man in her life and he needed no further passport to liberty-taking than that.

It was at Balmoral that this strange and devoted pair first met. He had been born the son of a poor Scottish farmer and joined the staff of the royal estate as a boy, working first as a stable hand and then as a gillie. At a royal picnic by the side of the Dee in 1856, Brown's duty was to make the tea. 'The best cup of tea I ever tasted,' remarked his grateful sovereign. 'Well it should be,' replied Brown, 'I put a grand nip o' whiskie in it.' From then on, he was her constant companion when she was at Balmoral – a situation that existed until 1861 and the sudden, devastating death of the Prince Consort.

For months Victoria was in a semi-catatonic state of shock. There were genuine fears for her sanity as she alternately wept and wailed or stared morosely at the vacant place beside her. It was her personal secretary who had the idea of bringing south the kilted figure of Brown who always cheered her so much when she was in the Highlands. At first Brown merely took her for walks or strode beside her pony and trap on her outings around Osborne in the Isle of Wight. Yet slowly he began to take her out of herself. He babied her, cajoled her, protected her from unwanted intrusions and offered her the kind of simple companionship she could find nowhere else. He was a welcome relief from all the fusses and demands of her family, each of whom was an almost unbearably poignant reminder of her dear Albert. Thus did Victoria come to rely on this blunt, reassuring presence to try and fill the aching vacuum in her life. In return, she made him her personal servant indoors as well as out, ordered that he should always sleep in the apartment next to hers and granted him the most extraordinary latitude.

The no-nonsense tone he adopted towards her was strongly in evidence when they set out on their perambulations together. As she emerged into the open air, she was quite likely to be greeted by the gruff Highland voice ordering her to 'go inside and get yer shawl, ye'll catch yer death like that,' or even, 'yer hat is crooked, woman, put it straight, will ye?' Far from being appalled at his manner, as her other staff and family were, Victoria was delighted and always obeyed. He was able to speak to her as no other man, however vaunted, could. On another occasion she turned up for their constitutional wearing her familiar widow's weeds. Brown was appalled. 'What are ye doin' with that auld black dress on ye again,' he barked, 'it's green moulded.' At this, the Queen, upon whose empire the sun never set, scuttled back indoors and changed. One dreads to think how he addressed her in less public circumstances.

Politicians also felt the rough edge of his tongue. When one stayed at Balmoral and declared his intention of doing a spot of angling, Brown shook his head. 'No, ye'll no be ganging fishin'. Her Majesty thinks it time ye did a bit o' work.' Even Gladstone was not beyond the servant's reproach. He was astonished, when he was disputing a point with Victoria at a Windsor dinner party, to receive a smart tap on the shoulder from Brown and hear the Scottish stage whisper in his ear, 'That's it. Ye've said enough.' With stories like this in general circulation, no one was a bit surprised to learn of his behaviour at another dinner function. Thinking that the Queen's health should be drunk and seeing that none of the high-born guests was going to do it, he ordered a glass of wine, called the startled company to silence and proposed the loyal toast himself.

An especial target for his abrupt manner was the Prince of Wales. He treated him as a mere child long after Bertie had reached manhood and rarely gave him anything but his most derisory attention. Once, when the Prince went to see the Queen at Windsor, he arrived at her quarters to find Brown seated in a chair outside her room and engrossed in reading a paper. 'What do ye want?' demanded the servant, of the heir to the throne. 'I wish to see the Queen,' replied Bertie. 'Ah,' said Brown, 'ye no seein' yer mother till five o'clock. Ye'll need to go and amuse yerself for two hours.' With a vigorous shake of his newspaper, Brown returned to studying its columns. Bertie was then in his late twenties and this incident turned his already intense dislike of Brown to out-and-out hatred. For several years in the late 1860s he refused to speak to his mother's servant and there was even talk that in 1868 the heir had hired a boxer from Aberdeen to rough up Brown.

Part of Bertie's resentment sprang from the pervading influence that Brown now had over the Queen. She hung on his every word, engaged and dismissed royal servants entirely on his say-so, was believed to discuss state papers with him (some of her more robustly imperialist views allegedly being his) and often summoned him several times a night to check 'all was well'. She also absorbed his ludicrously frugal ideas of domestic management and imposed them without question on her own household. Thus did those attending the wealthiest and most important court in the world have to use worn silverware, confine themselves to only one lump of sugar in their tea, sit before unlit fires and use squares of discarded newspapers in the loo.

The central role that Brown now occupied in the Queen's thoughts was made abundantly clear to even the dullest of her subjects with the publication of her *Leaves from the Journal of*

Our Life in the Highlands. The manservant emerged as the hero of the book and barely a page passed without a glowing reference to her beloved Brown. Long before this, however, the place and presumptuousness of Brown was drawing comment from the public. His critics called him 'The Shadow Behind the Throne' and in 1866 *Punch* gave satiric voice to what everyone had been previously saying behind their hands. In an item headed, 'Court Circular, Balmoral, Tuesday', their resident leg-puller wrote in an obvious parody of that column: 'Mr John Brown walked on the slopes. He subsequently partook of a haggis. In the evening Mr John Brown was pleased to listen to a bag-pipe. Mr John Brown retired early.'

The cloying relationship he enjoyed with his Queen also fed rumours that the pair had secretly married, thus earning Victoria the nickname 'Mrs Brown'. Once again *Punch* was spot-on, publishing a cartoon showing Brown putting his boots on the royal mantelpiece while a contented Queen looked on. There were even those who attributed his influence with her to the supernatural, claiming that he was not just a medium but the only one who could put her in constant touch with dear, departed Albert. This extravagant theory rests entirely on sup-position and the mysterious fate of Brown's diaries, which on his death were impounded by the Queen's private secretary and summarily burned at Victoria's request. No one ever knew why.

The innuendo about Brown's role at court was just reaching its climax when, in February 1872, a young Irish sympathiser called Arthur O'Connor broke into the courtyard of Buckingham Palace and lay in wait for the returning Queen. As her carriage wheeled to a halt by the entrance, O'Connor stepped forward with a pistol in his hand. Brown was equal to the occasion. Springing from his place, the 46-year-old royal minder threw himself on the lad and disarmed him. In that one instant Brown's public image was transformed and the criticism all but muted. The Queen presented him with a medal and he put it with all the other keepsakes that she had given him. Some years later she even made him the present of a house, the palatial Bhaille-na-Chaille near Balmoral. He mumbled his thanks but never occupied it. Instead, he went on serving his Queen day in, day out, with never a holiday and only a few afternoons and evenings lost to his taste for his native drink. Eventually, in August 1883, he caught a chill and died, aged 57.

For some time no one would dare tell Victoria, fearing that she would once more retreat into the grief-ridden madness from which Brown had previously rescued her. Yet they need not have worried; grief and mourning were a lifestyle to her now and, although deeply upset at the loss of Brown, she bore up sufficiently to supervise the fulsome tributes to his memory. A whole column in the Court Circular was devoted to his obituary, a statue of him was erected in the grounds of Balmoral, a two-foot-high commemorative brass plate was put up in the Royal Mausoleum at Frogmore, his cousin was appointed to his old job and busts of Brown began to appear on pedestals in every royal residence. Victoria even planned to write a life of her manservant until an agitated Dean of Windsor persuaded her otherwise. So she contented herself with commissioning even more busts, making his grave her first port of call when she visited Balmoral and refusing ever to sit down at meal-times unless the humble salt-cellar Brown once gave her was placed on the table.

With Victoria's own death in 1901, this veneration of Brown ended with a vengeance. Bertie's vengeance, to be precise; for the new King Edward VII now had a chance to get his own back for all those slights – real and imagined – of some 20-odd years before. Starting with the statue of Brown at Balmoral, the King had every trace of the hated manservant removed. The brass plate at Frogmore was unceremoniously unscrewed and Edward ordered that every bust of Brown should be smashed, breaking several of them with his own hands. Just to make sure he would never again have to feel those piercing Scottish eyes gazing at him in disapproval, the King also had destroyed hundreds of pictures and photographs of Brown. This was a shame. All these endless images of the lugubrious, bearded Scot standing stiffly besides the dumpy Queen hardly constituted a treasure trove but they would at least have been a record, and probably rather a touching one, of this most extraordinary servant: the royal minder whose devotion was more than reciprocated by his Queen.

> *'We sometimes forget that monarchs are just normal people trapped by abnormal circumstances.'*
>
> MICHAEL MACDONALD.

C

*'No race of kings has ever presented above
one man of common sense in twenty generations.'*

THOMAS JEFFERSON, 1787.

Prince Adolphus, Duke of Cambridge (1774–1850). Uncle of
Queen Victoria and an incessant barracker of clergymen. His
belief that every church service could benefit from the odd
interjection and his inability to speak at anything other than
gruff full-volume was notorious among nineteenth-century
churchmen. The sight of Adolphus in their congregation was
enough to make the most stolid men of the cloth twitch in
nervous anticipation, especially as they could never be sure
when and where the famous royal interruption would come.
Even a simple request of 'Let us pray' could be met with a
booming 'By all means' from Adolphus, always repeated, as was
his annoying habit, three times.

On other occasions, the Duke would feel impelled to add a
more argumentative twopennyworth. Once, for example, when
a royal chaplain offered up a special prayer for the relief of a
prolonged drought, Adolphus's loud voice could be heard
demanding, 'Oh God! My dear man, how can you expect rain
with the wind in the east?'

A frequent butt of these outbursts was the Rev W.J.E.
Bennett of St Paul's, Knightsbridge. In time he learnt to resign
himself to the fact that when he was reading the Ten
Commandments he was unlikely to get beyond number eight
before the eruption from the royal pew: 'Steal! No, of course

not, mustn't steal, mustn't steal, mustn't steal.' Yet even the Rev Bennett could not have expected the uncontroversial statement of 'For we brought nothing into the world, neither may we carry anything out,' to be met with Adolphus's riposte of 'True, true, too many calls upon us for that.'

Carol II (1893–1953). King of Romania, sexual athlete and football fan. In 1930 he called a temporary halt to the incessant traffic in and out of his bedroom so that he could address himself to the national problem of Romania's entry for the World Cup. He secured funding for the team's trip to Uruguay, persuaded the players' employers to give them time off and, as due reward for his efforts, insisted on the right to pick the squad. His selections did not do too well, however, losing 4–0 to the host nation and returning home after the first round.

Caroline (1768–1821). Uncrowned Queen of England whose vulgarity revolted her husband, delighted the mob and made her our most controversial consort. She remains the only one – so far – to have been barred from her own coronation.

Born in 1768 to the Duke and Duchess of Brunswick, it was obvious even in her teenage years that she had a red-blooded nature that was liable to lead her astray. Indeed, her parents were so afraid of what she might get up to that they appointed a governess whose chief duties were not educational but to act as a vigilante of the girl's morals. If Caroline so much as went from one room to another, the chaperoning governess would follow and if the princess danced then the prying old biddy would have to hail a passing guest and tail the princess all round the floor, lest she engage in indecent conversation with her partner. It was a wise precaution, for Caroline's earthy manners gave many a lad precisely the right impression.

Very little of this percolated back to England when George III and his advisers were canvassing the court of Europe for a suitable bride for the Prince of Wales, later George IV. In fact, Caroline's testimonials were so glowing and her portrait so flattering that the couple were married by proxy before her future husband had even set eyes on her. When he did, at the Duke of Cumberland's apartments in St James's, he was so taken aback by the disappointing reality of his bride that he rocked on his heels and said to a friend, 'I am not well, pray fetch me a glass of brandy.' The Princess was equally crest-fallen. 'Is the Prince always like that?' she asked. 'I find him very fat and nothing like as handsome as his picture.'

The truth is that the pair of them were hardly oil paintings – and especially not the ones they had exchanged. He was already beginning to distend from high living and she was short, stout and unwashed, with clothes and make-up like a cheap doll. Even at 27, she resembled nothing as much as an aging actress trying to impersonate a little girl – and not having much success. Nevertheless, on 7 April 1795, three days after their first let-down of a meeting, the couple were married at the Chapel Royal, St James's. She, for once, gritted her teeth and behaved with some dignity but he rolled up drunk, had to be supported throughout by the Duke of Bedford and at one point began tottering away from the altar until he was prodded back into place by the King. Later, at Carlton House, the Prince somehow managed to consummate the union before lapsing into a stupor. They never slept together again and the daughter born of their joyless wedding night was a constant source of ill-feeling between them.

Meanwhile, back at the honeymoon in Hampshire, things were going from bad to worse. It could hardly have been otherwise, for George had taken along his current mistress Lady Jersey and some of his drinking cronies, while Caroline responded by speedily reverting to type. Her Sunday-best manners began to slip and the coarse-grained floozie in her began to show through. By the time the couple went back to London, they were barely on speaking terms and were sleeping in separate wings of their house. The Prince refused even to eat with her. 'I had rather see toads and vipers crawling over my victuals than sit at the same table as her,' he said with some feeling. After little more than a year of this domestic attrition he signed a formal letter of separation, went back to Mrs

Fitzherbert and amended his will accordingly. 'To her who is called the Princess of Wales,' he dictated, 'I leave one shilling.'

Freed from the suffocating ill-will of Carlton House, Caroline moved to Blackheath and adopted an increasingly unconventional lifestyle. She held wild dinner parties, growing ever more fat in the process, and filled her house with children. Most of them were local orphans but some may have been the product of her affairs. The truth is somewhat elusive, particularly as she had a habit of playing at being pregnant by leaving off her corset and letting her impressive stomach flop forward. She also fantasised about leading the life of an anonymous citizen and when these feelings became overpowering, the Princess of Wales would go incognito to Bayswater, knock on doors until she found a room to let and live in humble circumstances for a few days.

Some of her ways were even more alarming. According to Lady Charlotte Campbell in her *Diary of a Lady In Waiting*, every night after dinner Caroline would model a wax figure of her husband wearing a large pair of horns. She would then take out three pins and stick them into the figure before melting it in the fire. Perhaps this was not altogether surprising, since her husband's agents constantly harried her in their efforts to find evidence for a divorce for the Prince. Her friends, however, remained loyal to her and she to them. She repeatedly turned down large sums to leave the country until, in 1814, the bored Caroline finally could resist the lure of Europe no longer.

It was now, at the age of 46, that she really loosened her stays and let rip. Many were the Continentals who were rather shocked to see the ample, rouged figure of the Princess of Wales roll up at their receptions in a short, girlish frock with ribbons in her hair and her gigolos in tow. That, however, was but the demure side of Caroline now. At balls in Geneva, Athens, and Naples she went topless, at Baden she added to the startling effect by wearing half a pumpkin on her head (explaining to the Grand Duke that it was 'the coolest sort of coiffure') and when in Rome she did as few Romans did and flirted with the Pope. Between all this and riding into Jerusalem astride an ass, no less, there were also lovers, chiefly an Italian called Bartolomeo Pergami.

The Prince's agents, who had followed her relentlessly on this gallivanting tour, could hardly believe their luck. They now felt they had more than enough evidence for a divorce should Caroline ever show her painted face in England again. That, however, was a public fuss the Prince preferred to avoid if he could and when he succeeded to the throne in 1820, thus making Caroline (albeit in absentia) his Queen, he offered her £50,000 to renounce her title and pledge never to visit his country again. Naturally she spurned the bribe and immediately set course for England, arriving back on an ordinary packet at Dover intent on claiming what was rightfully hers.

As she made her way to London, she was given a tremendous reception. The ordinary people had always considered her ill-used and many of them so detested George that they would have cheered the Devil himself if he had been ranged against their new King. Of course, as far as George was concerned, this was precisely who was rolling into town and he was determined to have her stopped before she could cause him any further embarrassment or, worse, bodge up his grand coronation by insisting on taking her place beside him and receiving her crown. Accordingly, a Bill of Pains and Penalties was introduced in Parliament, designed to strip her of all her entitlements. The second reading in the House of Lords was, in effect, a trial of the Queen and her morals.

It was, perhaps, the most thorough and public airing of dirty linen in British royal history. Every fibre of evidence garnered from her scandalous perambulations in Europe by George's agents was held up to the light and examined for stains: her dress (or lack of it), her flirtations and high jinks and, most important of all, her affair with Pergami. Her Italian servants, whose expenses were rather over-generously met by George, were called to the stand to tell through an interpreter of Pergami's sleeping next to Caroline, his attendance on her when she bathed and his nocturnal visits to her room. No detail was spared: not the hastily rearranged clothing, nor the crumpled sheets nor even Andrea Veronese's testimony of the less than romantic origins of their relationship: 'Her royal highness had heard of the enormous size of his machine and sent for him by courier.'

The defence, led by Lord Brougham, made Signor Pergami's physique sound less impressive, claiming that he was impotent. Caroline was equally adamant that there had been no hanky-panky and in a sharp reference to the illicit marriage of George and his then mistress Mrs Fitzherbert 30 years before, declared, 'I have only committed adultery with one man and he was Mrs Fitzherbert's husband.' In the end, the Bill could not amass sufficient votes for further passage and, amid wild scenes of public enthusiasm, was thrown out.

Yet the echoing cheers of the crowds only emphasised how hollow her victory was. Shorn by the 'trial' proceedings of any last vestige of dignity and ostracised by all but the most radical and discontented of the Establishment, she was Queen in name only. When she turned up at George's coronation and the ceremony that should have put a crown on her head, she was flatly refused admittance to the Abbey on the King's instructions. The nearest she got to seeing the ancient ritual was when she attended a re-enactment of the coronation at Drury Lane that evening. On her return to her residence in Hammersmith she felt unwell and within the month the only Queen of England ever to have her sex life put to the vote in Parliament was dead.

Catherine I (1684–1727). Queen of Russia, wife of Peter the Great and organiser of some exceptionally dull parties. Her rules for these gatherings stipulated that no gentleman was to get drunk before 9 pm and that no lady was to get drunk at any hour. Her daughter, Princess Elizabeth, and other young women of the court evaded these restrictions by holding soirees in men's clothing.

Catherine the Great (1729–1796). Empress of Russia and, if her parties were anything to go by, the most enlightened of all the enlightened despots. She was a proud and powerful monarch but when the day's ruling was done, she liked nothing better than to retreat inside her Hermitage, throw off all the trappings of royalty and relax with some friends. These social gatherings were Catherine's way of letting her hair down and she was very particular about how they were conducted. So particular, in fact, that she wrote out and displayed a list of dos and don'ts for her guests to observe. They still stand as probably the most sensible rules for party-giving ever devised.

These events were held in her main saloon, known as the Pavilion Hall and, as those invited passed inside, there above the entrance to the hall was a placard written in her own hand:

> 'Please be seated wherever you wish
> Your hostess hates all ceremonies
> Every guest in her home is free to do as he pleases.'

Nearby were pinned Catherine's 'Ten Commandments', also copied out in her own hand. Written 200 years ago, these rules, if their adoption was proposed for social occasions at Buckingham Palace today, would be regarded as scandalously revolutionary. Catherine, however, insisted that the highest and the lowest abide by them. They read:

'1). Leave your rank outside, the way you leave your hat and especially your sword.

2). Your order of precedence and your arrogance and any other such qualities, whatever they may be – leave them outside the door, too.

3). Be gay – without, however, breaking or spoiling anything.

4). Sit down, stand up, walk about as you please, regardless of who else is present.

5). Speak in a moderate voice, not too loudly, so that other people near you will not get headaches.

6). Discuss anything, argue anything, but without bitterness or hot temper.

7). Do not groan because of problems, do not yawn or cause yawns, do not inflict boredom or impose burdens on anybody else.

8). Innocent pranks should be met in the same spirit – what one person starts, others should join in and continue.

9). Eat well and with pleasure, but drink with moderation so that everyone, on going out the door, will be able to find his own feet.

10). Do not carry gossip from this room; what enters one ear should go out the other before it can go out through the door.'

Underneath, Catherine had written the scale of penalties for breaking these rules, which were all rigidly enforced:

'If anyone should behave contrary to the above rules, then, on the deposition of two witnesses, for each transgression each guilty person will drink a glass of cold water, the ladies not excepted, and read aloud a page of *The Adventures of Tolemaque, Son of Ulysses*. Anyone found guilty of two transgressions will learn by heart six lines of the same book and those found guilty of ten transgressions will never again be allowed inside the door.' Would that any modern royal showed even half as much sensibility.

Charlemagne (742–814). King of the Franks and ruler of the Holy Roman Empire, he sat on his marble throne for over 400 years. This, of course, he could never have managed without the assistance of his funeral directors. On his death they had his body embalmed and then dressed in the royal robes with the crown on his head, his sceptre in his hand and a suitably majestic expression on his face. This handsome cadaver was then propped up, sitting on his throne. There he remained until 1215, when the Emperor Frederick II had the corpse removed and buried in a gold and silver casket in the cathedral at Aix-La-Chapelle.

Charles I (1600–1649). King of England and midget. He stood a mere 4 ft 7 ins high in his stockinged feet, which meant that even before his head was cut off, he was the nation's shortest monarch. After his execution in Whitehall, this little body was taken to Windsor Castle where it was interred in the same vault that held the carcass of Henry VIII. Being so small it was soon mislaid and it stayed lost for nearly 200 years. Then it was rediscovered and a post-mortem was performed on Charles's remains by the royal surgeon, Sir Henry Halford. As a souvenir of his probings, Sir Henry took the fourth cervical vertebra which had been so neatly severed by the axe. For the next 30 years or so this morbid doctor shocked friends at dinner parties by using the vertebra as a salt-cellar – thus allowing Charles to serve his people at last. Alas, when Queen Victoria got to hear that part of her ancestor was being employed as a condiment-holder, she was rather unamused and she ordered the bone to be returned whence it came.

Charles II (1661–1700). King of Spain who seemed doomed never to enjoy life. He was known as 'Carlos the Bewitched' and although there was no direct evidence of any supernatural involvement, he certainly seemed to be rather unlucky, not least in the body he was given. He was something of a late developer, being unable to stand unaided until he was well past three, still breast-feeding in his fifth year and taking seven years to learn to walk. When he did grow up, his jaw was so deformed that he found it impossible to chew food and so had to swallow it in large lumps, thus playing merry hell with his other great complaint, indigestion.

Not surprisingly, Charles became a rather morbid individual with the passing years. Towards the end of his life he would summon a torch and descend into the dank vaults of the royal mausoleum to spend some time with his ancestors. When he got tired of gazing at coffins, he would summon an attendant and have the caskets opened up in order of their occupants' reigns, beginning with Charles I. He, alas, was much decayed and the features of Philip II were distorted but Philip III looked in far better shape, being nearly perfectly preserved. Sadly, though, he was even more delicate than he was in life and his remains crumbled into dust as soon as Charles touched them. Then it was on to the queens, whom he inspected one by one until he reached the body of Mary Louise, his first wife. This invariably proved too much and he had to be led away weeping. His health could only stand so much of this and in due course he joined the collection in the mausoleum on a permanent basis.

Charles IV (1748–1819). King of Spain whose interest in the affairs of state was commendably minimal. He once told Napoleon, 'Every day, winter and summer, I went shooting till 12, had dinner and at once returned to shooting until the fall of the evening. Manuel told me how things were going and I went to bed to begin again the same life the next day, unless any important ceremony prevented me.' After 20 years of this taxing routine, he abdicated.

Charles VI (1368–1422). King of France and royal fruitcake. After 1392 he was subject to repeated bouts of madness, during some of which he would smash furniture and tear his clothes. In his quieter moments, however, he imagined that he was made of glass and would break if moved. Under this undoubted handicap his country lost battles, territory and suffered a debilitating civil war.

Charles VII (d. 1167). King of Sweden and, despite the numerals after his name, the first king of that name to rule his country. Charles I, II, III, IV, V and VI never existed. Charles VII did – and he was assassinated.

Charles VII (1403–1461). King of France and, until his conscience was pricked by Joan of Arc, a dedicated pleasure-monger. Even while the English occupied Paris, the immature Charles amused himself with balls, entertainments and revelry, seemingly oblivious to the threat his country faced. One day a nobleman called La Hire came to the King to discuss the critical situation and found him engrossed in arranging one of his parties. Charles asked him what he thought of his elaborate plans. 'I think, sire,' said La Hire, 'that it is impossible for anyone to lose his kingdom more pleasantly than Your

Majesty.' Charles later pulled himself together and drove the English from all of France, except Calais.

Prince Charles Edward (1884–1954). Duke of Albany, grandson of Queen Victoria, brother of Princess Alice, Old Etonian and Nazi. While he was still in his teens he was plucked from the school, raised as a German princeling and, in 1900, became Duke of Coburg. During the First World War he enlisted in the Kaiser's army, was made a general and fought on the Russian front with the 1st Regiment of Prussian Guards and the 1st Saxon Hussars. After his country's surrender he lost his titles and became an increasingly enthusiastic activist on the extreme right. In 1935 he went the whole hog and joined the Nazi party.

A year later he was in London for the funeral of George V and, according to some reports, had the temerity to show up wearing a steel helmet and swastika armband. Yet his main purpose in attending was not to pay his respects, however eccentrically, to his late cousin, but to explore the possibility of an Anglo-German agreement. While staying with his sister at Kensington Palace, he met Anthony Eden, Duff Cooper, Astor of *The Times* and Neville Chamberlain. He also met the new King on several occasions. In due course he sent a report to Hitler. When war came he worked for the Red Cross but was still sufficiently tainted by his Nazi connections to be imprisoned by the Americans in 1945. He faced trial several times but was released in 1946 and retired to a small cottage where he died in 1954.

Princess Charlotte (1796–1817). The one and only child of George IV who, but for her agonised death in childbirth, would have succeeded him and supplanted Victoria as England's great queen of the nineteenth century.

In spite of an appalling childhood, during which she was buffeted between her dissipated father, restless mother and periodically deranged grandfather, she emerged as a merry young woman with an extraordinarily charitable heart. Her glowing good humour even survived her betrothal to the impoverished and emaciated-looking Prince Leopold of Saxe-Coburg. He was so poor that when he visited London in 1815 for the festival to celebrate victory over Napoleon, he could afford accommodation no more grand than rented lodgings above a grocer's shop in Marylebone High Street. At their wedding, when Leopold said, 'And with my worldly goods I thee endow,' Charlotte burst out laughing. They did, however, become devoted to each other.

Perhaps because of her own difficulties, Charlotte was a great patron of the down-trodden. After the Spitalfields riots, she helped set the area back on its feet by ordering 2,000 yards of silk from the mills there and even with something as prosaic as the royal meat contract she could be unusually sensitive. After she moved to Claremont House in Esher, several local butchers applied to supply her household. When she was told that these traders were wealthy men already earning a comfortable living, she asked if there were any other butchers in town. Only one, she was informed, but he was a very poor specimen and was in no position to supply meat to the royal table. Charlotte sent for him, lent him money so that he could compete with his well-heeled rivals and then awarded him her contract. It was England's immeasurable loss when this most worthwhile young woman perished in her dutiful attempts to produce an heir.

Prince Cherkassy (19th Century). A relative of the Russian royal family who lived in such mortal dread of boredom that at his estate on the heights above Cannes he employed 48 gardeners to change the plants in the flowerbeds overnight and so surprise him with a new arrangement each dawn.

Christian IV (1577–1648). King of Denmark, tireless reformer and an impressive swiller of booze. When he was on form he could drain some 30–40 goblets of wine a night. This he did in the happy knowledge that he could safely resort to the old soak's time-honoured excuse that it was 'purely for medicinal purposes', his court physician having written that 'It is good for people to drink themselves unconscious once a month. So doing gives the body greater ultimate strength, the flow of human water having been facilitated and the body likewise purged by sweating.'

Christian's drunkenness fascinated him and he went so far as to mark with a cross in his diary the days when he had to be assisted to his bed. A second or third cross would be added if he had been excessively drunk or partially paralysed. This diary was a charming document in which he also reported anything that caught his eye or fancy. For example: 'June 3 – Hans the lamplighter's Anna, who is 22 has just had twins. He is 88. I propose to investigate the matter.' Sadly, the outcome of this potentially riveting inquiry is not recorded.

Prince Christopher of Hesse (1901–1943). Brother-in-law of Prince Philip and a member of Hitler's SS. He had been impressed by the Nazis and was one of many young aristocrats and minor princelings whose membership helped to give the party a gloss of respectability in its early days. Soon after his marriage to Philip's 16-year-old sister Sophie in 1931, Christopher began his rise through the SS ranks. A mere ten months after being commissioned he was made Hauptsturmführer (Captain), then Sturmbannführer (Major) two months later. Within 18 months he had been created Obersturmbannführer (Lt. Colonel) and finally, in April 1936, he was promoted to Standartenführer (full Colonel). That same year he was also awarded his SS Sword of Honour.

In blazing this trail of spectacular preferment, he was considerably helped by his own brother, Philip, who was a confidant of both Hitler and Hermann Goering. It was through Goering that Christopher obtained his first real job for the Nazis and he was later head of the Abhordienst in Goering's Luftwaffe Research Office. This was the secret 'eaves-dropping' arm of the air force which tapped foreign diplomats' telephone calls and monitored their correspondence. In time it extended its sinister nose into the affairs of German citizens and became a prototype organisation for the Gestapo.

Yet unlike Philip of Hesse, who was implicated (albeit

indirectly) in the running of an asylum where the SS practised euthanasia on inmates, Christopher has never been linked to any atrocities. The SS records lodged at the Imperial War Museum, which list him under SS number 35903, do contain a large gap from 1938 to 1943 but there has never been evidence that he was anything other than a favoured time-server who indulged in some over-zealous snooping. Indeed, his family are animatedly insistent on the point. One of his sons, Prince Rainier of Hesse, told a British newspaper in 1985, 'A year before his death (1943), my father wrote to my mother back home expressing doubts about the whole development of Nazi Germany. He was pessimistic about the future and wanted to quit the party and the SS. He never did, presumably because he would have been treated as a deserter.'

Rainier also said that his father was merely an honorary member of the SS – a claim which, while one would not wish to contest it in this case, is made with such frequency by surviving relatives that one wonders why the SS was not disbanded through lack of interest. One thing, however, is certain: Christopher may not have been anywhere near the first division of Nazi uglies but, in the Thirties, this brother-in-law of Prince Philip prospered in an organisation which was busy killing opponents, suppressing trade unions and the Press, persecuting Jews and preaching a gospel of hatred and racial purity. Even honorary membership was incompatible with decency.

Fortunately for the British royal family, the moral dilemma of whether they should ever entertain Christopher never arose. He was killed in 1943 while flying with the Luftwaffe over Italy. Three years later, his widow married Prince Georg Wilhelm of Hanover and, although she had no contact with Philip for some time after the war, she now visits him regularly. As Prince Rainier has said, 'Our relationship with the royal family has not been damaged by my father's activities during the Second World War.'

Chulalonkorn (1853–1910). King of Siam whose Oriental ways translated rather awkwardly to Victorian dining-rooms. When he was entertained by the Duke of Portland in 1897, all present were somewhat taken aback by the loudness of the royal visitor's voice. Asked by the butler at the end of the meal if he would take port, sherry, claret or Madeira, he caused considerable alarm by shouting 'PORT!' at the top of his voice. It was, apparently, the custom in Chulalonkorn's native land for those of royal birth to make the most noise.

Matthias Corvinus I (1443–1490). King of Hungary and humorist. He once passed a law saying that all ladies in waiting should sit in his presence because their ugly faces were less of an eyesore that way.

Craterus (3rd Century). Brother of King Antigonus of Macedonia and a victim of precocious growth. He experienced infancy, youth, marriage, fatherhood and his dotage – all before he had attained his eighth birthday. Such accelerated development is not as preposterous as it may appear. There is the attested case of Philip Howarth of Canada who was born on 21 February 1806 and within a year had achieved the shape and development of a schoolboy. By the age of two and a half he was fully equipped for manhood, with his voice broken and sexual organs in full working order, and at three he weighed seven and a half stone and stood 3 ft 4½ ins tall.

> '*It is the lot of a king to do well but to be ill spoken of.*'
>
> ANTISTHENES.

Queen Alexandra, long-suffering wife of Edward VII and friend of The Elephant Man

Albert Victor, Duke of
Clarence and sometime Jack the
Ripper suspect

Bokassa I of the Central African
Empire wearing 4% of the
national income on his head
(Camera Press)

Boris III, Czar of Bulgaria and excitable railway enthusiast
(*The Mansell Collection*)

Alfred, Duke of Edinburgh, who supplemented his £25,000 a year by charging for introductions to his royal relatives

Edward, Duke of Kent, Queen Victoria's socialist father (*The Mansell Collection*)

Ludwig II of Bavaria, the Ruritanian monarch who lived in a world of make-believe (*The Mansell Collection*)

(Right) *Leopold II*, unloved King of the Belgians who bled the Congo dry for his own profit

(Below) *Queen Mary*, consort of George V and a formidable scrounger of objets d'art

Princess Michael of Kent, the Page Three Princess
— the tabloid man's dream *(Camera Press)*

The face that launched a thousand slips –
Prince Philip by his son Andrew *(Camera Press)*

D

'*I have always regarded and written of monarchy as
a profoundly corrupting influence upon our national
life, imposing an intricate snobbishness on our
dominant classes . . .* '

H.G. WELLS, 1944.

Robert Francis Damiens (d. 1757). Unemployed butler and
would-be assassin of King Louis XV of France. Despite the fact
that his feeble attempt only resulted in the superficial wounding
of the royal person, Damiens was tortured repeatedly, charged
with 'divine and human lese-majesty', no less, and then bar-
barically and publicly dismembered. Yet even after his flesh
had been picked, hot sulphur poured in the open wounds and
his limbs torn from his body by wild horses, the French
people's outrage was still not satisfactorily avenged. Every trace
of his existence had to be removed. The house where he was
born in Artois was razed to the ground, no other building was
allowed to be erected on the site and all his surviving relatives
were exiled. Typically, within three decades, the French had
second thoughts about their royal family and judicially murdered
the lot.

Darius (550 BC–486 BC). King of Persia who owed his crown
and kingdom to a horse. After the death of the previous Persian
ruler, the seven young nobles who formed the imperial council
met and agreed on the following novel method for finding a
successor: they would all retire that night and the one among
them whose horse neighed first at dawn the next day would be
the new king. Darius won, although it was not entirely a matter

of chance, since his groom made sure his master's horse would be in a frisky and vocal mood in the morning by providing him with a mare.

As a system of choosing a ruler, there is, on the face of it, a good deal to be said for this method. Darius reigned for 35 years, built the world's first highway network, created a primitive form of postal service, had a canal dug between the Red Sea and the Nile, established a coinage and enlarged his empire until it stretched from Bulgaria in the north to China in the east.

Demetrius Poliocretes (336 BC–285 BC). King of Macedonia and resourceful roué. When Lamia, the much-prized courtesan of Greece, demanded the sum of 250 talents (or £290,000) to sleep with him, he not only paid up but slapped a special tax on soap to cover his expenses.

Dmitri II (d. 1289). King of Georgia and known, quite rightly, as 'the Devoted'. He was executed by the Mongols after surrendering himself as a victim to save his people.

Don Carlos (b. 1545). Son of Philip II of Spain and the owner of a monumental temper. His paddies were inflicted on anyone who annoyed him but he reserved his special rages for those who were in no position to answer back. One such was the cobbler who made him a pair of boots that, when tried on, turned out to be a bit on the small side. Don Carlos then forced the poor wretch to stew and eat the offending footwear.

> *'The animal known as king is by nature carnivorous.'*
>
> MARCUS CATO.

E

*'The plain truth is that the antiquity of
English monarchy will not bear looking into.'*

THOMAS PAINE.

Edgar I (943–975). King of England and saint whose canonisation went through on the nod, despite his record of having seduced two nuns before he was even 16. The Church authorities, of course, were more impressed by his lavish patronage but they also admired his innate flair for retribution and justice, especially his valuable pioneering work in the fields of nostril-slitting, eye-gouging and ear-ripping.

Indeed, his special forte was making the punishment fit the crime, a talent he put to inventive use when he visited an Andover earlderman. As was sometimes the custom, the noble had been requested to supply his own daughter as the royal guest's playmate for the night. But to save her blushes, the earlderman had substituted a housemaid. She, to her credit, gave the unsuspecting King a thoroughly good time. So much so that when, in due course, Edgar discovered that she was a ringer, he not only awarded her the noble's house but also instructed that her former employer and his family should act as her servants.

Edward IV (1442–1483). King of England and, at a height of 6 ft 3 ins, by far and away our tallest monarch. His large body meant that he had an impressive capacity for tucking away food and this was no mean advantage for someone who loved his grub as much as Edward. Yet even with a frame as big as his, he frequently reached bursting point with food still annoyingly on the table. It was the age-old problem of the dedicated nose-bagger – how do you go on eating when you are full up? Edward, however, had a solution. 'In food and drink he was most immoderate,' wrote Dominic Mancini, a visitor to his court, 'it was his habit to take an emetic for the delight of gorging his stomach once more.'

Such manners seemed not to have the slightest effect on his career as a ladies' man, probably because they were offset by his easy-going charm and snappy dress sense. He seemed to have rather a thing about older women and he chased after them with such relentless vigour that a succession of widows and mature spinsters were brought to his bed. The observant Mancini noted, 'He pursued with no discrimination the married and the unmarried, the noble and the lowly; however, he took none by force. He overcame all by money and promises and, having conquered them, he dismissed them.' This insatiable fun-lover succumbed to a fever at the age of just 41.

Edward VII (1841–1910). **King of England, Emperor of India** and, among other things, a pyromaniac. It might seem strange but when he was the Prince of Wales he enjoyed nothing more than watching someone else's house burn down. He and his friends, Lord Hartington and the Duchess of Manchester, would dress up in old clothes and go many a street to see a particularly good fire. As far as they were concerned, the bigger the blaze the better and Captain Shaw of the London Fire Brigade was under strict instructions to notify the Prince's Marlborough House residence of any sizeable conflagration. The fire stations at Watling Street and Chandos Street were even said to keep a spare fireman's uniform for him.

Whether Edward was drawn by the thrill of seeing flames devour some poor wretch's home or just the excitement of a big event, we shall never know, but there was a somewhat malicious streak in his character. Nothing seemed to amuse him as much as the discomfort of others and he imagined himself to be at his most risible when filling his guests' beds with dead game birds, dried peas or, on one occasion, a live lobster. Sticky pear-drops infiltrated into the recesses of his friends' evening clothes never failed to raise a royal guffaw and oh how he laughed as he tipped his brandy over the sycophantic Christopher Sykes. Even the blind were fair game and once, when he saw the sightless Duke of Mecklenburg hove into view, he took the man's hand, placed it on the arm of the hugely fat Helen Henneker and said to the blind Duke, 'Now don't you think Helen has a lovely little waist?'

For a man who was supposed to be such an arch-diplomatist, Edward could be extraordinarily insensitive. This was especially true in matters of dress, to which he attached quite ridiculous importance. He was forever correcting guests about their attire and decorations and was quite prepared to ruin a newcomer's debut at court to uphold his precious standards. One doubts if an admiral's daughter ever forgot the time she arrived for a royal party in a dress which hung an inch above her ankles. 'I am afraid you must have made a mistake,' the King said tartly, 'this is a dinner, not a tennis party.' Exit embarrassed girl, feeling about as tall as her disputed hem.

Of course, as far as his own appearance was concerned, no one was allowed to pass comment. When Sir Frederick Johnstone was rash enough to call him 'Tum-tum' to his face, Edward cut him dead, for he was especially touchy about his weight. He had good reason to be. In 1905 his waist measurement was no less than 47 inches and most of this was self-inflicted. It was, in fact, layer upon layer of lard, laid down over the years by pigging vast amounts of fodder. A typical day's intake when he was at Sandringham went something like this: breakfast – bacon and eggs, haddock, chicken, toast and butter; elevenses – a bowl of turtle soup; luncheon – a multi-course event; tea – poached eggs, petits fours, preserved ginger, rolls and scones, hot cakes, cold cakes, sweet cakes and short-cakes; dinner – never less than 12 courses and maybe more. Often a large cold chicken would be placed by his bedside so that he could refresh himself after a hard night's prowl.

It was not just the sheer quantity of food that did the damage (although anyone who could ship several dozen oysters in minutes, as he did, will sooner or later have a date with the doctor), it was the richness of it as well. In amongst his itinerary for dinner was invariably some form of game and not just a simple roasted bird either. His chef took grouse, partridge or pheasant and stuffed them with such a sequence of fillings that they were like a gastronome's Russian doll. A pheasant, for instance, might be implanted with a snipe or woodcock, which in turn had its innards replaced by truffles. The whole thing was then coated in some exotic and glutinous sauce. The King also adored Côtelettes de becassines à la Sauvoroff, which took longer to pronounce than to eat. These were snipe, boned and halved, stuffed with foie gras and forcemeat, moulded into small cutlets, grilled in a pig's caul and served on silver dishes with small slices of truffle and Madeira sauce.

Readers with delicate stomachs may care to leave us at this juncture and rejoin at the next item, for another of Edward's favourite dishes was ortolans. These were small garden buntings, a relative of the yellowhammer, which were trapped live in nets in the South of France, caged in darkened rooms where they were fattened up on millet, then roasted, served in threes in a rich sauce and eaten by hand from the feet upwards. Perhaps the most memorable dish associated with Edward was one whose invention neatly combined his two great interests – his stomach and his loins. He was dining at the Cafe de Paris in the 1880s and, to make the evening go with a swing, the chef, Henri Charpentier, had devised a pancake sauce of maraschino, curacao and kirschwasser. Not surprisingly, this combustible fluid ignited in the chafing dish. The chef was aghast but Edward, who never knowingly spurned a good solid pudding, ate every last pancake. In honour of the Prince's companion, the dish was christened 'Crêpes Suzettes'.

No doubt the lady showed her appreciation later that evening. In this, she would have been no different from all the rest of the unending stream of high-born ladies and low-slung courtesans who serviced 'Edward the Caresser', as Henry James called him. The details of these liaisons are too tedious and well-worn to bear repetition here. All, that is, except one incident from the second decade of his marriage when the royal philanderer received his come-uppance at the hands of a small boy. It took place in 1875 when the Prince paid a sneaky visit to his French mistress, Princess Jeanne de Sagan, at her residence in Mello. Not long after he arrived, Edward steered the lady towards her bedroom and was soon heavily engaged in reacquainting himself with her charms. Who then should come along but de Sagan junior? Perhaps attracted by what his childish ears thought were cries for help, he had rushed into his mother's boudoir next to the bedroom only to see a pile of clothes, unmistakably those belonging to the Prince, lying on her chair. He was disgusted; so disgusted, in fact, that he gathered every single garment into his arms, ran to the nearest balcony and hurled every last stitch of them into the fountains below.

Moments later, Edward came padding out of the bedroom, his face a study in smug satisfaction. Then he saw the empty chair. A stray sock led his gaze along the carpet to the window. It was open and he could hear voices below. Raised voices, they were, with a touch of panic in them and when he peeped round the curtains he saw that they belonged to a group of servants frantically fishing some clothes out of a goldfish pond. His clothes, in fact.

The Prince was beside himself with fury and was still ranting and raving when, a short while later, he left the house in borrowed trousers that were far too tight. To us voyeurs, a century on, this is one of the most pleasing episodes of Edward's life. Even for a king, he stood on his own dignity too much to be likable and one cannot help feeling that, for his own good, this great stickler for correct dressing should have been caught with his trousers down a bit more often.

Edward VIII (1894–1972). The third best King of England we had in 1936. Although his apologists would protest at the suggestion, his attitude to the monarchy was probably contained in one of the many emotional outbursts he made while Prince of Wales. 'What does it take to be a good king?' he once rhetorically asked his then mistress Freda Dudley Ward, 'you must be a figurehead, a wooden man! Do nothing to upset the Prime Minister or the Court of the Archbishop of Canterbury! Show yourself to the people! Mind your manners! Go to Church! What sort of modern man wants that sort of life?' He certainly did not but then one doubts if life as Mrs Simpson's consort was really any more appetising.

St Edwold (9th Century). Brother of King Edmund of East Anglia who, on tiring of being the subject of forelock-tugging and blind obedience, renounced his royal lifestyle and became a hermit. His cell was on top of a hill four miles from Cerne in Dorset and there, sustained by nothing but bread and water, he sat at his devotions until his death.

Edwy (940–959). King of England and a thoroughly impatient youth. The 15-year-old ruler caused something of a stir at his coronation banquet by slipping out of the hall to join his sweetheart Elgiva in an ante-chamber. When the Abbot of Glastonbury and a bishop went to look for him, they found their new monarch heavily engaged on the couch with his red-blooded companion and her equally enthusiastic mother. The crown of England was lying discarded on the floor. The two clerics managed somehow to prise the threesome apart, gave them a sharp lecture and then dragged the King back to his place at high table. Edwy later had his revenge by exiling the abbot but never quite got the hang of being king and was deposed in 959.

Lord Effingham (18th Century). Deputy Earl Marshal of England and the man who presided over the worst organised coronation ceremony in British history. That George III was crowned at all on that late September day in 1761 remains one of the deep and abiding mysteries of monarchy.

Even before the great day dawned the gremlins were at work

– which is more than can be said of the men who had been engaged to put up the decorations. Outraged at their pay and conditions, they had downed bunting and had refused to stick up so much as a piece of ribbon until their grievances had been met. The dispute dragged on and only last-minute arbitration got the lads back up their ladders and the garlands in their place, or at least approximately so. Thus, by coronation morning, the stage for Britain's foremost pageant had been somehow set. All it needed was for the King to occupy it; something he would no doubt have done bang on time had not Lord Effingham managed to mislay both the royal canopy and the Sword of State, neither of which were small objects. The ensuing delay of some hours meant that the procession to Westminster Abbey did not start until midday.

Once at the Abbey, things went from bad to worse. A succession of decrepit old clergymen droned on and on interminably and the Bishop of Salisbury, whose grasp on reality was evidently far from firm, made repeated and puzzling references to the number of years that the King had already sat on the throne. To George, weighed down by his heavy robes and bored visibly to distraction, this must have felt like the literal truth. Unfortunately for him, only when the last old wind-bag had had his say did the ceremony come to a blessed conclusion. It had lasted six hours and meant that the return procession was conducted at dusk, something of an annoyance, to say the least, for the waiting crowds. A glimpse of their newly crowned monarch through the deepening gloom seemed poor reward for their patience.

By the time the King and all his guests arrived at the banquet, the Lord High Steward, Lord Talbot, was on the verge of a nervous collapse. His condition did not improve when it was discovered that there had been a fearful mix-up over the seating arrangements, leaving some of the most exalted standing at the back of the hall and their far more inferior brethren lording it at the high tables. The barons of the Cinque Ports and the Knights of the Bath were, apparently, particularly difficult to placate.

The incident, however, that made the day one that Lords Effingham and Talbot would really remember concerned the entrance of the King's Champion. This, in theory, is the moment of time-honoured drama when the holder of that ancient office comes mounted on a charger to the coronation assembly and throws down the gauntlet in a ringing challenge to the king's enemies. The essence of his role is to look brave, heroic and dignified and, to ensure such an appearance, Lord Talbot had spent hours rehearsing the knight and his horse at Westminster Hall. Imagine, therefore, milord's abject horror when, come his grand entrance, the King's Champion backed into the hall and presented his horse's flatulent rump to his sovereign. It was said that Lord Talbot heard the ensuing laughter ringing in his ears for the rest of his life. The King alone was sympathetic but, in the end, with the horse beginning to deposit visible signs of nervousness on the floor, even he was moved to complain. Lord Effingham's reply was priceless. 'It is true, sire, that there has been some neglect,' he said and then, without thinking, added, 'but I have taken care that the next coronation shall be regulated in the exactest manner possible.'

Elizabeth (1709–1762). Empress of Russia who was ruthlessly determined to be the star fashion turn at her court. She was so obsessed with never being outshone that she not only plundered her treasury to buy vast numbers of gowns but also introduced new laws to make things difficult for her rivals. It was, for instance, illegal to receive the latest French fashions before she did and it was treated as a crime against the state for a lady to wear dresses of the same pattern as those of the Empress.

Avoiding such duplication was by no means easy. Most queens and empresses have a wardrobe but Elizabeth had more of a warehouse and inside was a huge collection of clothes. It was so big that when only part of it was hit by fire in 1744, no fewer than 4,000 dresses went up in smoke. By the time of her death in 1762, Elizabeth had accumulated so many outfits that she left over 15,000 dresses (some never worn), two large chests full of silk stockings, two more bulging with garters and ribbons and more than 1,000 pairs of shoes. Small wonder, then, that despite changing her costume up to six times a day, she was said never to have worn the same outfit twice.

Elizabeth of Hungary (1207–1231). Daughter of King Andreas II and a paragon of royal saintliness. As the wife of Louis IV, Landgraf of Thuringia, she astonished even his well-behaved court with her piety, hatred of pomp and good works. After her husband's death on the Crusades in 1227, she was forced out of her home by her brother-in-law and decided to give herself totally to a life of self-denial. She put on a nun's garment and lived in a cottage at the foot of the hill below her old castle, from where she devoted herself to the care of the poor and the sick. Elizabeth spent her days in incessant prayer, cleaning the homes of the poor and fishing to help feed them. She gave all her annual allowance of 500 marks to the poor and met her own meagre needs from the income she derived from carding and spinning. She died, worn out, aged only 24 and four years later was canonised.

Elizabeth (1837–1898). Empress of Austria and a stunning royal beauty. Yet her looks, however striking, were not nearly so breathtaking as the lengths she went to to improve and preserve them. Not for her the half-hearted diet or the quick going-over with soap and water; instead she subjected herself to every cosmetic torture known to woman – and a few that had hitherto not even been imagined. As a result, she held for decades her position as the most attractive and stylish royal in the world – a kind of nineteenth-century Princess Diana.

As with that lady, nature had been more than kind to Elizabeth. She had a magnificent head of chestnut hair, finely proportioned features, a lustrous complexion and an extraordinarily trim figure. It was this slender shape that was at the heart of her most outlandish obsessions. Trim was not good enough; nothing less than perfection, with an 18-inch waist and everything else to match, would ever satisfy Elizabeth. To achieve this, her diet verged on the self-destructive. Breakfast consisted of a single dry biscuit taken with unsweetened black tea, although later in the morning she would allow herself a glass of meat juice. This was freshly extracted from several pounds of fillet beef by means of a special apparatus that she always carried with her. She would then have nothing more until she dined in the evening. This was a more varied meal, often just iced milk, raw eggs and a glass of Tokay, sometimes nothing at all and occasionally a plate of whatever food she was currently swearing by. Once, when she was staying at Combermere in England, it was turtle soup, which meant that live turtles had to be brought to the house every day. This, of course, was in addition to the cases of sea water that had to be imported from the Welsh coast to the estate each morning so that the Empress could have her warm salt-water baths.

Naturally there were times when she could not help deviating from this strict dietary regime but she was always quick to correct any backsliding. She weighed herself twice a day and if she was even a few ounces over what she believed to be her top weight of 7 stone 10lb (hardly normal for a woman of over 5 ft 6 in in height in mid-Victorian times) then she immediately confined herself to the skimpiest of rations. If a starvation diet of oranges and raw meat juices did not do the trick then she resorted to a slimmer's draught of the whites of half a dozen eggs mixed with salt.

Elizabeth supported these outrageous efforts with a fearsome programme of exercise. She took a daily walk of anything up to 20 miles, rode incessantly and even had gymnastic equipment installed in her private apartments at Laxenburg so that she could begin each day with a workout. She was, indeed, truly hyperactive. When staying in England she often hunted six days a week and back home in Austria she was so fearful of boredom setting in that she had a little circus built in one of the courts of the Hofburg so that, when the mood took her, she could put on a circus dress and ride and perform tricks on the backs of her superb horses. Even when she had no choice but to lie down, as in the bath or in bed, the figure-conscious Empress still managed to press on with her beauty and fitness treatment.

She bathed daily in distilled water but if she felt her body was in danger of losing its unique suppleness then she would immerse herself in warm olive oil – a practice not without its perils, as a narrow escape with oil heated to almost boiling point once proved. At night she retired to a plain iron bedstead (so good for the deportment) and, in an effort to preserve the slenderness of her waist, often slept with wet towels around her middle.

There was little point in having such a remarkable figure if it was never shown to advantage and no detail of her apparel was too small to be overlooked. When hunting at Combermere, Elizabeth summoned a local tailor to the house each morning for the sole task of sewing the skirt of her riding habit to her figure-hugging bodice, so that there would not be the slightest crease around her 18-inch waist. These pernickety attentions, however, were as nothing compared to the fuss she made over her hair. It was, admittedly, magnificent: long chestnut tresses which fell down to below her knees and were regarded by her as nothing less than a valued part of the Austrian national heritage. However, this was small consolation to the poor individuals who had to maintain it in all its glory, for brushing these locks, an operation that lasted several hours each day, was a far from simple affair. First a white tablecloth was laid upon the floor, then a chair placed on the cloth and, only when the Empress was finally seated, could the brushing commence. Great care had to be taken because if so much as a single hair fell upon the cloth then Elizabeth would be upset for the rest of the day. She had such a phobic fear of anything snagging in her hair that she insisted her hairdressers had no rings on their fingers, cut their nails short and wore gloves at all times.

There was nothing ordinary about the way this hair was washed. The shampoo was 20 bottles of the best French brandy mixed with the yolks of a dozen eggs and Elizabeth forbade the use of any artificial drying method. Instead she put on a silk robe and walked up and down until all trace of dampness had gone. Mercifully, her complexion required a less complicated pit-stop. She was mostly content to use a simple toilet cream, although there were the occasional nights when she wore a mask lined with raw veal and the odd evening when she would smear her face and neck with crushed strawberries.

However, even these ministrations could not ward off the debilitating effects of her constant dieting and as she neared the age of 50 her skin tones began to deteriorate. Yet she was still a remarkably youthful figure and although she once said that 'Life will be worthless to me when I am no longer desirable,' she led too restless a life to be thought of as conventionally vain. There was her hunting and riding and her walking and travelling, some of which she did incognito or, at least, unannounced. Few Victorian families strolling along the promenade at Bournemouth or Cromer, for example, probably ever knew that the tall lady dressed in brown alpaca who sat on the beach staring out to sea and writing poetry was the Empress of Austria.

Indeed, as one who had always inspired admiration rather than love, she increasingly became a rather lonely figure as she moved from haunt to haunt. She had never been very willing to play the public role of the Emperor's wife and by her mid-forties she had effectively ceased to act out the part in private either. Nor could she count on the love of her two children if she had wanted to. She had taken little interest in their upbringing, save chipping in with the odd eccentric idea, such as when she suggested that the nerves of her son Rudolph might be trained to withstand shocks by having pistols fired off suddenly near his ear.

So as she moved into late middle age, Elizabeth's life was more and more that of the introverted and wealthy tourist. Yet, however and wherever she travelled, her erect, slender figure was still unmistakably that of the Empress Elizabeth and as she boarded a lake steamer at Geneva one day in September 1898, an Italian anarchist with a grudge against royalty had no difficulty in picking her out. He moved in and with the iron file he had bought for a few sous in Lausanne market, he stabbed her in the chest. Somehow she managed to stagger a hundred yards but the file had pierced her heart and she collapsed and died, aged 61.

Enil-Bani (d. 1837 BC). Ruler of the ancient kingdom of Sumer and Akkad who ascended the throne by a most unusual route. He was a gardener in the service of King Erra-Imitti and, as luck would have it, chosen as the 'king for a day' as part of the court's new year festivities. This, however, was not a cause for much celebrating in the Enil-Bani household. The custom was that each mock king would be allowed 24 hours of fun and games but after it was over he would then be the star turn at the next human sacrifice. Such a fate seemed in store for the unlucky gardener until, halfway through his day of glory, Erra-Imitti obligingly dropped down dead. The local wise men put their heads together and decided that since Enil-Bani was already on the throne, he might as well stay there; and he did, ruling well for 24 years.

Eric II (d. 1104). King of Denmark and known as Eric the Memorable. Unfortunately no one can now remember why.

Ernest II (1818–1893). Duke of Saxe-Coburg-Gotha and Prince Albert's wicked older brother. Unlike the workaholic prig who became Queen Victoria's adored consort, Ernest was a man of more earthy tastes. All he asked of life was a bellyful of food, a hunting field by day and an accommodating wench at night and, since his word was law in the little kingdom that he ruled, he was rarely disappointed. While his brother was busying himself, helping his wife rule her great empire and organising his grand schemes, Ernest went assiduously about the business of pleasure. As a result, the only great exhibition Ernest ever made was of himself. By late middle age he resembled nothing as much as a crotchety bulldog in a frock coat and was so gross that he needed special chairs built for him. It must have seemed to Queen Victoria a cruel injustice that while her lean, thrifty husband pegged out at the age of 42, his debauched brother, who was kept afloat only by the good offices of several low-grade money-lenders, went on to a ripe old age of 75.

About the only thing that the two siblings did have in common, apart from their parentage, was the fact that both married women who worshipped the ground on which they walked. Ernest's wife was Princess Alexandrina of Baden, a nervous little creature who blinked almost continuously. He returned her adoration with calculated indifference, flaunting his lady friends and forcing Alexandrina to live in a humble apartment up in the roof of Schloss Kalenburg. Despite this, she would hear no ill spoken of her husband. When he died she made sure that his current floozie was taken care of and, in a curious echo of Victoria's veneration of Albert, Alexandrina even declared that the little villa that Ernest had used for his assignations should be left just as it was when last he panted on its couch. She insisted, she said, 'because it was there that my beloved Ernest lived such happy hours'. A forgiving nature, indeed.

Ethelbald (d. 860). King of Wessex; he complicated the royal family tree no end by marrying his 15-year-old stepmother, Judith.

Ethelred (968–1016). King of England. Unready he may have been but at times that was the least of his problems. When he was a child his mother Elfrida beat him so severely with a large candle that he developed a phobic fear of them. For the remainder of his life he refused to have the wretched things carried in procession before him.

> *'That the king can do no wrong is a necessary and fundamental principle of the English constitution.'*
>
> BLACKSTONE'S LEGAL COMMENTARY, 1760.

F

'Wait till I'm king, I'll get you.'

THE YOUNG PRINCE FAROUK.

Farouk I (1920–1965). King of Egypt, road hog, racketeer, glutton, pickpocket, womaniser and, ultimately, overweight playboy in exile. He was, in fact, the king who never grew up. If he wanted something he would take it, whether it was Winston Churchill's pocket watch (purloined from the great man's waistcoat and only returned under protest) or a beautiful woman married to someone else. Instant gratification was his motto and he lived, and in the end, died by it. He liked fizzy drinks and so would swill down over 30 bottles of orange pop a day; he wanted pornography and so had rooms full of it. Similarly if he did not like something then he would want it immediately removed. Lions, for instance, once featured in a series of nightmares he had, so one morning he went down to Cairo Zoo and shot every one of these beasts in their cages. This typically petulant gesture, incidentally, brought him no relief from the dreams.

Equally childish was his desire to use the highways of Egypt as his own personal backyard and race his cars untroubled by any restrictions. Very early in his reign, the local police stopped him while he was on one of his ton-up sorties and so, to avoid this happening again, he had all his 100-plus cars painted fire-engine red and made it illegal for anyone else to own a vehicle of that colour. He could thus speed along, safe in the knowledge that when the police saw a red blur whizz past them, they knew not to give chase. If any other motorist tried to pass him then he would shoot at their tyres. He was also very sensitive about the accidents he caused and once jailed a newspaper editor for running a story that Farouk's car was always shadowed by an ambulance to pick up casualties.

Yet his infantile nature was perhaps most readily apparent in his desire to possess bright and sparkling objects, regardless of their use to him. What he could not buy, he would steal and he even had an old lag sprung from Tural prison to teach him the rudiments of pickpocketing. Like some latter-day Artful Dodger, he practised with a suit into which tiny bells had been sewn and in time he became highly skilled. At receptions and parties he would move among the company, brushing against the dignitaries and their ladies and then slipping off into an ante-room where he would empty his pockets of watches, wallets, lighters and powder compacts. Eventually an entire warehouse was filled with these items, which even included the ceremonial sword, belt and medals stolen from the body of the Shah of Persia as it passed in state through Egypt in 1944.

There was almost no temptation he was able to resist. When German residents fled Cairo at the start of the war and left their homes unoccupied, Farouk organised nocturnal looting parties to strip them of their contents. He also ran countless schemes to rook his own people. One such scam was known as 'Farouk's Treasure Box' and involved one of his confederates contacting a businessman with the suggestion that the King would appreciate the gift of a box of chocolates. The man would then go to Ahmed Naguib's, the suggested shop, and find that although the chocolates were cheap, the box was a good deal pricier. It was, to be precise, a jewel-encrusted casket and hit the till at £650. Not wanting to risk the royal wrath, the businessman would cough up and Farouk would duly receive the present, wolf down the chocolates, return the box for the next mug to buy and transfer the £650 into his account.

Some of his other fiddles were positively mundane by comparison: monkeying around with import duties to hinder his commercial rivals, making his income tax-exempt and selling one of his yachts, the *Fark el-Behar*, to the government, persuading them to refit it luxuriously at public expense and then commandeering it for his pleasure jaunts. For the honeymoon of his second marriage in 1951, however, he surpassed himself, asking for the wedding gifts in gold and then having them all melted into ingots and packed into the hold of his yacht. He was away with his 16-year-old bride for no fewer than 13 weeks, living it up so freely (he flew his barber from Italy to Paris just to give him a shave one morning) that the trip cost £1,000 a day.

This proved to be one of his final flings as King of Egypt. Despite occasional and highly publicised gestures of charity, he was deeply unpopular and in 1952 was almost nonchalantly deposed by Colonel Nasser. His parting shot, as he went into exile with his 29-strong retinue, was typically immature. 'It isn't easy, you know, to govern Egypt,' he said. Fine words from a king who had once appointed a man Minister of Justice because he liked his moustache.

While Farouk headed for the playgrounds of the Mediterranean, his country's new government began to go through his effects and what they found astounded them. Among the trinkets and swag from his larceny and obscene novelties and magazines from his pornography collection, there was a wondrous hoard of genuine treasure: 8,500 coins and medals in gold, 164 in platinum, the largest stamp collection in the world, 1,261 works of art in gold and silver, a library of rare books, hundreds of valuable clocks and watches, four drawers full of solid gold fountain pens, diamond-studded dice, Fabergé items and case upon case of ancient Egyptian artefacts. There was enough, in fact, to keep the men from Sotheby's busy for three months while they logged it all. When they had finished, the contents of Farouk's grottos raised over £700,000 at auction – the equivalent of many millions today.

By the time these items went under the hammer, the ex-king was settled in a villa near Rome. He was only 32 but with his weight rising inexorably towards 20 stone, he looked far older.

In his head, however, he was still the same immature Farouk. He slept, ate large and sickly meals, lazed about, raced his cars, went night-clubbing in the company of his two Albanian body-guards and had rows with his wife. In 1954 she divorced him and the big fat overgrown kid consoled himself with a succession of shapely gold-diggers. That there was still quite a lot of precious metal left for them to mine was demonstrated by an 18-year-old former Miss Naples called Irma Minutolo. In return for allowing him to make a close study of her and her 42-inch chest, she was installed in his city flat, had her singing lessons paid for, was launched into society and, when it was all over, walked off with a trunkful of goodies and four cars.

Yet playing sugar-daddy to such women came cheap compared to his other hobby of gambling. He once lost £25,000 in one night at Deauville Casino and was always game for any flutter – baccarat (at which he was quite capable of winning or losing up to 50 million francs in just a few hours), slot machines, poker or even the football pools, which he did under the name of Mr Omar. With losses that sometimes ran to over £1 million a year, Farouk eventually had to trim his staff to 12 and cut his transport fleet down to three cars and a small yacht.

These dwindling possessions were no substitute for all the toys that had amused him while he was king and, as the tenth anniversary of his exile came and went, he began the descent into torpor. Now in his forties, he would spend most days in a darkened room, stuffing himself with chocolates, drinking fruit juices and doing nothing more taxing than watching television. He could still, however, raise the energy for a girl and on 17 March 1965 he took his latest, Annamaria Gatti, to his favourite French restaurant. The 45-year-old Farouk tucked away a dozen oysters, lobster thermidor, a treble portion of roast lamb, chips and string beans, a great mountainous helping of chestnut trifle and two oranges. Then he died. He was the last King of Egypt, the Final Pharaoh, and he left for posterity not only the memory of his childish antics but also his one recorded outburst of genuine wit. 'Soon there will only be five kings left,' he once told ex-King Zog of Albania, 'Spades, Hearts, Diamonds, Clubs and the King of England.'

Maria Fedorovna (1847–1928). Empress of Russia, aunt of George V and a soft-hearted old soul. She once saved the life of a condemned man by moving a comma in a warrant signed by her husband Alexander III. He had written 'Pardon impossible, to be sent to Siberia', but after Maria had edited the document it read 'Pardon, impossible to be sent to Siberia'. The man was duly released.

Ferdinand I (1861–1948). King of Bulgaria and an amateur naturalist of some note. He was a good enough zoologist and botanist to write the standard work on the flora and fauna of Brazil and he also built up a vast personal aviary which contained every known species of bird found in his land. A love of wildlife did not, however, stop this shifty-looking monarch from ruthlessly trying to exterminate every owl in Bulgaria. He believed them to be harbingers of doom – a superstition that, in its way, was no more daft than his insistence on always wearing gloves to ward off evil spirits and never doing anything remotely adventurous on the 13th of each month.

Frederick I (1754–1816). King of Wurtemburg who was so fat that, at the 1815 Congress of Vienna, a semi-circular piece had to be cut out of the mahogany negotiating table in order to accommodate his stomach.

Frederick VI (1768–1839). King of Denmark whose tricky start in life was followed by a most bewildering childhood. The youngster's miseries began not long after he had uttered his first cry, when royal etiquette dictated that the entire court should troop past the foot of his mother Matilda's bed and pay homage to the little prince. The strain of being pleasant to several hundred nosy wellwishers just hours after her confinement nearly killed the Queen. Danish protocol's next piece of child-care wisdom was the tradition that the royal baby had to be wet-nursed by all the women of the court in strict rotation according to their rank.

Soon after the society dames had finished playing pass-the-parcel with him, the infant was given his own retinue of servants. Seizing this chance to build up a nice nest egg of royal favour for the future, these forelock-tuggers enthusiastically granted young Frederick's every whim. So chronically was the little darling indulged that within a few years he had become a petulant, ungovernable weakling; capable of screaming and stamping his feet but scarcely able to stand upon them. He was well on the way to being even more limp-wristed and touched than his notorious father, Christian VII.

At this point in his already confusing life, his mother's lover, the court physician Dr Struensee, came on the scene. He decided that what the boy needed was not molly-coddling but the smack of firm discipline and a taste of the outdoor life. In no time at all, the little prince's world was turned upside down with a rugged and character-forming programme. Out went the velveteen suits and rich food and in came a tunic of light, silken material and a simple diet of boiled rice, vegetables, bread, potatoes, milk and water. There was to be no more sulking about the palace but a strict regime of cold baths twice daily and eight hours of manly exercise in the open air each day. All Frederick's spoilt little companions were sent packing and in their place came just one ordinary playmate, an illegitimate boy named Karl.

Not only did Struensee dismiss all the prince's fawning servants and replace them with a few hard-bitten old retainers, but he also forbade even this undemonstrative bunch ever to show Frederick any affection. When Struensee's own valet once picked up the boy from a bad fall and tried to comfort him, he was immediately sent to prison. Neither was there anything as namby-pamby as meals served indoors on a plate. Except during the very depths of winter, Frederick's food was usually hidden away in secret places or holes in the garden and the boy had to use his own wits and instinct to unearth it. More often than not he succeeded but there was one famous occasion in

October 1770 when he failed to return after going to forage for his lunch. After several hours' absence, even his Spartan minders were moved to mount a search party and eventually he was found, lying on the ground, unconscious from exposure.

Mercifully, the story has a happy ending for Frederick recovered and not only survived the rigours of the vicious outward bound school but, through it, acquired sufficient character to cope admirably with his mother's exile, Struensee's execution and his father's frothing insanity. The boy who at one time seemed destined to turn out all wrong, grew up to become one of his country's better kings.

Frederick William I (1688–1740). King of Prussia who recruited and maintained the strangest battalions in military history. They consisted of two units of 600 grenadiers, each of whom was handpicked and, in some cases, transported thousands of miles at the King's expense just so they could join up. They wore gorgeous blue and scarlet uniforms, had a huge bear for a mascot and were drilled until they could manoeuvre in their sleep. Yet what made them unique was not their prowess but the fact that they were truly head and shoulders above the rest of his army; for these guards were all human giants. In an age when the average man measured off at something under 5 ft 6 ins, these soldiers were all over 6 ft and the celebrities among them were nearer 7 ft. Frederick William doted on them and in time this military gimmick became an obsession. He spent millions on them, went to absurd lengths to bring prized specimens to his colours and yet never ever risked them in battle.

Initially the recruits were volunteers: Germans lured by the promise of a uniform and regular meals, and foreigners who were sent as goodwill gifts by their rulers. Peter the Great of Russia, for instance, sent 50 a year and the Turkish sultan was similarly generous. When this supply did not meet the Prussian King's demands, he hired recruiting agents: furtive individuals who hung around taverns, waited for a big lad to be in his cups and then dropped the king's schilling into his stein. It was only a matter of time before these unscrupulous agents got tired of watching big, hulking Germans swill beer and opted instead for lurking behind hedges and waylaying their victims with a quick bang over the head with a mallet. The King, too, got rather carried away and began offering a bounty which increased with the height of the captive and inflamed his agents to further excesses.

Things were now getting out of hand. In Prussia a rural pastor died of shock when one of Frederick William's recruiting parties burst into his church and made off with his taller communicants, while in Rome several desperados broke into a monastery and abducted a gangling monk as he knelt praying in his cell. Clergymen seemed to figure in more than their share of such incidents and matters came to a head when a huge Dutch preacher was hauled off in mid-sermon together with four of his congregation. Holland nearly declared war over the affair and the King was forced to tell the kidnappers to lie low for a while. Still, there was always bribery – £6,000 bought him a 7 ft 2 in Irishman called James Kirkland – or, failing that, eugenics. The King's idea was that if you got a very tall man and a great beanpole of a woman and mated them, they would produce offspring of quite astounding height. For a while there was a brisk trade among the bounty hunters in large and imposing women but the lack of a quick return meant the King soon lost interest in this method. What he wanted was not the promise of giants tomorrow but the sight of them performing today and it was to this end that he directed most of his personal attention.

The Potsdam Giants, as they were known, were indeed a stirring sight. Dressed in blue jackets with gold trim and red lapels, scarlet trousers, white stockings, black shoes and tall red hats that added a further foot to their already looming stature, they were drilled to perfection and attained a rate of fire almost double that of other soldiers. On closer inspection, however, they were less impressive. Great height does not mean towering intellect and some of these freaks were, frankly, feeble-minded. Desertion, too, was virtually epidemic and it was perhaps just as well that these units never went on active service. All they were really fit for was to be the live toy soldiers in Frederick William's parade-ground games.

The King was determined that in time his son should step into his jackboots and the efforts he made to breed military interest into the lad were, to say the least, thorough. Hardly before the child was weaned he was being woken each morning by the thundering discharge of a cannon beneath the nursery window and, by the age of five, Frederick the Younger had been made to learn by heart all 54 movements of the Prussian drill code. His governor was a 60-year-old general and, under the auspices of this old buffer, the boy was now given his own company of cadets to drill. He was but six years old. Within twelve months, this Junior Reichsmarshall Kit was extended by the addition of a miniature arsenal.

No doubt there would have been many boys who would have revelled in playing soldiers with such realistic accessories, but little Frederick was not one of them. He bitterly resented his martial upbringing and took refuge when he could in books and music. His father was horrified and tried to beat any vestige of culture out of him. If he found his son studying Latin, he had him publicly flogged and when the boy was discovered reading a novel in some bushes rather than stalking deer, his father beat him with his rattan cane and made him kiss his boots. Those who abetted this interest in culture came in for similar treatment. A girl who accompanied Frederick on the piano while he played the flute was arrested and flayed through the streets of Potsdam by the public executioner.

His son's resigned acceptance of this brutality enraged the King almost as much as the boy's bookishness. 'If my father had treated me as I treat you,' he once stormed at his heir, 'I wouldn't have put up with it. I would have killed myself or run away.' Finally, in August 1730, the King's son took him at his word and, in the company of his friend, Hans von Katte, tried to flee to England. They were captured, the Prince was imprisoned in the fortress of Kurstrin and von Katte was court-martialled. On the King's orders, his son was woken one morning and held at the window of his cell while von Katte was decapitated by sabre in the courtyard below. Frederick fainted just before the moment of execution.

His son, however, was not the only person Frederick William persecuted. To while away the evenings after a hard day's unpleasantness, the King organised gatherings of his cronies, which he called the Tobacco College. This met every night at 6 pm and was a kind of bully-boys' Atheneum. Smoking and drinking were the excuses that brought them together but the main item on the agenda was always a good hearty session of vindictiveness. The principal target was one Jacob Paul von Gundling, a harmless, bumbling court historian. The King would send articles to learned journals that insulted von Gundling from beginning to end and would then summon the old historian to read them aloud to the Tobacco College. Not content with that, this bunch of Hooray Heinrichs also once set fire to von Gundling and, on another occasion, produced at their meeting a monkey dressed up in a copy of von Gundling's clothes, declared him to be the historian's natural son and made the unfortunate man embrace him before the entire company. In 1731 von Gundling died; but even then the humiliations did not stop. The King ordered his body to be clothed in a dress of state and placed inside a large wine cask and, despite the objections of the clergy, this was how von Gundling was buried.

Nine years later Frederick William himself died. He had suffered from a milder version of the disease that so affected the mind of George III of England but no amount of sleepless nights and urine retention could possibly excuse the terrors that he inflicted on his son, his historian and countless tall men the length and breadth of Europe.

Frederick William II (1712–1786). King of Prussia and, despite being subjected to the warped upbringing described above, one of the best-adjusted monarchs in history. He had, above all, a healthy contempt for the trappings of royalty. A crown to him was 'merely a hat that lets the rain in', and he was never one to allow his head to be turned by public displays of enthusiasm for him when he paraded through his capital. 'Put a monkey on a camel,' he once said, 'and you'll get much the same response.'

This level-headedness was obvious from the moment that Frederick acceded to the throne. His first acts were to throw open the state granaries to the poor, to introduce religious freedom and abolish flogging, torture and censorship. He also set about establishing the most cultivated court in Europe and soon his sharp mind and ready patronage were drawing some of the best writers and philosophers of the age to his palace. Among them was Voltaire and the French writer was sufficiently taken with his benefactor to hail him as 'The Solomon of the North'.

This compliment was only a marginal exaggeration of the King's wisdom and perhaps nothing better illustrated the quality of Frederick's intellect than his incisive denunciations of hunting – then a conventionally royal pastime. In a comprehensive attack on both the activity and those who pursued it, he wrote, 'The butcher does not kill animals for his pleasure but merely because human society requires them for food; whereas the hunter kills them only for his pleasure, which is detestable. The hunter, therefore, should be placed in the scale of society below the butcher.'

Some might think that with his liberalism, hatred of the hunt, passion for the arts and refusal to identify with Prussia's tradition of boozy swagger, Frederick was the very realisation of his father's worst fears for him. Yet he was no teetotaller (preferring even his coffee to be made with champagne) and as a military commander he was one of the bravest and the best, leading his army with profitable success in both the War of Austrian Succession and the Seven Years' War. It was these triumphs, rather than his worthy character or enlightened reforms, that earned him the title of 'The Great'.

His one true oddity concerned snuff, which he adored and consumed with undisguised relish. More than 2,000 lb of Spanish snuff was always kept in store for him and during his lifetime he must have sniffed his way through many times that amount. Lord Malmesbury said, 'One could hardly approach the King without sneezing.' On his death he left over 130 richly decorated snuff boxes, worth no less than £1 million.

Fuad I (1868–1936). King of Egypt who, throughout his reign, fought a dogged rearguard action against his servants' unhygienic habits. Fuad had something of an obsession with cleanliness but even a less fastidious ruler might have baulked at some of the unwholesome practices of this household. You could, for example, hardly blame him for making daily inspections of his kitchens, especially after he once found a servant making the royal cup of tea by straining the leaves through an old sock. The rich variety of bad smells that hung around the palace was a further source of irritation. His capital Cairo might stink like an abattoir in a heatwave but he was damned if his own personal quarters would do the same. So if he detected even the merest whiff of an unpleasant odour, he would chase from room to room armed with an eau-de-cologne spray until he had located and eradicated it. He was also a keep-fit fanatic and began each day by leaping out of bed and performing half an hour's physical jerks in front of the mirror.

His passion for clean living did not, however, extend to his business dealings. In these Fuad was little better than a back-street racketeer and between 1917 and 1936 he built up a vast land-holding by a mixture of intimidation and corruption. His favoured methods were anything but subtle: if he decided to purchase a tract of land he would summon the owner to his palace and ask him how much he wanted for his property. If the man was unreasonable enough to ask the market price then the King would send in the government valuers, an obliging body of men whose speciality was to assess even the most fertile land at scandalously low prices. Acting on this corrupt advice, Fuad would often offer £30 an acre for land that was actually worth 20 times that price. If the owner still seemed strangely reluctant to part with his land and livelihood then the government surveyors would be called in and they would threaten to divert irrigation channels away from the man's land. That usually did the trick and contracts would be duly exchanged. By these and other nefarious means, Fuad eventually owned one seventh of all cultivatable land in Egypt.

Ensuring a ready market for the produce of these royal estates was never a problem – the King simply ordered his officials and police to stop all the fruit and vegetable lorries entering big cities until his goods had been sold. The profits were, of course, enormous, especially as his workforce were paid less than half the going rate. Fuad could soon afford countless royal residences and over 100 cars, including ten Rolls-Royces. By the time of his death he was able to leave a fortune that measured in excess of £45 million.

> '*It is more kingly to enrich than to be rich.*'
> PTOLEMY SOTER, King of Egypt, 290 BC.

G

'Those who see and observe kings, heroes and statesmen discover that they have headaches, indigestion, humours and passions, just like other people; every one of which in their turn determines their wills in defiance of their reason.'

LORD CHESTERFIELD.

Mohandas Karamchand Gandhi (1869–1948). Indian nationalist leader, modern saint and a highly original present-giver. When Princess Elizabeth and Prince Philip married in 1947, Gandhi decided that the very thing for a young couple setting out on life's great adventure was . . . a loincloth. It was knitted, naturally, by his own hands and at the subsequent display of wedding gifts at St James's Palace, duly took its place alongside the fish knives, butter dishes and tea-caddies. In due course, when Queen Mary went for a private nose around these goodies, she was aghast on looking down and seeing Mr Gandhi's little offering nestling on a table. 'How indelicate,' she said, 'what a horrible thing.' Call it coincidence if you like, but within the year Gandhi had been assassinated.

George I (1845–1913). King of Greece, Prince Philip's grand-father and roller-skating enthusiast. His favoured venue for this activity was the grand ballroom of his Athens palace, where he would thread his way in and out of the ornate pillars with the rest of his family, in order of seniority, following on behind.

George II (1683–1760). The last King of England to lead an army on the battlefield, he was also an eternally optimistic dirty old man. On no occasion was this more apparent than at a

'Come-As-You-Fancy' ball at the Haymarket on 1 May 1749 when Elizabeth Chudleigh, the Duchess of Kingston, turned up in a topless body stocking with only a garland of flowers to cover her charms. George took this tantalising costume to be nothing short of an open invitation and, panting hard with excitement and his eyes out on stalks, he began edging his lecherous way towards her. When he reached the saucy Duchess, he was in such a lather of anticipation that, without wasting any time in conversational pleasantries, he simply bent his head to her ear and quietly asked if he could fondle her breasts. He could hardly believe his luck when she gave him a knowing wink, took his hand and said that she would guide it to a much softer place. She then put his hand on his own head.

Apart from a somewhat over-active libido, George also had a foul temper and a fanatical hatred of his own son, the ill-fated Prince Frederick of Wales. He once said of him, 'Our first-born is the greatest ass, the greatest liar, the greatest canaille and the greatest beast in the whole world and we heartily wish he was out of it.' Soon after these intemperate words were uttered, Fred was indeed dead, killed by a ruptured ulcer at the age of 45. George lived on for another nine years before he himself died, killed (indirectly at least) by the constipation that had racked so much of his later life. Seated in the royal lavatory one Saturday in October 1760, he strained so hard to overcome his affliction that he suffered a fatal seizure, thus making him the only English king actually to die while seated on the throne.

George III (1731–1820). King of England whose character has been remorselessly assassinated for the last 200 years. In popular histories he has been variously portrayed as a slobbering lunatic who could not control himself, let alone his family; a power-besotted despot who treated his ministers like dirt; a bungling incompetent who lost us the American colonies and, not infrequently, a disastrous mixture of all three. In fact, although he must take some blame for the political failures of his long reign, he was a decent and hard-working man who treated his poorer subjects with kindliness and whose so-called 'madness' has been distorted out of all proportion. Were it not for him and his virtues, Britain's monarchy might well have come a lot nearer to sharing the fate that befell the French crown.

Yet the popular vision of George remains that of the royal fruitcake ranting around Windsor Castle, suffering from a host of amusing delusions. Was it not he, for instance, who believed that beef grew like vegetables and tried to prove his point by planting 4 lb of it in the castle's kitchen garden? Did he not for a time insist on ending every sentence with the word 'peacock'? (A tricky one, this, since it allegedly came on just as he was about to read the King's speech to Parliament. A quick-thinking minister solved the problem by agreeing with His Majesty that 'peacock' was indeed an excellent word with which to conclude sentences but counselling that kings should not let mere subjects hear it. He urged that it should be whispered and the result was a pronounced pause after each sentence, but nothing worse.) And surely it was he who threw the Prince of Wales against a wall at a state banquet, thought he could see Germany from his Windsor bedroom and once had to be forcibly restrained from riding his horse into a Weymouth church?

The answer is that no one can now tell which of these colourful anecdotes is truth and which is fiction. Many people at the time, the Prince of Wales's cronies among them, had a vested interest in exaggerating the King's mental wanderings and were not averse to a little factual embroidery. Once, it was said, George stopped his carriage in Windsor Great Park, stepped down, bowed to a tree, shook one of its branches as if it were a hand and began to address it as the King of Prussia. The story, however, is somewhat less impressive when one considers that it originated from a royal page who had been sacked.

What is certain is that the King's insanity has been totally misrepresented for the last two centuries. He was not even mad in the conventional psychiatric sense, but suffering from a hereditary disease called porphyria. This condition disturbs the process which creates red pigment in the blood and, in chronic cases such as George's, the entire nervous system, including the brain, becomes poisoned. The symptoms are bloodshot eyes and discoloured urine, accompanied by extreme agitation and sleeplessness, sufficient in his case to upset periodically the balance of the mind.

This illness was not the perpetual shadow over his reign that it is often thought to be. He had a brief attack in 1788 but until he was over 70 he had been incapacitated for no more than a total of six months. Only in 1810, when he had been on the throne for 50 years, did he become permanently insane. This sad, final descent, when he wandered the corridors of Windsor, white-bearded and blind, hugging a pillow-case that he imagined was his dead baby son Octavius, could hardly have been delayed or eased by the primitive treatment that he had received for his attacks. In the absence of understanding or cures, all that could be offered by the men from a private asylum who took charge, were the straitjacket, threats and a cruel metal restraining chair.

If the nature and extent of his 'madness' has been unduly inflated down the years, then so have his virtues been minimalised. George's active sympathy for his ordinary subjects was, for his period, nothing short of remarkable. In the severe winter of 1785, for instance, he was out walking on his own when he met two pathetic-looking little boys. Both were far too young to know who he was and, before he had a chance to tell them, they burst into tears and begged him for food. As they spoke to the King, they told him that their mother had been dead for three days and that their father was now lying ill on a bed of straw. George immediately asked the boys to lead him to their cottage and when they arrived he saw the pitiful scene with the father stretched out on the family's one bed, still clutching in his arms his dead wife.

The King was so moved he could barely speak. He gave the boys what cash he had and rushed back to his lodge and ordered a messenger to return with food, clothing and coals. When the father recovered, George sent for him and told him that henceforth the boys would be fed, clothed and educated at his personal expense. Nor was this an isolated case of royal charity. He regularly gave ten fat oxen to the poor of Windsor and in

1794 had a mill built in the grounds at Windsor for the grinding of corn which was then sold to the poor at a cheap rate.

He even showed kindness to those who wished him ill. In 1786 a woman called Margaret Nicholson tried unsuccessfully to stab him and, as she was led away, his first concern was for her safety. 'Pray do not hurt the poor woman,' he cried out. This, and her subsequent removal to Bethlehem Hospital, was in stark contrast to the fate which befell those who made similar attempts on the lives of Continental monarchs, such as M. Damiens, for example. George even sent money and messages of goodwill to Henry, Bishop of Frascati, the Stuart claimant to his throne – a striking act considering that the Jacobite rising of 1745 was still very much within living memory.

Typically, George also showed generosity to those who rivalled him in his grand passion of book-collecting. Despite being possessed by an overwhelming urge to amass the best of all possible libraries, he still gave orders that his agents at auctions were never to bid against a scholar, professor or any person of moderate means who wanted a particular book for his own use. Although never an intellectual (he collected volumes rather than read them), George still stands out among our far-from-bookish monarchs as a man with a genuinely inquiring mind. He was a patron of Herschel and other scientists, founded the Royal Academy, supported Handel and was a great encourager of the new agriculture, earning himself the nickname of 'Farmer George' and contributing to the 'Annals of Agriculture' under the pen-name of Ralph Robinson.

The King was also an intensely moral man. He was faithful to his wife and dutiful in his religion and his irreproachable court was a valuable antidote to the excesses of the earlier Hanoverians. In fact, George should probably be recognised as the founder of the modern concept of the royal family being a healthy example to the rest of the nation of clean-living domestic decency. Unfortunately, in George's case, the idea did not survive his offspring's childhood. Judged by their actions in later life, it seemed as if his sons could not wait to burst from the confines of their pious, over-protective parents and begin leaving a trail of bastards and unpaid bills all over Europe. George simply never knew how to handle these unruly young men once they had outgrown the nursery. Domestically it was his biggest failing and one that will always be a handicap to even the most enthusiastic of his rehabilitators. Kindly, upright and much put-upon though the King may have been, any man responsible for foisting a wayward specimen like George IV on history can never be regarded as being entirely on the side of the angels.

George IV (1762–1830). Probably the most unpopular king ever to sit upon the English throne. Others may have been murdered, run out of the country or simply executed, but none before him, and certainly none since, have ever been subject to such universal and unqualified condemnation. Once he turned 40, he could hardly go anywhere in London without hearing boos and catcalls, at his coronation he felt so threatened by the mob that he surrounded himself with a bodyguard of hand-picked prizefighters and in the second half of his reign his increasing unpopularity, combined with his physical deterioration, meant that he lived the life of a virtual recluse. And when he died – a dropsical, cherry-brandy-swigging invalid, painted up and addicted to laudanum – *The Times* dressed its best page in a black border, cleared its editorial throat and said this of him:

'The late king had many generations of intimates with whom he led a course of life, the character of which rose little higher than animal indulgence . . . There never was an individual whose passing was less regretted by his fellow-creatures than this deceased king. What eye wept for him? What heart has heaved one sob of unmercenary sorrow? . . . If George IV ever had a friend – a devoted friend in any rank of life – we protest that the name of him never reached us.'

What inspired the author of this obituary to sharpen his pen to such a vindictive point was a view of George that was then shared by millions of his fellow subjects: that their King was a walking compendium of every vice that money could buy and most that it could not. He was, to begin with, a womaniser who had first cheated on his wife and then rejected her as his Queen.

He was also an insensitive spendthrift who, while children starved in the fields, lavished over £¼ million on his coronation and 50 times that on his own comforts. Furthermore, he was a glutton, filling his face at 12-course banquets, swilling up to three bottles of wine at one sitting and breakfasting on more food than most men ever saw in a week. He was also a preposterous dandy, rouging his cheeks and corseting his bulk (20 stone at its peak) into expensive and gaudy clothes. He thought nothing of spending over £1,200 on a single outfit, during the eight years of the Regency he bought no fewer than 500 shirts and, when an invalid in 1829, was still acquiring clothes at such a rate that he was £10,000 overspent on his dress allowance in the first half of the year alone.

What is more, when it came to politics, George was nothing more than a turncoat, feigning support for the Whigs as a young Prince but backing the Tories when regent and King and sliding ever more surely into the reactionary camp. He was a snob, too, an ingrate who spread malicious rumours about his father's illness, a liar who claimed he had fought at Waterloo and ridden the winner of the Goodwood Cup, a drunkard, an idler who on his death left no fewer than 48,000 state documents unsigned and, of course, he was also a shameless and incorrigible debtor. From the moment he left the royal nursery be began owing money and by the time he was but 24 years old, his slate had reached the considerable sum of £269,878 6s 7¼d. Thereafter the figure escalated beyond the point where any such precision could be applied: in 1788 it was fully one quarter of the annual civil expenditure of the realm, then there was a grand clearance of the sum by the King, followed by a rapid growth to £400,000 in 1792, £500,000 in 1794 and, finally, £650,000 in 1795. Sixteen years later a certain amount of belt-tightening and some ad hoc donations from the Treasury had only reduced the sum outstanding by £100,000. After this date, when as Regent and King he splashed out almost unchecked on such essentials as chandeliers costing £11,000, the amount by which he exceeded his income ceased to be calculable by conventional mathematics.

Suffice to say then, that when George's subjects identified him as the devil incarnate, they did at least have plenty to go on. Yet however accurate they may be, caricatures are not portraits and in reality George IV was not quite as black – or in his case, as scarlet – as he was often painted. As a youth he was good-looking, witty and demonstrably the most intelligent of his line and although he had dissipated most of these talents by the time he was called upon to use them, there were at least sufficient remnants to set something against his glaring faults. There was, for instance, his personality, which when not befuddled by alcohol, could still produce conversation of a distinctly unroyal brilliance. He had, too, a showman's flair for the ceremonial, as demonstrated by his coronation and his visit to Edinburgh in 1822 when he walked the length of Princes Street dressed in the Stuart tartan. This, and his appearance in Ireland the same year, were particularly brave steps given the rebellious feelings in both provinces – akin, nowadays, to the Queen going on unchaperoned walkabout in Argentina. He was no doubt helped by the fact that, despite a 55-inch waist and a figure so heavy that he had to be winched on board a horse, he could still cut quite a dash in uniform, albeit with the aid of straps and corsets. Above all, as a stylist and connoisseur, he retained a sharp and imaginative eye almost to the end. Much of the royal art collection was acquired by him and in his buildings his bequest was perhaps even greater: the refurbishment of Windsor Castle and Buckingham Palace and the building of Brighton Pavilion and large parts of central London (hence, of course, Regent Street).

George even had a few traits which could be described as virtues. He cleared the debts of friends, cared deeply for his sisters, bought paintings from struggling artists at prices way above their market value and showed at times when King an unexpected degree of clemency. He abolished the flogging of female prisoners (a decidedly wet attitude for the age), constantly harassed his Home Secretaries with reprieves for condemned criminals and was uncommonly considerate to his servants (until his dotage when he began dismissing them for staring at his bloated and invalid person).

George's tragedy, perhaps, was that these decent impulses never lasted very long, nor were they spread very far about his kingdom. They were there, however, and the Duke of Wellington, who served George as soldier and first minister, was in no doubt about which part of the King's many-sided personality was the dominant one. 'He was,' he declared, 'the most extraordinary compound of talent, wit, buffoonery, obstinacy and good feeling – in short a medley of the most opposing qualities, with a great preponderance of the good.' The old campaigner was probably applying a bit too much spit and polish to his master's image but no more, perhaps, than was necessary after the dreadful scuffing it had received from the man at *The Times*.

George V (1865–1936). King of England and, without doubt, Britain's most tattooed monarch. It was during a stopover in Tokyo on one of his youthful voyages that George was first illustrated. An elaborate pattern of dragons in red and blue was etched on him and this design was later extended by experts in Kyoto and Jerusalem. Years later, at Queen Mary's suggestion, Britain's leading tattooist, George Burchett, was called in to make some improvements to what was no doubt known as the royal tattoo. These engravings meant that parts of the King resembled the postage stamps of which he was so inordinately fond. In time he built up the world's largest collection of British and Empire stamps. There were a quarter of a million of them in 325 albums, all stored in a special room at Buckingham Palace. He devoted each Tuesday to the study and cataloguing of these items, logging the price of each purchase in a special code under its hinge.

His other great passion was shooting. George owned the sporting rights to over 30,000 acres at Sandringham and elsewhere and it seemed at times that his mission in life was the extermination of every living thing on these estates. In the 1899 season alone, for example, 12,100 pheasants were shot and the wonder is that this total was not higher, for he was a talented and tireless marksman with such enthusiasm for slaughter that throughout his life he recorded his daily bag in his diary.

However, there was one bird who was safe to take the most outrageous liberties with him and that was his pet parrot, Charlotte. This ill-humoured and, in time, moth-eaten specimen was given the virtual run of the palace and was even encouraged by George to make a thorough nuisance of itself at the meal table. At breakfast, for instance, it was allowed to scratch around among the plates, poking its beak in the marmalade and interfering with the royal boiled egg. Evidently George had not heard of psittacosis. The Queen also raised no objection to the presence of Charlotte on the table, although her tolerance may have had something to do with the fact that the King was quick to cover up the indiscretions of his feathered friend. His sleight of hand with the condiments when the bird messed would, by all accounts, have done credit to Oxford Street's best three-card trickster.

The parrot and his love of shooting are reminders that while George may have been a king, his instincts were those of a retired naval officer turned country squire. He had something of a fetish about correct dress, rowing constantly with his eldest son over turn-ups on trousers and once saying to him at breakfast, 'I hear you were not wearing gloves at the ball last night. Please see this does not occur again,'; he had a deep-rooted contempt for booklearning, with the spelling to match ('wrung up on the phone' and 'sollicitor', for example); he had a fierce temper, prompting Lord Mountbatten to describe him as a 'martinet' and to add that he was 'gruff and unbending in matters of form and etiquette'; he had the social prejudices of the century he was born in, saying once of a homosexual, 'I thought chaps like that shot themselves,' and insisting, 'I won't knight buggers'; he was proud, ordering the destruction in 1924 of a painting of him by Charles Sims because he thought it made him look like a ballet dancer and, above all, he had a real John Bull-ish attitude to abroad, believing that the borders of hell were situated just a few hundred yards south of Dover.

And yet in spite, or more probably because, of these

prejudices, the British people adored him. They loved him for his stoical sense of duty, for the solid domestic example that he and his wife set (his one sexual dalliance was before his marriage, with a girl that he visited in Southsea), for his bluff dignity, for the sacrifices he shared with them during the Great War and, at the other end of his reign, for his Christmas broadcasts. A year before the King died, this accumulated affection for him poured out in the celebrations for his Silver Jubilee in 1935. In the main they consisted of the usual parades, street parties and municipal feastings and meant a field day for the manufacturers of vol-au-vents, bunting and cheap mugs. A few local dignitaries, however, still had the flair to mark a royal milestone with some originality. In Southport, for instance, the town's magistrates decided that the best way to salute the King's 25 years on the throne was to allow children over 14 in to see films licensed for adults only. It is hardly surprising, then, that George's best-known remark is the cursing of a seaside resort.

German courtier (17th Century). A Teutonic sycophant who once turned to Ernst Ludwig, the Landgrave of Hesse-Darmstadt, and said, in all seriousness, 'If God were not God, who should more properly be God than your serene highness?'

Gustav III (1746–1792). King of Sweden and an early campaigner against caffeine. He was convinced that coffee was a poison and, to prove his point, conducted a novel experiment with two convicted murderers. He sentenced one to drink coffee every day, the other to drink only tea and appointed two doctors to oversee these vital tests. He then sat back to await the result, confident that the coffee-drinker would soon be dead and thus proof of the fatal effects of the dreaded beverage.

In due course there was indeed a death – one of the doctors, to be followed shortly by his colleague. Next to go was the King, murdered at a masque at the Stockholm Opera in 1792. Meanwhile, the condemned men kept on drinking until finally the first of them died, aged 83. He was the tea-drinker. Despite this somewhat inconclusive experiment, the following 30 years saw Sweden twice enact laws for coffee prohibition.

Gustavus IV (1778–1837). King of Sweden and religious maniac. As a child he had been subjected to a fearsome regime of cold baths, corporal punishment and Bible study. The Book of Revelations was an especially regular text and so intensely did the youthful Gustavus pore over its pages that he even began to believe himself to be one of the mysterious beings alluded to in that most difficult of scriptures.

Eventually he was persuaded to address himself to more mundane matters like marriage and, in due course, he was betrothed to Princess Fredericka of Baden. She had not been given too detailed a description of her intended and so could be forgiven a thrill of anticipation when, just hours after their wedding ceremony, the young King took her arm and led her to their apartment. Imagine, therefore, her surprise, when, as soon as they were alone, she was guided by him not to the connubial divan but instead to a chair, ordered to sit down and handed a Bible. Obeying her husband's instructions, she opened it at the Book of Esther and began solemnly reading out loud its cheerless first chapter, which details the dire punishments that await a wife who does not immediately bend to her husband's will. Princess Fredericka's wedding night was concluded by a sharp reminder from her wild-eyed spouse that any failure to jump to wifely attention every time he barked, would be attended by the same penalties as those meted out to the biblical woman.

Gustavus's opening gambit rather set the standard of joy and companionship that could be expected from this marriage and, in time, he and his wife were divorced, he was deposed and then, finally, exiled. Travelling under the name of Count Gottorp, he rambled all over Europe, living on only £96 a year in whatever accommodation he was offered, including, for a short while, a small apartment in Hampton Court. He survived in this fashion for the last 26 years of his life, consoled only by his literary pursuits which eventually bore complicated fruit in the publication of his book, *Reflections on the Aurora Borealis and its Connection with Diurnal Motion*. It was not a best-seller.

Maharajah of Gwalior (1886–1925). Indian Prince whose fabulous wealth allowed him to indulge his every whim. This was particularly apparent in the fixtures and fittings of his palace, which included not only baths of solid silver and a Persian carpet that could accommodate 2,000 people, but also, to serve his dinner guests, a food-carrying model train.

This railway was the Maharajah's pride and joy. It consisted of 250 ft of track (whose rails were, naturally, made of silver) which stretched in a loop from the kitchens to the banqueting hall, around the tables and back again. On this line ran an electric model engine (silver again, of course) and a number of specially designed wagons. At a certain point during banquets, this locomotive would chug slowly out of the kitchen doors, pulling its trucks loaded with desserts, sweets and decanters of port and brandy. It stopped at each place setting, allowed the amazed diner to remove what he wanted and then moved on. It worked perfectly, except for the time when the control panel short-circuited and the locomotive went berserk, spraying gravy, roast beef and a green pea purée over the horrified guests. Still, the train was an ingenious piece of one-upmanship on his fellow maharajahs who had to be content with only bewigged flunkeys to wait at table.

For his next trick, however, he managed not only to outdo his neighbouring princes but also the great white Empress back in England. Gwalior was an ardent admirer of Victoria and when he heard that she had a huge chandelier in Buckingham Palace, he decided that he wanted an even bigger one. He agreed a design, ordered it to be made by the finest craftsmen in Venice and sat back to await its delivery. He then began to be bothered by a nagging thought: would the palace roof stand the weight of the crystal monstrosity? For days he would peer up at the ceiling, anxiously turning the question over in his mind. Finally, he could stand the agonising no longer and resolved to settle the matter for once and for all. So he selected his heaviest elephant, had her strapped into a cradle, hoisted up by a crane and then lowered onto the roof to test its strength. To his relief the roof held, the elephant survived the shock and the chandelier was duly installed.

To a man as rich as Gwalior, sparing no expense for life's little luxuries was never a problem. Yet unlike many other wealthy princes, he was equally quick to cough up when duty called. During the Great War he funded the British military effort to the tune of £2¼ million and even organised and financed a hospital ship called *Loyalty*. Duty also dictated that he erect some kind of memorial to his mother when she died but he was so devastated by her death that the finished project went far beyond a normal expression of filial affection.

Outwardly, there was nothing strange about the memorial – just a large pavilion in which was placed a life-size marble statue of the dead parent. What made it unusual was that instead of being left to its own petrified devices, the stony likeness of his mother was then treated exactly as the old girl had been when she was alive. Every day female attendants would bathe and dress it, hang jewellery upon it and even dab perfume in its nooks and crannies. Food was served to its feet dead on the dot at meal-times, a band serenaded it with a repertoire of favourite songs and, if the weather was especially hot, a fan would be brought out to waft cool air on its face. These bizarre marks of respect were observed daily until the Maharajah himself died in 1925, whereupon his remains were cremated and the ashes placed in a mausoleum opposite his mother's pavilion.

> '*Monarchy is the gold filling in the mouth of decay.*'
> JOHN OSBORNE.

H

'The kingly office is entitled to no respect. It was originally procured by highwayman's methods; it remains a perpetuated crime, can never be anything but the symbol of a crime. It is no more entitled to respect than is the flag of a pirate.'

MARK TWAIN.

Abdul Hamid II (1842–1918). Sultan of the Ottoman Empire whose entire life was dominated by the constant fear that he was about to be bumped off. For Abdul Hamid, normal security precautions were not enough; everything about him – his palace, clothes and food – had to be arranged so that even the slimmest prospects of assassination were eliminated. He wore chain mail under his tunic, a steel-lined fez on his head and hired not only a food taster but a clothes sampler, too, whose daily task was to try on the Sultan's garments in case they had been doctored with poison. All his documents had to be baked in an oven and disinfected before being placed before him, his water well was strictly patrolled and every cow which provided his milk was given an individual round-the-clock armed guard. He also built himself a palace that was more like a vast booby-trapped strongroom than a residence and he even refused to have a telephone installed there because he feared some fiend would send a lethal current down the line to him. All in all, when it came to paranoia, Abdul Hamid was in the hall of fame.

This was unfortunate. Of all the places and ages in history to be cursed with a persecution complex, it was not Turkey in the late nineteenth century. The country was positively crawling with plots and conspiracies and in the capital, Istanbul, treachery and mischief were cooked up in every home along with the kebabs. When Abdul Hamid came to the throne he gazed about him and grew decidedly twitchy. Everywhere there were sinister looking ne'er-do-wells with hooked noses, cruel mouths and furtive eyes (people much like himself, in fact), and he suspected they were no more scrupulous than he was. Each one was a potential assassin, he thought, and the only thing to do was to make himself so inaccessible that not even fresh air could get to him. So it was that he came to build Yilditz.

The security precautions began even before a stone was laid. With a maximum of secrecy, a site formerly occupied by two graveyards was acquired and Abdul Hamid began planning his hideaway with 12 hand-picked architects – not one of whom was aware of the existence of the 11 others. The same strictures applied to the hundreds of workers, and the men who were building the harem, for instance, were never allowed to meet those employed on the private zoo. The whole operation was divided up like the cells of a revolutionary organisation and for months on end the clandestine work went on. When it was finished, what Abdul Hamid had was not so much a palace as a security compound – and a pretty large one at that. Covering a vast area a mile beyond the palace of Dolmabache, the huge barrack-like Yilditz was an extraordinary honeycomb of nearly 100 buildings with a high wall on one side and the Bosphorus on the other. False facades, guards and secret service agents covered the front and fortifications protected the approach from the sea, which was also regularly and anxiously scanned by the Sultan himself through one of the many powerful telescopes permanently trained on it.

Inside, many of the rooms were used as stores and stockpiled with clothes, guns, food and even toys, as if Abdul Hamid was laying in for some anticipated siege. The various habitable quarters, between which he moved at deliberately irregular intervals, were fitted with the most absurd hotch-potch of furniture. Turkish couches, French chairs and English tables were all jumbled up together, the one common pattern being that in each room these tasteless articles were arranged so that visitors could only enter in single file, which the Sultan always thought less threatening. A good many rooms were mirrored (all the better to detect a movement behind him) and most were connected to other rooms by a series of secret passages. With every fresh outbreak of unrest in his empire, this warren was extended and yet more wooden doors were replaced by steel ones.

Even with all this, Abdul Hamid was not prepared to rely solely on the marksmanship of his guards to deal with intruders. In many rooms he ordered the fitting of innocent-looking cupboards. These always faced the door and, at the touch of a switch by the Sultan's couch, their glass doors would be flung open, revealing a pair of pistols inside which would fire automatically. These, of course, were in addition to the loaded guns he kept handy in all rooms and the two revolvers which hung by his bath. In a place so bristling with firearms, accidents were bound to occur and, sure enough, did. The saddest, perhaps, was one day when a gardener made an unexpected movement as he salaamed and the jumpy Abdul Hamid turned and shot him in the head before anyone could stop him.

This chronic mistrust of even the most harmless situation pervaded every aspect of his household. His food was prepared in kitchens which had bars on the windows and bolts on the doors and if he was feeling especially vulnerable to poisoning, he would not only call in extra food tasters but also lay down his fork or spoon (which could always be coated in fatal substances, couldn't they?) and insist on feeding from the cupped hand of a harem girl. Not surprisingly, for a man so eaten up with suspicion, he was a martyr to indigestion. Yet however bad the griping pain, he would never deviate from his cautious routine with medicaments: hundreds of pills would be removed from their wrappings in front of him and shaken into a bag, in which Abdul would rummage and select one at random. He was, above all, a coward who could not even bring himself to look under his divan last thing at night but instead always asked one of his concubines to shine a candle there.

Besides people and poisons, Abdul Hamid was also afraid of words and imposed a rigorous censorship on the Turkish press. One of the first blanket bans concerned reporting acts of regicide, with the absurd result that when the King and Queen of Serbia were brutally murdered in 1903, the Istanbul papers said they had died of indigestion. In time, Abdul even outlawed the use of individual words and 'freedom', 'revolutionary', 'republic' and 'assassin' were all on the proscribed list, along with 'dynamite', whose similarity to the word 'dynamo' caused him to confuse the two and issue a blunt refusal to extend the local electricity grid beyond the walls of Yilditz. 'Bomb' was also illegal and when the Emperor and Empress of Germany visited in 1898, the chef who wrote the words 'Bombe Glacée' on the menu was sacked on the spot.

Yet try as he might, he could not seal himself off from every form of attack. He may have initiated some reforms and modernisation in his empire but, as his reign wore on, reports of his army's appalling atrocities and the reclusive Abdul Hamid's misgovernment combined to fuel discontent. He did not help himself by having less and less to do with his ministers and taking instead the counsel of such characters as a slave he bought in a market, one of his cooks, a bootblack, a circus clown and a Punch and Judy man. In 1908, despite holing up at Yilditz and sending lookalikes to the mosque in his place, Abdul Hamid was deposed. He went into exile taking seven of his harem but leaving behind sackfuls of gold coins, boxes of gems, notebooks detailing all his secret foreign investments and wardrobes full of bullet-proof garments. Ten years later, the old Sultan who had spent so much of his life in mortal dread of a sudden death, passed peacefully away in his 77th year at his villa in Salonika.

Hartmann (1613–1686). Prince of Lichtenstein and one half of the most prolific royal couple in the world. His better – and longsuffering – half was Countess Elizabeth zu Salm-Reifter-scheidt and together this devoted pair produced no fewer than 24 children, 21 of whom were born alive.

Herr Hecht (19th Century). A footman who shook the Victorian royal family to its roots by seducing Queen Mary's young cousin.

She was the 19-year-old Princess Marie of Mecklenburg-Strelitz, one of the more minor branches of German royalty. Her family maintained perhaps the most rigid and hidebound court in all Europe and it was this that helped bring about the girl's downfall. The problem was the lamps which, according to the household's ludicrous protocol, could not be handled by the maids but had to be delivered to the bedside by a male footman. Hecht was allocated Marie's lamp and soon he was bringing a little light into her life in more ways than one.

The result was that she was pregnant, he was dismissed and royalty throughout Europe was pop-eyed with outrage. None of them, of course, could believe that any relative of theirs was capable of doing such a thing willingly, let alone with a servant. Queen Victoria thought that Marie must have been drugged, the girl's mother was convinced that Hecht had ravished her, while the future King George V and the German Emperor favoured hypnotism.

No one emerged with much credit from this fiasco. Hecht sold his story to the newspapers and Marie's family not only banned the very mention of her name but also insisted that the child of this shocking liaison was farmed out. Ironically, about the only shred of compassion came from Queen Victoria and George's wife Mary, both normally thought of as our two most po-faced royals. The old Queen declared that the family's treatment of Marie was 'wicked' and Mary went considerably out of her way to be seen with the unfortunate girl.

Henri I (1767–1820). Emperor of Haiti and megalomaniac who rose from obscurity to create an absurd Ruritanian kingdom in the middle of the Caribbean Ocean. Like all such instant states, it resembled a film set – pretentious glitter up front but very little substance behind – and nothing illustrated this better than the visit of Sir Home Popham, the Commander-in-Chief of the British West Indies Squadron. He had come to review the Emperor's household troops and from a terrace outside the opulent royal palace, Sir Home watched open-mouthed as rank upon rank of superbly uniformed and drilled soldiers, all more than six foot in height, marched past for inspection. On and on for more than six hours went the parade until the British admiral, aghast with admiration, declared that he must have seen 60,000 troops, plus their guns and ammunition trains.

Of course, he had not seen anything like that number. The review platform only looked over part of the palace roadway and as soon as each file of men had passed from view, they broke rank and ran hell for leather round the back of the palace to take their place in the rear of those coming up. All Sir Home had seen for six hours was but one company of men performing sneaky laps of the building.

The man who masterminded this deception had been born Henri Christophe in Grenada. He was the slave son of a slave and ran away to sea at the age of 12. After working as a ship's captain's servant and billiard-marker in a tavern, he bought his freedom, joined the army and fought his way up from cook to general. He modelled himself on Napoleon and, in the confusion following the break-up of the newly independent Haiti into two states, he seized power and had himself crowned Henri I in a hastily-built cathedral in 1811. He rapidly set about giving himself all the trappings and pretensions of the most ostentatious of European monarchies. He rode about in an elegant London-built carriage pulled by four greys and surrounded himself with a retinue of officers dressed in gold lace, silk stockings and white breeches. When they first saw him, his poor and primitive subjects, most of whom were African slaves or the descendants of slaves, must have wondered if they were on the right island.

It was a good job they never got near the comic-opera palace; for here was Henri's off-the-peg aristocracy, newly founded and luxuriating in such splendidly ridiculous titles as the Duc de Marmelade and the Comte de Limonade. To make sure that his daughters, the fancily-named Amethiste and Athenaire, could hold their own in such exalted company, he even had two American dames imported to teach them deportment and other social graces.

There was never any shortage of places for the girls to

practise their new skills. Henri built no fewer than 15 ornate palaces on his tropical island, plus a vast cathedral and the huge fantasy castle of La Ferriere. This was a parody of the medieval fortress with massive crenellations, bulbous towers and walls that were nearly 30 feet thick. Along its imposing battlements sat 365 bronze cannon – every one of them trained on the sea to bombard would-be invaders – and the entire thing was set on the crown of a mountain over 3,000 ft above sea level.

The money for all this nonsense, and for the purchase of land in the interior of his island, came from Henri's rake-off from the export boom he helped bring about by opening up his state to Europeans. It was true that he diverted some of this gold into founding schools, setting up poor and sick relief schemes and starting a primitive form of workmen's compensation, but most of the cash found its way into the royal coffers. Few states, let alone a seething stew of intrigue like early nineteenth-century Haiti, could tolerate such a ruler and in 1820, faced with mounting discontent, Henri shot himself before his people could have the pleasure of deposing him.

Henry I (1068–1135). King of England who managed to find time between founding the Exchequer, re-conquering Normandy and dealing with an uppity Church, to sire no fewer than 24 children – most of whom were born the wrong side of the sheets. Despite several commendable attempts at an improved total since, this remains, as far as one knows, the British royal record.

Henry III (1551–1589). King of France and a celebrated namby-pamby. He was originally the King of Poland but in 1574 his brother, Charles IX, died and Henry succeeded to the French throne. When he arrived in Paris, his new subjects could hardly believe their eyes. Something about his appearance at a court fete told them that he was definitely not as other men are. It was not just his rouged cheeks, nor the fact that his hair and beard were dyed and scented with violet powder. Nor was it even the emerald and pearl pendant earrings that he wore.

What really gave the game away was that he was dressed in a gown of pink damask, the eye-catching lines of which were rather attractively set off by billowing sleeves tied with gold thread.

There were, of course, those courtiers who were anxious to reassure each other that Henry's costume was but a satirical fancy dress especially run up for the occasion. However, the awful truth was soon apparent. Far from being a prank, Henry's get-up was only a marginally exaggerated form of his everyday dress. He did usually stop short of putting on a skirt but he habitually wore outrageously feminine clothes, powdered and painted his face, carried a fan, wreathed himself in jewellery, curled his hair, swapped beauty tips with his wife Louise and slept every night in a cosmetic face mask. Occasionally he suffered pangs of remorse for this vanity and then, as penance, he would go barefoot to church, whipping himself the while, with only sackcloth to cover his dainty skin. Yet it was never long before he was togged up once more in his glamour gear, pouting and preening in front of his applauding circle of boyfriends.

In keeping with this effeminacy was his incessant fussing over his little lap dogs, of whom there were no fewer than 2,000. All lived a life of canine splendour but his favourites were especially pampered, wanting for nothing and sleeping each night in a velvet-cushioned apartment next to the royal bedchamber. Henry doted on these yapping animals so much that when he went for a walk, he could not bear to leave any of them behind. So he had built a large but light basket, richly lined with crimson silk, into which anything up to 30 dogs would be crammed and then carried behind their master on his promenades. Cats, however, he could not abide and he developed such a phobic fear of them that he would faint if one came near. With such important distractions as these, he concentrated only fitfully on his nation's affairs and a well-meaning patriot assassinated him in 1589.

Henry IV (1553–1610). King of France whose eventful life

seemed to conform to some strange numerical pattern. He was the 14th king of France, had 14 letters in his name Henri de Bourbon, his birthdate was 14 May 1553 (which adds up to 14), his first wife Marguerite de Valois was born on 14 May 1552, the Parisians rose in revolt against him on 14 May 1558, he won the battle of Ivry on 14 March 1590 and a great military and ecclesiastical demonstration was organised against him on 14 May 1590.

None of these coincidences was, of course, prima-facie evidence of some diabolical force at work in his life, even to someone as normally superstitious as Henry. But they ought, at least, to have suggested to him that 13 May 1610 was not the best date to stage the coronation of his second wife, especially when he had been warned that he would not long survive the event. Naturally enough, he didn't. On 14 May his heart was duly pierced by the dagger of Ravaillac the assassin.

Henry V (1820–1883). King of France, he came to the throne as a 10-year-old boy on 2 August 1830 and was persuaded to vacate it precisely one week later. At least he considerably out-reigned his predecessor, Louis XIX, who spent 55 years waiting to inherit the throne, sat on it for a few hours and then abdicated. This is believed to be the shortest reign on record.

Hercule I (1562–1604). King of Monaco who made a distinctly unregal departure from this life when he was thrown off the cliffs near his palace by his disgruntled subjects.

Prince Leopold Alexander of Hohenlohe (1794–1849). German Prince and relative of the British royal family who created a sensation in nineteenth-century Europe with his controversial faith healing. To this day no one is quite sure whether he was an inspired mystic with extraordinary powers or simply a devious trickster with a nice line of patter.

The evidence of his early life certainly leans towards the prosecution, suggesting, as it does, that he had a rather eccentric idea of vocation. He was born the eighteenth son of

Prince Karl Albrecht and was ordained a priest in 1816, despite being expelled from one seminary for 'levity'. For the next few years this young man of God moved in a distinctly mysterious way, cribbing his sermons from a well-known anthology, absconding from Vienna with his church's collection money but always scrupulously distributing every pfennig of his ill-gotten gains to the poor.

Then, in 1821, came the key event in his life. He met a peasant and faith healer called Martin Michel and shortly afterwards took him to try and cure Princess Mathilde Schwartzenberg, a 17-year-old cripple. To the amazement of one and all, she was healed and the city of Wurtzberg went crazy. Somehow, in their delirium of joy, they hailed Prince Leopold as the cause, and the halt and the lame for miles around began streaming into the city, seeking health at the magical hands of the royal priest. Hysteria ensued and the Prince (who, let it be said, was hardly unwilling to have himself cast in the role of miracle-worker) was swamped with sufferers from all manner of distressing conditions. Not everyone, however, rushed to join in the acclamation and it is at this point in the story that the wheat of truth becomes rather difficult to separate from the chaff of legend. Everyone in Wurtzberg stampeded to take sides and objective observation was trampled underfoot.

The local papers, who supported the Prince, rushed out reports of the blind seeing, the lame walking and the deaf hearing; among them none other than the Crown Prince of Bavaria, the future King Ludwig I. The papers also published the account of an eye-witness called Herr Scharold who claimed to have seen the Prince cure stroke victims and numerous cases of rheumatoid arthritis. Doctors and fellow priests, too, came forward to testify.

The sceptics, however, were unimpressed. 'What about the Prince's visit to the city's hospital?' they scoffed. Here the royal priest had called half a dozen lame men to hobble up to him and then told them to throw away their sticks and walk. Sadly, when the cripples followed his instructions, they just crumpled into a dishevelled heap and the kindly nuns who ran the establishment had to spend several minutes unravelling the tangled limbs. The more persistent of his critics also claimed that his failures were not only legion but his so-called successes were, in fact, quite bogus. They cited the case of the girl with hearing not a whit impaired who was brought before the Prince one day. He assumed a glassy stare, mumbled a few words, clapped his hands over her ears, cried out 'You are cured,' and when the bewildered girl said 'Pardon?' his followers burst into ecstatic applause.

So it was hardly surprising that when he moved on to practise his faith healing at Banberg, the burgomaster there, a chap called Hornthal, insisted on the appointment of a commission to verify any possible cures. The Prince was now performing in front of invited and doubting audiences and, try as he might, no cures were effected. He had better luck at the baths of Bruckeman but despite more cures, the enthusiasm for Prince Leopold and his amazing properties was now past its peak. In an effort to rally his cause, he drew up a detailed account of over 100 healings that he claimed to have worked, had them attested by witnesses and then sent this document to the Pope. His Holiness took no notice and neither did the people of Vienna when he turned up there. The Prince could take a hint and, telling people that his healing gift had deserted him as quickly as it had arrived, he attempted no more cures. Instead, the royal priest settled for a quiet life as a career churchman, spending his time preaching, helping the needy and writing slender little devotional works. In 1844 he was made Bishop of Sardica and five years later he died aged 55.

Humayun (1508–1556). Moghul Emperor and a slave to superstition. Unlike most of his contemporaries, who were content to placate the fates by periodically reeling off a few verses of mumbo-jumbo and avoiding one-eyed dogs, left-handed virgins and the like, Humayun allowed his every move to be governed by strange signs and portents. He believed, for instance, that unspeakable calamities would ensue if anyone entered a building with the left foot first and if anyone ever dared cross a threshold in anything but the approved manner, then he would make them go back and re-enter correctly. This and similar foibles may have been inconvenient and aggravating to his immediate circle – especially on well-attended state occasions – but at least the disruption was confined to them. This could hardly be said of his attempt to reorganise the whole imperial bureaucracy along astrological lines, an eccentric policy which succeeded in rendering the administration of the great Moghul Empire well-nigh powerless.

His first act was to divide the public offices into four departments, each named after an elemental force. Thus the Earth Department looked after agriculture and architecture, the Water Department was responsible for canals and the royal wine cellar and the Fire Department took charge of war. Thus far, there was a kind of silly logic to the scheme, but this all rather fell apart when Humayun came to the Air Department, for this was a dustbin of all the things that did not fit in elsewhere. It had jurisdiction over anything from the wardrobe to the stables and the kitchen to the camels, etc. Having set these curious lines of demarcation, which had to be rigidly observed, Humayun then caused further havoc by decreeing that the governing planet for each type of business or pleasure would determine on which day of the week it was dealt with. These celestial accidents also dictated the colour of the clothes that the Emperor would wear that day. So on Sundays he dressed in yellow and attended to the affairs of state; Mondays were reserved for merry-making, for which he wore green; Tuesdays were when he dressed in red and dispensed justice of a quite shocking severity, and so on. However urgent the business, it had to wait for its proper day; nothing would ever tempt him to deviate from the timetable.

When not engaged in the auspicious duty of the day or sitting in the middle of his astrological carpet doling out forfeits to his courtiers, Humayun could invariably be found trying to foretell his own future. His favoured method was to shoot arrows into the air and divine from their flight and destination what the fates had in store. Sometimes he would mark half the arrows with his name, the other half with that of the Shah of Iran and attempt to tell from the way that they fell to earth which of the two nations would be more prosperous. These strange practices brought him much comfort, but like all superstitions they proved to be of very limited practical use. Had the fates and spirits to whom he had shown so much respect been doing their job they would no doubt have found some way of contacting him with the message: 'Steer clear of the library roof on the 24th of Jan.' They did not, however, and Humayun went there on that day. As he walked down the steps, he heard the call to prayer, turned to bow, tripped on his robe, fell and died from his injuries three days later.

7th Nizam of Hyderabad (1884–1967). Indian Prince and, among other things, a resourceful dirty old man. Not content with having the run of a huge harem, which at its height totalled over 200 women, he also felt the need to spice up his sex life with a spot of voyeurism. Fortunately his wealth enabled him to play Peeping Tom in some style. He had concealed cameras installed in the guest bathrooms at his palace of Falaknuma and he spent many a happy hour gloating over the results. When he died, thousands of candid photographs of visiting dignitaries and their wives were found among his collection of erotica.

This taste for sex through the keyhole rather than on the couch was one of the many surprises about the man. Contradiction seemed to flow through his veins. He was, for example, so wealthy that he could afford to donate £25 million to the British Exchequer for the prosecution of the First World War, yet so mean that he only offered dinner guests one cigarette and, when they departed, would smoke the dog-ends left in the ashtray. The Nizam, regarded by many as the richest man in the world, also fined dinner guests who were late and, despite cellars full of gold bars and trunks full of rubies, wore in private nothing more grand than crumpled cotton pyjamas, camel-skin slippers bought for a pittance in the local bazaar and a battered old fez.

Yet anyone who concluded from this shabby outfit that he was not a proud man would be very much mistaken. He demanded and received an extraordinary level of deference from his courtiers and, as a result, they barely moved a muscle without his express consent. If one of them wanted to leave Hyderabad for even an hour they would have to obtain the Nizam's written permission and this required a degree of grovelling that would have shamed a galley slave. Their request had to be made on special notepaper on which had been printed an address to the Nizam that left no compliment unpaid, nor any royal boot unlicked. It read:

'After kissing the Threshold of Your Throne it is humbly submitted to the Great and Holy Protector of the World, Shadow of God, Mighty Holder of Destinies, Full of Light and Most Elevated Among Creatures, the Exalted, may God's Shadow never grow less, may God protect Your Kingdom and Your Sultanate, most respectfully I beg to submit . . .' Then, after all this tripe there was a blank space where the courtier would make his humdrum pitch, scribbling something like, 'Can I go to Poona races tomorrow?' or 'Mother has beri-beri, must go home to slop out.' If the subject was lucky, the request would then be granted.

When Indian independence came, the Nizam had to say goodbye to this life as a mortal god. After watching the new state take possession of his 200 cars and cart away his millions, he settled down to a life of quiet retirement at his palace of King Kothi. There, drinking 40–50 cups of coffee a day and subsisting on an annual allowance of a mere £400,000, he passed the time away until his death at the age of 83 in 1967.

> *'Everyone likes flattery; and when you come to royalty you should lay it on with a trowel.'*
>
> BENJAMIN DISRAELI.

I

*'Insanity occurs in about five per cent
of royalty – five times that of the
rest of the population.'*

F.A. WOODS.

Ibrahim the Mad (1616–1648). Sultan of the Ottoman Empire and probably the most vindictive old pervert ever to sit on a throne. His fixations about certain objects and odours were a constant trial to his court and so gross were the demands that he made upon his harem that even this fine and long-suffering body of women were driven to protest. No wonder, then, that he was eventually deposed at the instigation of the father of one of the girls whom he had most comprehensively abused.

In appearance, Ibrahim was the very picture of the pleasure-monger. His body was puffed up from years of self-indulgence, his turban invariably leant on his head at a drunken angle and he always reeked of ambergris, drenching his beard, kaftan and even his curtains in this suffocating perfume. He had his beard encased in a network of diamonds and the weather had to be exceedingly hot for him not to be wearing some garment made of sable. In fact, he had something of a fetish for this fur, dressing himself and his courtiers in it and having the walls of his apartments covered in the stuff so that he could run his hands over the pelts when he felt the need. He even had his cats shaved so they could all be kitted out in sable coats.

His sexual tastes were hardly less strange. He had one room in his inner sanctum covered with mirrors and here he would make his women strip naked and pretend to be mares while he frolicked among them, acting the part of the stallion at stud. It may have been only horseplay to him but there must have been times when his 'mares' longed to see the man with the gelding irons show up. In time, Ibrahim became so jaded that it was only by means of such elaborate tableaux that he could be roused to perform with his harem at all. His life now became a desperate search for new experiences to stave off his increasingly frequent fits of impotence. His harem informant, Sechir Para, was despatched in a jewel-studded coach to procure attractive girls for him, thus earning her the title of 'The Filthy Sultana' and, when he tired of her beautiful discoveries, he turned to something rather different.

He became convinced that the more there was of a woman, the more fun she was likely to be and so he had his agents comb the empire for the fattest woman they could find. They found many prize specimens but the best was a vast, billowing Armenian woman and, after making appropriate arrangements for her transportation, they brought her back to the capital in triumph. Ibrahim was delighted and after hours of endless fun in her capacious arms, he showered her with riches and made her the Governor General of Damascus. It seemed now as if only the most daunting sexual challenge could ignite his torpid interest and his next urgent impulse was to possess the daughter of The Mufti, one of the most vaunted and sacred of Turkey's religious leaders. Here indeed was an unscalable romantic height if ever there was one and only Ibrahim was surprised when The Mufti disdainfully rejected his panting overtures. By now the Sultan was not so much on heat as boiling over. His libido was firing on all cylinders and, not to be denied, he had the girl abducted and taken to the harem where he introduced her to some practices which can only be described politely as 'experimental'.

Ibrahim's need for novelty and the harem's squeaks of protest hardly made for a congenial atmosphere at court. Suspicion was quick to take root and when he was told that one of his concubines had been unfaithful, he decided that the only way to make sure that the culprit was punished was to put all

280 girls to death. Drowning was the chosen method and group after group of the harem were manhandled into sacks which were then tied up and weighted with stones, loaded into boats, taken to the Bosphorus and then tipped into the water. Only one girl survived, her sack having become untied, allowing her to struggle free, hail a passing boat bound for France and so subsequently spill the dreadful beans in Paris.

When rumours of the great harem drowning began filtering back to Istanbul, The Mufti and all the others who had suffered at Ibrahim's hands took the chance to avenge his barbarities. The guards were despatched to the palace, where they removed the gibbering Sultan to a quiet corner and, with a quick twist of a bowstring, brought his appalling reign to an end.

Lord Inchcape (20th Century). English peer who was understandably amazed to be offered the crown of Albania. There he was one day in October 1921, minding his own business and just about to settle down to family lunch at his castle in Ayrshire, when a special messenger arrived breathless from London. 'My lord,' said the emissary, 'you have just been offered the throne of Albania.' For a moment, Inchcape was struck dumb. Then he spoke. 'Good heavens,' he said, 'where is it?'

Eventually an atlas was found and, sure enough, there was the generous little kingdom, wedged in between Yugoslavia and Greece on the Adriatic coast. Although the place undoubtedly existed, Lord Inchcape had no idea why its people should want him as their monarch. He was rather inclined to believe that it was all some elaborate hoax. Not until the following day, when a letter arrived, did he accept that the offer was genuine. The letter was signed by the English representative of some influential Balkan interests and was one of the most ludicrous documents in the history of royalty. It read:

'I do not know if this is the first time in your career that you have been offered a kingdom . . . Perhaps next time you are cruising in the Mediterranean you would feel drawn to put in at Valona or Durazzo in order to express your sentiments, whatever they may be in connection with the offer which I am now seriously putting before you. In any case, if you turn it down entirely perhaps you would feel called upon to suggest the name of some Englishman or American with administrative powers who would like to take up the cudgels on Albania's behalf, thereby securing an honourable position as Albania's king.' With typical British understatement, Inchcape replied, 'It is a great compliment to be offered the crown of Albania but it is not in my line.'

This put the Albanians and their friends in something of a fix and to find a king they began trawling in some even stranger waters. Among the candidates were Colonel Aubrey Herbert, on whom John Buchan based the character Greenmantle in the novel of that name, and the celebrated sportsman C.B. Fry. There are two versions of what happened to Fry's candidature: one that he rejected the offer out of hand, the other that he was keen but blew his chances by shipping too much whisky at his interview with an Albanian bishop. As soon as the newspapers reported that the field was once again open, there was a rash of applications, including one from a naval cadet and another from a dancing instructress. Finally, the country's president, Ahmed Bey Zogu, ascended the throne and reigned under the splendid title of King Zog.

M. L'Isle-Marivault (d. 1590). An excessively devoted subject of the effeminate King Henry III of France. He was so upset by the premature death of his royal master that he vowed he would survive him no longer than he could possibly help. Rejecting suicide as dishonourable, young L'Isle-Marivault decided instead to die in a blaze of glory, avenging the late king. So in 1590 he issued a public announcement that he would fight to the death anyone who asserted that Henry's assassination was not a great calamity. A youth called Marolle took him up on his offer and suitable arrangements were duly made. When it came to the combat, L'Isle-Marivault put up a flamboyantly ineffectual performance, succumbed to the first thrust of Marolle's lance and died the martyr's death that he had so earnestly sought.

Moulay Ismail (1672–1727). Emperor of Morocco and the most prolific stud in history. According to *The Guinness Book of Records*, which takes an unhealthy interest in such matters, Moulay fathered no fewer than 548 sons and 340 daughters – a grand total of 888 children. His productivity may at first glance appear to be surprising, until one realises that even in the seventeenth century there was precious little else to do in Morocco. More astonishing is the fact that he was the last of his line to reign – something for which he could hardly be held responsible.

Ivan IV (1530–1584). Czar of Russia whose nickname of 'The Terrible' does not even begin to do justice to his staggering appetite for slaughter. For most of his reign it seemed as if he was hell-bent on nothing less than a systematic cull of his people. If he was not ordering the execution of individuals by the ghastliest means imaginable, then he was laying siege to cities and subsequently making the most awful meal of butchering the inhabitants. As a result, his reputation for psychopathic violence grew so intimidating that he scared some of his subjects literally to death. In 1569, for instance, a young girl was so horrified to hear she had been chosen as his third wife that she collapsed and died from shock; and later, when Ivan bore down on a castle in Livonia, the occupants chose to blow themselves up rather than fall into his hands.

It was probably the most prudent policy; for, as the city of Novgorod discovered in 1574, Ivan was not the kind of caller to encourage. He had become convinced that this, Russia's most Westernised city, was fomenting a rebellion and he set out from Moscow determined to snuff out all dissent. On the way, he stopped to burn the city of Tver and kill many of its people; so, by the time he arrived at Novgorod, he was nicely limbered up for the task ahead. His first action was to erect a wooden wall all around the city to prevent its inhabitants from fleeing. Then he had a special platform built and, for the next few weeks, he sat back an watched as 1,000 people a day were taken out and executed. Alas, this method proved too slow and so he ordered mass drownings in the Volkhov river. Men, women and children were tied to sleighs, which were then run into the freezing waters. Any who broke their fetters and surfaced were pushed back down beneath the ice with long poles. Eventually, even Ivan tired of the carnage and he moved on, leaving an estimated 50,000 dead.

It was, perhaps, no more than should be expected from one who spent his boyhood throwing dogs from the 200-ft-high towers of the Kremlin wall or riding his horse full tilt into crowds of innocent Muscovites. By the age of 14, this beardless little charmer was sufficiently hard-boiled to seize power from his guardians and order 30 of the more uppity boyars to be hung on roadside gibbets. Any further protesters were beheaded, imprisoned, thrown to the dogs (sometimes by Ivan himself) or, if they had merely been insolent, had their tongues cut out. So it went on until the time came for him to take a wife. As may be guessed, the patient wooing of a maiden's hand was not Ivan's style and instead he chose a more direct method. In 1547 he issued a circular to all nobles ordering them on pain of death to send their marriageable daughters to Moscow. Nearly 1,500 turned up and they were housed in a huge building, sleeping 12 to a room. Here midwives examined them and physicians questioned them while Ivan, unseen behind a grille, eyed them up and down, weeding out the less promising specimens. Gradually this vast cattle market was whittled down to just ten and then finally he made his selection – Anastasia Zahkarina Koshkina.

Amazingly, considering how they met, he grew to love her deeply and she, together with his mentor, a monk called Sylvester, had a decidedly calming influence on him. Over the next dozen years his rages and cruelties decreased, his conquests made him the hero of his people, he reformed the legal code, established trading links with England and even became quite bookish. Piety, no less, reared its head and in 1555 he ordered the construction of St Basil's Church in Moscow (an act which inspired the persistent legend that he was so pleased with the work of the architects that he had them blinded so they would never be able to design anything more beautiful. This, however, is a libel on a ruler who was, at that time, hard-working, far-sighted and even cultured and only marginally more vicious than his contemporaries.)

Then, in 1560, came the turning point in his life. Anastasia died and Ivan lost all restraint. He ranted, raved, refused to see his children, smashed his furniture, banged his head on the floor in full view of the court, ordered virgins to his bedroom and there debauched them. His old cruel nature, with its violent tempers and barbaric whims, resurfaced and, until his final years, raged unabated. Suddenly no one was safe – not from the long, iron-pointed staff he carried and with which he was always liable to lash out; nor from the fatal orders he was apt to bark in his highpitched voice at the slightest provocation. There was no telling what he would do next. He would set bears on people just to see what would happen, put them under the ice for some imagined show of disrespect, have peasant women stripped naked and used as target practice by his Orichnik marksmen and once, for a joke, tipped boiling soup over a jester and, when the man squealed, stabbed him to death.

His sense of humour was strange indeed and never more so than when some English and Dutch women laughed at him during one Moscow festival. In his fury he had them sent back to his palace, where he ordered them to undress and file into a great hall. After a few moments, the doors opened and a team of servants threw onto the floor 45 bushels of shelled peas, which Ivan then ordered the naked ladies to pick up – one by one. When they had finished, he gave them all wine and told them to be more careful in future. On another occasion he demanded that the inhabitants of a city deliver him a cart full of live fleas. As well he knew, he could have set them no more irritating task and, sure enough, the people finally sent word that not only were they unable to capture the elusive insects but they were now also infested with the wretched things. When Ivan had finished cackling, he fined them 7,000 roubles.

If he really wanted to enjoy himself, he would go down to the dungeons of his fortress of Alexanorov and watch the prisoners being tortured. Here was a sadist's paradise – everything from racks to flaying implements, iron cages to pits for live burials.

And if he wanted a particularly lively session, he could always order the victims to be pitted against bears. Strange to think, then, that the man who revelled in all this and laid waste city after city during his Reign of Terror, also had a little bedroom secret: Ivan, the Butcher of Novgorod, would insist that every night he had a bedtime story and even kept three ancient blind men whose sole duty these soothing yarns were. Perhaps these old wrinklies shoved the odd moral into their tales, for as Ivan moved towards his last years, he experienced the occasional bout of remorse. His foaming temper was never long hidden, however, and when he argued with his son and heir in November 1581, something inside the old czar once again snapped. At the height of their ruckus, he raised his iron-pointed staff and brought it crashing onto Ivan junior's temple. His son fell to the floor and five days later was dead.

When Ivan realised that he had killed the man who would have succeeded him, his mind gave way completely. For weeks afterwards he wept, tore out his hair and beard, wandered through the corridors calling for his dead son and beat his head on the Kremlin walls. He was now a broken man. For the next two years he gradually slipped into lassitude until, in March 1584, he died aged 53. He had enlarged Russia, modernised parts of it and brought his country into the wings of the European stage; but his warped nature had always been ready with the sabotage. In the end, it was somehow typical of his reign that one moment of blind rage should mean that he was followed not by his capable son, Ivan, but by his feeble-minded idiot of a son, Feodor.

> *'Kings climb to eminence over men's graves.'*
> AUSTIN DOBSON.

J

Jacques I (20th Century). A wealthy and eccentric sugar magnate who at the turn of the century suddenly proclaimed himself 'His Imperial Majesty, the Emperor Jacques I of the Sahara' and claimed that vast desert as his kingdom.

His real name was Lebaudy and his adventures began when he loaded his yacht *Frasquita* with stores, arms, his family and friends and set sail for North Africa. The second day at sea was a confusing one for all on board. In the morning Jacques issued an order that the crew should address him as 'Captain' but in the afternoon he announced that he would rather be known as 'General'. It was all the same to the crew; they were so well paid they would have been prepared to call him 'Your majesty' and bow and scrape accordingly. This was just as well, because before the sun went over the yardarm that was precisely how Jacques was demanding to be addressed and treated. By the time the ship docked at Cape Juby in the summer of 1903, the king had become an emperor and His Imperial Majesty Jacques I was declaring that the Sahara was his and he would build his capital at Troya.

Now setting up an empire, especially in the world's largest desert, is a fairly substantial undertaking and at first the Imperial family had to be content with large tents for their royal residence. Eventually, however, a prefabricated palace arrived from England and they were able to live in something like the manner to which they thought they ought now to be accustomed. Britain also provided Jacques with portable stables, which were intended to house the results of his most ambitious project of all. He had long since decided that, as the horse was fast but could not cope with the shifting sands while the camel possessed the opposite characteristics, a hybrid between the two animals (which he would call a che-val) would be the perfect means of transport around his new kingdom. Yet despite the most explicit and imperious commands from Jacques, the beasts refused to show anything other than purely academic interest in each other and the special stables remained empty.

This was not his only problem. The Morocco government and the Hague Tribunal were not entirely happy about this half-baked adventurer simply rolling up and commandeering millions of square miles of desert, infertile and inhospitable though it was. They put the matter in the hands of their lawyers and soon the writs were piling up outside the tent of Jacques's Minister of State. His Imperial Majesty was beginning to realise that being an Emperor was not all pomp and circumstance and cross-breeding camels. He needed to find somewhere where he could still have all the fun of being treated like royalty without any of the responsibilities. In 1903 he found it – the Savoy Hotel in London. So his court moved from the Sahara to the Strand, taking with them their Emperor and his almost unmanageable megalomania. After issuing an edict that 'in my absence from the throne, all usurpers will be strictly dealt with', Jacques settled down to a life of pampered indolence, punctuated with the occasional outburst of petulance. He once, for example, had two of the hotel's pageboys dismissed for daring to address him as merely 'Mr'. Fellow guests also had much to put up with and one, a Mr Redding of Chicago, had cause to complain to the management that 'the Emperor of the Sahara stole my coal scuttle'.

After a few years of living high on the hog in the Savoy, Jacques's money ran out and he disappeared back into obscurity. He was still, however, behaving imperiously to the end and his last recorded act as Emperor was to despatch to the French Prime Minister a cheeky formal protest against the lack of an invitation for the Sahara government to attend the Algeciras Conference of 1906.

James I (1566–1625). King of England and one of the least successful silkworm farmers in history.

It was in 1609 that James decided that he would single-handedly found a British silk-weaving industry. So, at a cost of £935, he imported 10,000 mulberry trees, had them planted on the site where Buckingham Palace now stands and sat back to await the first bales of fabric. Yet even for kings, the business is not quite as simple as that. What James did not know was that there are two types of mulberry tree – *morus alba,* upon which silkworms spin to their hearts' content and *morus nigra,* a fruit tree which they avoid like the plague. Sure enough, James had planted the wrong one.

After repeated, and, to him, mysterious crop failures, James began to lose patience with the idle worms and, finally, interest in the project altogether. Most of the trees were felled, the land became a pleasure garden and, eventually, the site for a royal residence. Today, in the south-west corner of Buckingham Palace gardens, stands a lone black mulberry tree – a gnarled memento of James's doomed silkworm experiment.

Jehangir Khan (1569–1627). Moghul Emperor and a hard taskmaster. When a royal attendant accidentally broke a china cup, he ordered the poor man to fetch him an identical replacement – all the way from China. Normally, however, he valued cups for what they contained, as he was a great drinker. In his late twenties he was sinking 20 cups of double-strength distilled spirits a day and when he ascended the throne this boozing had reached such an heroic scale that he was actually depicted on Moghul coins holding a drinking cup. This was something of a deceit, in fact, because by then this dipsomaniac was in such an advanced state of delirium tremens that others had to hold the cup for him. The court physician later ordered him to cut his alcoholic intake by more than half and he increasingly turned for his pleasures to sadism, taking revenge on the spoilsport doctor by shooting blunt arrows at him.

Jerome I (1784–1860). King of Westphalia, youngest brother of Napoleon Bonaparte and an incorrigible spendthrift. Using the meagre resources of this small German state, he lived in such unadulterated luxury that he even took to bathing in red wine. It was not a habit that anyone, let alone a king, could hope to keep secret and, when word leaked out, his subjects declined to drink wine of that type for fear that it was their monarch's bathwater rebottled. This was not idle fancy. According to his biographer, the claret that was used for the royal ablutions was sold off in job lots to a cafe called Murray's in Konigstrasse.

Jerome was probably only capable of such excess because he had undergone such a comprehensive apprenticeship as a wastrel. Even as a child, his indulgences required a hefty subsidy and he soon learnt to be an unprincipled scrounger of funds. At the age of 15 he once demanded a loan of 500 francs from his Uncle Fesch and, when the old man hesitated, Jerome threatened to slash his favourite Van Dyck painting. It was no bluff. Only the uncle's frantic flourishing of the cash stopped the youngster's sword just inches from the canvas.

By 23, his career was already an impressive testament to his frivolity and utter unreliability: he had fought a duel, thrust himself at women relentlessly, pursued an outrageous naval career and been on a disastrous trip to the United States. Here he not only spent three times his annual income inside three months but also illegally married the daughter of a Baltimore businessman, whom he was then forced to renounce in farcical circumstances. Uncharacteristically, he afterwards corresponded with her for seven years and seemed genuinely to love her and the child she bore him.

Hoping that high office would miraculously reform this wayward youth, Napoleon made him Imperial Prince, then married him off to Princess Catherine of Wurttemburg and, finally, in 1807, created him King of the puppet state of

Westphalia. Sadly for his elder brother, Jerome now scaled new heights of extravagance. He dressed like a dandy on a chocolate box, purchased 150 carriages for his own personal use, maintained a vast household who were paid the highest salaries in Europe, showered expensive gifts on his mistresses, had his famous baths, held masques and balls practically every night and, when he went on his travels, bought up all kinds of foreign gold coins, which he then had melted down and minted into his own pretentious coinage of 'Jeromadors'.

His taste in women was totally indiscriminate: married or single, young or mature, they were all the same to him. Nor was he too fussy about where and when these liaisons were consummated. If the mood was upon him, which it invariably was, and a girl was to hand, then even the royal box at his own personal theatre was deemed suitable, regardless of the performance taking place on the stage below. He usually had the decency to hold himself in check until the interval but, since the next act could not begin until Jerome signalled he had finished, the intermission was often excessively long. Sometimes he would choose as his playmate an actress from that night's play, thus complicating the stage manager's life no end. On one such occasion a naked limb appearing over the parapet was misconstrued as the King's permission to proceed and the curtain went up with the actress still very much in Jerome's grip. When it came to her cue, the performance had to be stopped while she adjusted her dress, left the box and made her way to the wings.

In 1814 the entire Napoleonic edifice began to crumble and Jerome was forced to flee to Switzerland. Although he later managed to marry the wealthy Guistina Pecori and see out his remaining years in some style, his days of comic opera royalty ended then, at the age of 30.

Joanna I (1326–1382). Queen of Naples and an early feminist. This enlightened woman once issued a decree that no man must force his wife to have sexual intercourse more than six times a day. It is possible that her four marriages were, in part, a search for a husband who was at least capable of breaking her own law.

Joanna (1479–1555). Queen of Castile who adopted a refreshingly spirited attitude to her husband's infidelities. Most royal wives of the time just meekly accepted their partner's wanderings or else retaliated by doing a little discreet straying themselves. Joanna was different. She was not only deeply in love with her husband Philip the Fair but was also possessed of an intensely jealous nature, which was not improved by Philip's flaunting of his fancy women. So when she came upon him making sheep's eyes at a girl in Brussels and running his fingers through her magnificent hair, something snapped inside Joanna. She marched straight over to the guilty pair, harangued her rival at the top of her voice and then sent for the court hairdresser whom she ordered to cut off every inch of the girl's flowing locks.

Her husband swore at once that he would have nothing more to do with Joanna and he not only increased his flirtations but also, shortly afterwards, had his wife locked up in a room in the castle. Far from souring her feelings for Philip, this action of his served only to make her pine for him all the more and she continued to do so until his premature death at the age of 28 in 1506.

Joanna's devotion to him now passed from the soppy to the insane. Her mental balance had never been robust and the loss of her husband completely and permanently unhinged her mind. For the remaining 49 years of her life she did little more than maintain a deranged vigil over Philip's coffin, sometimes ordering it opened so that she might gaze at his embalmed body, at other times merely content to stare endlessly at the casket. Henceforth she ventured out only at night, behaviour that she explained in one of her rare lucid moments by saying, 'A widow who has lost the sun of her own soul should never expose herself to the light of the day.' Saddest of all was that Philip's death did not even free her from the obsession that every woman had designs on him and she never allowed any female, nuns included, to go near his remains. Only her own death in 1555 liberated her from this pathetic existence.

John (1167–1216). King of England and, according to every child's book of history, the original bad hat. However, despite his gluttony, loss of the Crown Jewels in the Wash and alleged persecution of the mythical Robin Hood, his royal descendants do owe him a debt of gratitude. He was, after all, in 1207, the first of our monarchs to use the royal 'we'.

John I (1296–1346). King of Bohemia who, despite being completely blind, insisted on hurling himself into the thick of the fighting at the Battle of Crecy. He had lost the sight of one eye in a skirmish against the Lithuanians in 1336 and incompetent medical treatment had robbed him of the sight of the other in 1340. He did not, however, lose his appetite for a good punch-up and when the French and English faced each other at Crecy in 1346, the 50-year-old warrior was helped into his armour, mounted on his horse and led into the fray. He perished but the Black Prince so admired his valour that he adopted John's three-feathered emblem and motto ('Ich dien') as his own and they have remained those of all Princes of Wales ever since.

John II (1455–1513). King of Denmark and ex-king of Sweden whose enjoyment of a Passion play was comprehensively ruined by the cast's ill-disciplined performance. The entertainment in question was a late medieval smash-hit called *The Mystery of the Passion* and John, who had been deposed from the Swedish throne in 1501 but still kept the Danish one, thought he would while away an evening of his semi-retirement by seeing the production.

All went well for a time and the audience was just settling down to enjoy the re-enactment of the Crucifixion when the players began making several alarming departures from the stage directions. Now, as everyone but the most abject heathen knows, when Christ is on the cross a Roman soldier called Longinus plunges a spear into His side. So at this point in the play, the authors had duly requested the actor playing Longinus to make a few menacing thrusts with his weapon. Unhappily, 'Longinus' rather exceeded this brief. Whether it was from a misplaced zeal for realism, revenge for some dressing-room acrimony or an effort to give his cameo role some substance is not known; all that is certain is that 'Longinus' proceeded to give 'Christ' a flamboyant skewering and the leading man slithered from his cross and fell dead on the stage.

Even the most experienced and level-headed of casts would have had difficulty in bringing the play to a successful conclusion now. This, however, was not the most experienced and level-headed of casts and when the awful realisation of what had just happened sank in, they rather lost their grip. Uproar ensued and the stage became awash with overwrought theatricals. In the midst of all this mayhem, 'Longinus' obviously thought it would be best if he made himself scarce but, in seeking to exit hastily stage right, he only succeeded in crashing into 'Mary', sending her flying. He then lashed out at 'St John', who had been manfully trying to restore order, and, while the gallant apostle fell injured, he attempted to pick his way through the bodies to the wings.

It was at this point that ex-king John entered the fray. Outraged at the sight of this cast of sacred characters cutting themselves to pieces, he unsheathed his sword, leapt onto the stage and, with a single blow, took off 'Longinus's' head. The rest of the audience were not far behind him and, in the heaving ruckus that followed, John was unfortunately torn apart. Anyone who has difficulty in swallowing this yarn, as I did, is referred to John Timbs' *Historical Ninepins* (see bibliography).

John IV (1604–1656). King of Portugal whose deafness prompted the design of a most unusual throne – a large and comfortable chair which also served as a hearing aid. Courtiers wishing to speak with the King would step forward and bellow their message into an opening in the throne's hollow arms. The sound would then reverberate along a flexible pipe whose trumpet-like ending the deaf sovereign held to his ear.

The Boy Jones (b. 1823). The most famous and persistent example of that most extreme breed of royal groupie – the Buckingham Palace intruder. He was the son of a respectable trader who, for some reason, developed an obsessive fixation about the young Queen Victoria. As events were to prove, Jones was only able to satisfy this strange fascination by playing Peeping Tom to his sovereign at the closest possible quarters.

His activities first came to light on 14 December 1838 when George Cox, a Buckingham Palace porter, saw a shadowy figure moving about in the Marble Hall just after 5 am. The alarm was raised and after a long chase by the staff, sentries and police through the palace and across the gardens, a young boy dressed as a chimney sweep was arrested. It was Edward Jones and if his mere presence in the palace caused a sizeable stir, then his subsequent court appearance was a sensation.

The 15-year-old Jones told the examining magistrate, Mr White, that a year previously he had met a man who requested that he accompany him to the palace. 'I went and have been there ever since. I got my victuals in the kitchen and I thought myself very well off because I came to London to better myself.' He even added that when the Queen met with her ministers, he hid behind furniture and heard every word of their deliberations. By now Mr White was open-mouthed. 'Do you mean to tell me,' he asked, 'that you have lived in the palace upwards of 11 months and been concealed when Her Majesty held a council?' 'I do,' replied Jones.

Not surprisingly, he was sent for trial to Westminster Sessions and by the time these proceedings came to court, some hard details had emerged about this mysterious young intruder. He had, for instance, only been a stowaway in the palace for three days and the escapade was entirely his own work. His former employer, a builder, came forward to report that Jones talked incessantly of the royal family and had often been seen feverishly making sketches of the exterior of Buckingham Palace. This was proof that Jones had prepared for his jaunt by extensively casing the joint but despite this, and the fact that he had taken some articles of clothing at the palace, opened two of the Queen's letters and tried to make off with a regimental sword, Jones's counsel, Mr Prendergast, was sufficiently skilled to portray the venture as a youthful prank and so win an acquittal. The offence, promised Mr Prendergast, would not be repeated.

Wily advocate he may have been, but Mr Prendergast was no judge of character. Two years later Jones was at it again. On Monday 30 November 1840 his slight figure shinned over the palace walls about halfway up Constitution Hill, picked a way through the gardens and slipped in through a window. He stayed a short while and then, fearing discovery, retraced his steps and made off into the night. He had, however, revived his taste for life at the palace and the next day he re-entered by the same route and began to settle in. During the day he hid in cupboards and under beds, occasionally peeping out to catch a glimpse of the royal family and then at night he would emerge to go skulking round the palace and forage for food. He even spent some time seated on the throne.

By his third day Jones had grown sufficiently confident to make his camp in Her Majesty's dressing-room and it was here that he finally gave himself away. Shortly before midnight, on 2 December, Mrs Lilly, nurse to the newborn Princess Royal, heard noises. Other staff were alerted, a search mounted and there, under a sofa which had borne the royal backside not two hours before, was discovered the dishevelled and dirty figure of Jones. This time the authorities were not so forgiving and, after questioning, he was consigned for three months to a house of correction and the treadmill.

Being detained at Her Majesty's pleasure in so unpleasant a place had not the slightest effect on Jones's enthusiasm for his monarch. Within hours of his release from Tothill Fields on 2 March 1841, he was once again trying to re-enter the palace. It must have been obvious now to even the most slow-witted official that Jones was in the grip of a compulsive obsession with the royal family and, when he gave his parents the slip two weeks later, there was no doubt about where he would turn up. Sure enough, at 1 am on 15 March, as a sergeant of the palace police passed the Grand Hall on his nightly patrol, he saw a young man peeping out through the glass doors. Despite extra police posted in the palace, Jones had still managed not only to break in but also to steal cold meat and potatoes from the kitchen and sit undisturbed in a royal apartment while he ate. The result was three more months in a house of correction, this time with the added horrors of hard labour.

By now he was something of a celebrity and after his release one music hall thought he would be such a strong attraction that they offered him £4 a week to appear on stage. He declined, preferring instead to hang around the gates of Buckingham Palace where he must have constituted one of the clearest cases of loitering with intent in legal history. This time the authorities were taking no chances and they sent him off to sea. It worked and, apart from a brief incident some years later (when he jumped ship at Portsmouth and headed for London and the palace before finally being frogmarched back to HMS *Warspite*), he was never heard of again. Jones is not forgotten, however, and the peculiar spiked railings on top of the walls surrounding the palace still stand today as a memorial to him. The Prince Consort ordered their erection directly as a result of the escapades of Jones – the youth who broke into Buckingham Palace no fewer than five times. No doubt Jones would be pleased to know that the railings have not been a total success and his spiritual descendants still occasionally break through the cordon and go snooping around the royal apartments.

Sir Mahabat Khan Babi Pathan, Maharajah of Junagadh (20th Century). Indian Prince and the best friend a dog ever had. Such was his fondness for these animals that he not only kept vast quantities of them but also spent an alarming percentage of his state's income on maintaining them in lavish splendour. Nothing was too good for his dogs, particularly his favourites, and in the end this absurd pampering became so notorious that Junagadh was probably the only place in the world where the common children grew up wanting to be treated like dogs.

At its height his pack numbered over 800. Yet although there were a lot of them, the last thing they had to worry about was where the next bone was coming from or whether there would be enough pavements to foul – every possible need was met.

This was especially true of his most favoured pets, who enjoyed a remarkably cushy existence in a luxurious apartment block. Each dog had its own room, complete with electric light and, of all things, a telephone. Not that they ever had to resort to that to summon room service; all they had to do to fulfil their dearest wish was to raise a languid paw and their own personal servant would come running.

Of course, even these conditions could not ward off the occasional spot of trouble with distemper and for this eventuality there was a hospital, consisting of three white-tiled wards supervised by an English vet. Never, one imagines, was neutering more sympathetically performed and this excellent establishment lost very few patients. Those who did not pull through, however, could be sure of a good send-off in a lined casket and a stirring rendition of Chopin's Funeral March to accompany the cortege.

The cost of running this canine paradise when it was at its peak was £2,300 a month (no less than 11 per cent of the state's revenue) and the Maharajah also spent large sums on competing with fellow dog-lovers to buy Cruft's champions every year. These pedigree specimens became the mainstay of his breeding stock and many hours of intense study and thought went into deciding precisely who would mate with whom. The actual encounter was, of course, a rather brief and unromantic affair with just enough time for an introductory sniff, the essential business itself and a quick retreat, before the man with the bucket of cold water moved in. However, when he came to cross his favourite bitch Roshana with a splendid golden retriever called Bobby, the Maharajah felt that these normal arrangements were a little too basic. He decided that if they were going to mate then they should at least be married first and he ordered preparations to be made for a dog wedding in the grand manner.

When it eventually took place, the event was a full-blown state occasion. There were 50,000 guests in attendance (the viceroy himself was sent an invitation but politely declined), a procession of elephants and a guard of honour for the bride and groom. Both looked the part – she perfumed and covered in jewels and he wearing gold bracelets on his legs and a cummerbund of embroidered silk around his middle. After the ceremony there was a formal banquet with young Bobby and his wife seated on the Maharajah's right hand and thus given precedence over all the other royalty that were present. Then, when the last bone had been picked clean, it was off to the bridal suite where, in the most tasteful of surroundings, the union was consummated. Sadly for Bobby the fun and games ended there, for once he had served Roshana and therefore his purpose, he was bundled back to the kennels. She, being a more favoured animal, spent the rest of her life lolling on velvet cushions in her room.

Yet all good things must come to an end and, as the days of the Raj drew to a close, even the highly conservative Maharajah was forced to apply the choke-chain to his costly obsession, cutting down his pack to a mere 300 dogs. He did his best to defy the inevitable and his state was one of the last three to submit to the new Independent India. When he could resist no longer, he took a few of his best-loved pets with him and fled to Pakistan. After that, a dog's life in India was never quite the same again.

> '*The world is growing weary of that most costly of all luxuries, hereditary kings.*'
>
> GEORGE BANCROFT, 1848.

K

'Good kings are the only dangerous enemies that modern democracy has.'

OSCAR WILDE.

Maharajah of Kapurthala (1872–1949). Indian Prince who apparently believed himself to be the reincarnation of Louis XIV. So, to make his former self feel more at home in the foothills of the Himalayas, he hired a French architect to build him a complete replica of the Palace of Versailles. Designers and experts in objets d'art were called in to make sure that all the fixtures and fittings of the great palace were faithfully reproduced. The Maharajah also insisted on French being spoken at court, engaged a cordon bleu chef from Paris and even forced his Sikh servants to abandon their traditional dress in favour of powdered wigs, silk coats, breeches and buckled seventeenth-century style shoes.

George Karageorgeovitch (20th Century). Prince of Serbia whose wild antics became such a trial to his fellow countrymen that in the end he was placed under lock and key. His violent nature was apparent from the first moment his family were rash enough to unleash him on decent society. Sent as a young prince to learn some semblance of manners at the court of St Petersburg, he carried on so badly that a Serbian minister had to be despatched from Belgrade to reason with him. George took one look at the emissary and knocked him out cold.

When he arrived back home, his behaviour was even less acceptable. At plays and the opera his habit of stamping and yelling abuse at the performers gave such offence that he was soon barred from every theatre in Belgrade, and his arrogance in restaurants was so overbearing that it once sparked a major diplomatic incident. He had sent an aide to a table where some foreigners were dining with the message that his royal highness found their faces so disagreeable that he would be obliged if they would turn and face the wall. Unfortunately, the diners were the Austrian ambassador and his party. Only the most abject grovelling from the Serbian Foreign Office prevented relations between the two countries being severed completely.

It seemed at times that his irresponsibility knew no bounds. Minutes after taking delivery of the first car ever seen in Serbia, for instance, he caused the country's first ever road accident. Not that George was driving at the time, for as the car gathered speed, he took his hands off the wheel and abandoned ship, so to speak, and the vehicle, which contained his brother Alexander in the back seat, careered out of control and into a tree. Apparently, if it had not been for Alexander's great presence of mind, he and several onlooking royals would have perished simultaneously.

It was this lack of concern for the life and limb of others, combined with his foul temper, that was eventually George's undoing. In 1909 he was forced to renounce all rights to the throne after an ugly incident with a royal servant. George had been so enraged at some minor dereliction of duty by a groom that he had flown at the man and kicked him to death, no less. Several years later, while serving as a commander of the Serbian army, he was to prove so impetuous that, even by the standard of First World War generals, he was conspicuous for his eccentric ideas of strategy. After the war, the Serbs decided to take no further chances, marched him off to the lonely castle of Nish, locked him up and threw away the key. For the next 20 years he lived in solitary asylum, subsisting mainly on the eggs he collected from the hens in the castle yard. Then, in 1941, invading Nazis released him. To his credit he would have nothing to do with them, went underground and only surfaced in the late 1940s. He saw out his remaining years pottering about in a villa on the outskirts of Belgrade, living on a pension of £30 a month provided personally by President Tito.

Karl Friedrich (1728–1811). Margrave of Baden-Durlach and the holder of the European all-comers record for the longest reign. He succeeded to his throne aged 10 in 1738 and departed it on his death 73 years later.

Edward, Duke of Kent (1767–1820). The father of Queen Victoria and yet the very last sort of person one would think responsible for spawning this great British symbol of moral rectitude. He not only lived in sin with his French mistress but was an incurable spendthrift, an unrepentant debtor and, just for good measure, an avowed socialist to boot. The one quality he possessed that was recognisable in his daughter was his sense of discipline but even that was way out of focus and earned him a reputation for brutality that was unparalleled even in the army of his time. Indeed, so cruel was his regime as Governor of Gibraltar that he had to be forcibly retired from the post not once, but twice.

This fourth son of George III owed his addiction to unbending discipline not so much to his upbringing but to his military training under the strict Prussian system. By the time he was first appointed to Gibraltar in 1790 he was the most fanatically severe commander of men since Lt. Col. Martinet himself. Everything had to be run with unblemished precision and if it wasn't then Edward would erupt. The slightest sign of tarnish on an officer's button or scuff on a soldier's boot would send him into a bug-eyed rage and earn the offenders punishments that other commanders reserved for high treason. Within a year the government thought it prudent to remove him to Canada.

Here he was, if anything, worse and many of the Royal Fusiliers who were serving under him preferred to risk the appalling consequences of desertion rather than hang around and be beaten bloody for minor misdemeanours. The Duke's response was typical. As the number of absconders rose then so did the quantity of lashes inflicted on each captured deserter. The limit was finally reached when a poor Frenchman called La Rose failed in his bid to leg it to the United States and safety, was brought back and sentenced to receive no fewer than 999 lashes. Edward watched and counted every one. The subsequent plot to assassinate him failed only narrowly in its objective.

The strange thing was that out of uniform and off the parade ground he was as nice as pie, showing an interest in social work and transforming Nova Scotia. By 1802 the government thought he was ready to make a good fist of the Gibraltar job once more. How wrong they were. Within days of arriving on the garrison island, Edward had made his usual sweeping and impulsive judgement. The place, he decided, was swarming with slackers and shirkers and he was determined they should mend their ways. Soon the smack of firm discipline was ringing round the Rock. But the problem was not so much his rigorous enforcement of King's Regulations, fearsome though it was, but his ludicrous extension of them. Code after code of new orders were issued, eventually filling over 300 closely-printed pages. These laid down the law not only on the length of a man's whiskers and beard but also on how every minute of the day should be spent. No detail of island life was too piffling to be excluded and Edward's orders even devoted a sturdy paragraph or two to the carrying of umbrellas by off-duty officers.

One particular aspect of his men's scant leisure time concerned him above all others – drinking. He was adamant that it should be suppressed and, heedless of the ill-feeling that would be stirred up, closed half the Gibraltar wine shops and barred his men from those that remained. They were allowed in only if they were served beer, a concession made less impressive by the fact that the beer was supplied by a brewery under Edward's control and was about as intoxicating as Tizer. As if this was not enough to keep the boozing in check, there was also a parade before lights out to ensure that no one was drunk. The final straw came on Christmas Eve 1803 when Edward ordered the men confined to barracks and quashed the traditional merry-making privileges for Christmas Day. Enough was enough and the mutinous mayhem that followed brought the Duke's career as a colonial governor to a swift and merciful conclusion.

Back in England, Edward was free to devote himself to his other interests – his mistress, his homes and charity. The woman in question was Julie de St Laurent, a Frenchwoman whom he had met in 1791 while in Canada. They lived together for nearly 30 years, making him the most domestically settled of all George III's sons. Yet their life was not without its complications and chief among these were Edward's debts. From the moment he left his first posting in Gibraltar owing £20,000, these had remorselessly piled up and the expensive hobbies he now pursued in London only added to the burden.

The major drain on his purse was definitely Castle Hill Lodge, his fabulous, folly-like residence in Ealing. This outrageous house was approached by a long fenced drive which was illuminated at night by hundreds of brilliant lamps. All along it was a system of bell signals, operated so that visitors were always met by six liveried staff when they arrived at the door. Their surprise at this was as nothing compared to their reaction to the home's contents. In every nook and cranny there were mechanised devices of all kinds – clocks, model songbirds, musical boxes, organs with dancing horses etc – and the corridors were lit by a fantastic collection of coloured lights. In every guest room there were hidden doors which opened onto closets containing perhaps the biggest shock of all: little models of rustic scenes complete with miniature rippling brooks and fountains.

Edward insisted that his staff were on duty 24 hours a day and for this he required huge numbers of servants. They included not only a band to serenade the Duke at breakfast but also a resident hairdresser to ensure that all below stairs were perfectly bewigged. Indeed, his royal highness was most particular about tidiness, even giving his gardeners instructions that no fallen leaves were to remain on the ground for longer than 15 minutes.

Besides this strange house, Edward's principal concern was his charities. By 1811 he was the active chairman, patron or president of no fewer than 53 different organisations. Apart from the usual worthy bodies, they included the National Society for Delivering Poor Married Women In Their Own Habitations, societies for the 'instruction of the infant heathen' and 'conversion of the Jews' and the exquisitely titled 'London Corresponding Board of the Incorporated Society in Scotland for Propagating Christian Knowledge in the Highlands and Islands' – a thankless task, indeed.

Edward had always brought a sense of social justice to these good works and gradually his conviction drove him further and further to the political left. After many years' tireless work for his charities he finally declared, 'It was evident to me that no charitable provision or establishment could remedy the evil of a depressed working class.' Under the tutelage of Robert Owen, the pioneer radical, Edward became a socialist. The two had met in 1815 and later that year the Duke announced, 'I am a full and devoted convert to your philosophy in principle, spirit and practice.' He presided at Owen's lecture meetings, lobbied on his behalf and carried the creed of socialism into the highest reaches of the Establishment, albeit in a low-keyed way.

Meanwhile, his debts went on mounting. By 1807 they had reached £108,200 and half his annual income was devoted to servicing the interest alone. Over the next few years he made heroic efforts to trim his outgoings but in 1816 he gave up the hopeless fight and, as an economy measure, decamped with Madame de St Laurent to Brussels where life was cheaper. Not that one would have known it. He took over the city's largest house, had it and its grounds extensively altered and seemed to live just as imprudently as before. He did not cut down on his work for his favourite causes and had to employ four secretaries to deal with his enormous postbag of 150 letters a week.

Then came the death of his niece Princess Charlotte in childbirth. Suddenly England was without a royal heir of the next generation and looked to Edward and his brothers to provide one. With indecent haste, they all began scuffling over Europe to find brides to begin the race to the succession. While Mme de St Laurent hied to a nunnery, Edward's eye was caught by the widowed Princess Victoire of Saxe-Coburg. He married her and returned to England just in time for their daughter Alexandrina Victoria to be born. Unfortunately, the Duke died while she was still an infant, succumbing to a feverish chill at Sidmouth, Devon in January 1820. It is difficult to avoid a tinge of regret that the future Queen Victoria was thus robbed of the educational influence of this, Britain's most left-wing royal.

Prince George, Duke of Kent (1902–1942). Fourth son of King George V, uncle of our present Queen and one-time drug addict. The details of this phase in his life are somewhat elusive; since most authorities, when they come to this subject, prefer to cough nervously, shuffle their feet and pass on as rapidly as possible. Those who dare to raise the matter seem to agree that, at some time in his twenties, he was encouraged to experiment with funny substances by an American girlfriend. Thereafter, however, the sources get thinner and begin to diverge. David Duff, in his *Queen Mary*, is almost alone among royal biographers in providing further details, suggesting that following the drug-taking and departure of his girl, the Prince suffered a nervous breakdown and was taken off to Fort Belvedere for a cure by his brother David.

A suggestion that the matter was more serious even than this comes from J. Bryan III and Charles J.V. Murphy in their *The Windsor Story*. According to their version, the Prince's brush with drugs – abetted by a rich South American roué who was sent packing from the country by the Prince of Wales – led him 'to the brink of suicide'. Wales talked him into seeking treatment and, they write, 'He leased a secluded house in the country, staffed it with experienced attendants and sent Kent there until he had conquered his addiction.' Although no source speculates about what the substance may have been, the South American connection and the drug fashions of the Twenties suggest cocaine, which was known to the fast set as 'joy powder'.

One thing is certain, the Prince never touched drugs again. He married Marina in 1934, fathered the present Duke, Princess Alexandra and Prince Michael and was on the verge of taking up an appointment as Governor-General of Australia when war broke out. In August 1942 this, arguably the most intelligent and gifted of George's sons, died when the plane taking him to Iceland crashed into a mountain in the north of Scotland.

Khosru II (591–628). King of Persia who lived in such pampered splendour that, when he went on a journey, 1,000 slaves watered the roads before him and another 200 walked on ahead to scatter perfumes.

Kublai Khan (1215–1294). Emperor of China who was most particular about his little lady friends. His staff had to go to the most outrageous lengths to ensure that each of his concubines was fit to slip between the royal sheets. Not for them a quick reconnoitre around the local clip-joints, followed by a swift harvest of the most likely-looking items. Instead, they had to devise an almost unbelievably complicated talent-spotting and vetting service. Only then could their emperor be certain that he was getting his hands on the finest and most unspoilt goods.

The selection process began more than two years before the girls were actually required to perform for their emperor. Gimlet-eyed agents would be sent out with detailed specifications to scour the Tartar province of Ungut, whose women were held to have the most beautiful and fair complexions in all China. Several hundred girls would be collected and they were taken to a central point to be examined. The serious weeding-out would now begin, for this throng of lovelies had to be whittled down to a mere dozen or so. The connoisseurs who did the judging were all men who had made a close study of the female form and, by trial and error down the years, they had gradually got the whole business off to a fine art. What could easily have become an indelicate leering and probing session was now a serious academic procedure. The girls were evaluated in carats, just like precious stones. Each feature – the hair, mouth, face, teeth, legs and no doubt other bits and pieces – were all appraised separately and given a certain number of carats. These were totalled up and the girls who had been awarded 20–24 carats were then taken back to the court for the next stage.

It was now that the Khan himself would get in on the act. His practised eyes would give them the once-over and more girls would be eliminated, thus leaving about 30–40 hopefuls for the final heat. This was a most rigorous and searching test. First they were subjected to an intimate physical inspection, the purpose of which was to ensure that no one had previously sampled their 24-carat charms. Then they were each placed in the care of a noble's wife whose task was to see that they had no aggravating personal habits or hidden imperfections. This was a full-time job for the wives and even involved sleeping beside the girls to make sure that they did not snore or toss and turn in the night and that they were free from unpleasant bodily odours or bad breath. If the girls survived all this with their sanity – and everything else – intact, then they were chosen as part of the new intake of the Khan's harem.

The girls could now share the Emperor's bed – and when he said share, he meant just that, for he always had them in batches of five. They formed squads of this number and they would cater to his every need for three days and nights, after which the next team came on duty. With the assistance of these enthusiastic shiftworkers, he managed to father 47 sons and innumerable daughters. Nor did all this excitement unduly shorten his life. Attended by servants who were so considerate that they stuffed silk napkins in their mouths lest their low-born breath contaminate his food, the great Khan lived to the remarkable age, for a thirteenth-century roué, of 79.

'*What is a king? A man condemned to bear
The public burthen of the nation's care.
From the first blooming of his ill-taught youth
Nourish'd in flattery, and estrang'd from truth.*'

MATTHEW PRIOR, 1718.

L

'There is not a crowned head in Europe whose talents or merits would entitle him to be elected a vestryman by the people of any parish in America.'

THOMAS JEFFERSON, 1788.

Lapetamaka (18th Century). King of Tonga who claimed it was his duty to deflower every native maiden on his island. For some reason his subjects believed him and in his prime he was said to be capable of exercising the royal prerogative up to eight times a day. His claims that he had never in his life slept with the same woman twice should be treated with some scepticism, since a career such as his is likely to induce chronic forgetfulness at the very least.

Vittorio di Martine Valperga Lascaris (20th Century). The king of the royal pretenders. Most claimants in history have confined themselves to eyeing up only one crown but Vittorio dismissed this approach as unambitious. He traced his royal lineage back over 1500 years, included among his forebears more than 100 emperors and armed with this crowded family tree, pursued a claim to no fewer than a dozen kingdoms. At his peak in the 1950s, this Milanese had declared designs on the crowns of Britain, Turkey, Bulgaria, Jerusalem, Cyprus, Armenia, Slovenia, Bosnia, Dalmatia, Toplitsa, Dardania and Albania. The nearest he came to any form of recognition was from the Turks, who, when they heard of him, banned him from entering their country.

Leopold the Unloved (1835–1909). King of the Belgians, cousin to Queen Victoria and royal racketeer. His most outrageous scam was to found a company ostensibly to develop and Christianise the Congo but, in reality, to bleed the territory dry for his own profit. Judged by these sordid standards, the venture was a success. He used the Congo Free State as his personal fief and, in 15 years of uninterrupted exploitation, made £400 million in gold.

His native subjects were less fortunate. Each village had to provide a set quantity of slaves or rubber or sometimes both, and if they did not come up with their quota then the most terrible reprisals were taken. Babies were thrown into rivers to discourage family life, communities were robbed of all their menfolk and, in some places, wholesale slaughter took place. In Bosira in 1884, for instance, Leopold's company agents responded to a shortfall of rubber by taking 1,800 prisoners and shooting the lot. When villages did gather sufficient rubber, it was weighed on rigged scales and fetched only one fortieth of the market price. In just over 20 years the atrocities, beatings, starvation and disease reduced the population of the Congo to just half its former 20 million.

Leopold, meanwhile, continued to rake in the cash, taking care never to inquire too closely into his company's methods. By the time the rest of the world woke up to what was going on, investigated and forced Leopold to sell the Congo to the state of Belgium, the damage was done and the skinflint king had salted away the profits. He spent the remaining years of his life in the Riviera and other playgrounds, occasionally tossing some conscience money in the direction of research into sleeping sickness. Finally, in 1909, while reclining in his sick bed, he married his latest floozie, a Parisian streetwalker, and died not long afterwards. He left not a penny of his millions to his family.

London, Brighton and South Coast Railway (1841–1923). A company who were so determined to suck up to King Edward VII that when he travelled on one of their trains, they not only cleaned and polished the locomotive until it gleamed but also ordered that the coal in the tender be given a coat of whitewash.

Louis XIV (1638–1715). King of France who was the object of such close and incessant attentions that he could not even go to the loo without an audience. Not that there was anything intrinsically fascinating about his majesty's bowel movements, it was just that court protocol demanded that the King was waited upon at all times. Indeed, about the only activity he accomplished unaided was to make love to his mistress and even then there would be courtiers hovering anxiously outside the door, monitoring each sigh from within.

His lack of privacy began the very second he opened his eyes each morning. At that instant, a bevy of courtiers would spring to their allotted tasks, Louis XIV would be helped from his bed, rubbed down with rosewater and spirit of wine, shaved and dressed. This last process was a far from simple matter, involving, as it did, a dozen nobles up to the rank of duke, each one of whom had charge of the clothes for a certain part of the royal body. These duties were jealously guarded and the demarcation disputes that often arose in the royal household would have done credit to the most recalcitrant trade unionist. Once, for instance, it took three days to settle who was responsible for dusting the royal bedsheet, there being some doubt as to whether the item constituted linen or furniture. It was, perhaps, best for all who might have become concerned that his Royal Highness only took a bath three times in his adult life, each occasion being prompted by a change of mistress.

This hidebound etiquette ensured that from the beginning of his elaborate morning toilet to the completion of its repetition in reverse at night, the King was followed everywhere by a swirling wake of nobles, their ladies and sundry hangers-on. So great was his retinue that even the shortest regal promenade in the gardens took on the appearance of a vast tribal migration. It could, one supposes, hardly have been otherwise, for Louis's palace of Versailles was home for more than 5,000 – each of whom led a life which was totally dictated by the movements of his majesty. His nickname of the 'Sun King' may have originated in a costume he wore at a ballet but its continuing relevance lay in the fact that everything, but everything, revolved around him.

On no occasion was this more apparent than at meal-times. Even his food was accorded royal status and it was not only escorted from the kitchens by an armed guard but, as it passed down the corridors, courtiers would doff their hats, sweep to the ground in salute and murmur reverentially, 'La viande du Roi'. As a precaution against poisoning, there were also officers appointed whose task it was to wipe the royal napkin, spoon, plate, knife, fork and tooth-pick with a piece of bread, which they then had to swallow. This operation, however, was a marvel of efficient manning compared to the waiting at the King's table. It took, for instance, no fewer than three noblemen, including a prince of the blood, to present Louis with his napkin and so numerous were these and other acolytes that they had to form a jostling queue to serve him. Needless to say, he hardly knew what a truly hot meal was.

As with any other royal activity, feeding time also meant that there was a large throng in attendance whose only purpose was to gawp at the King. Their numbers were often swelled by Parisians who paid 25 sous to take the twice-daily coach service from the capital to the palace. These visitors and the thousands of Versailles residents made sure between them that Louis was surrounded by his subjects in all but his most intimate moments. It was a prospect that made his fellow monarchs shudder. 'He is on such continuous display,' said King Frederick of Prussia, 'that if I was the King of France, I would hire a stand-in.'

Louis XV (1710–1774). King of France and an impatient lover. He was so anxious to lose no time travelling between his apartment and his mistress's on the floor above, that in 1743 he had the world's first lift installed. It was at his palace of Versailles and although the contraption was fixed to the outside of the building, it operated within the privacy of a courtyard. So every time that Louis felt the urge, he clambered into the 'Flying Chair', as it was called, gave a signal and, by means of a carefully balanced arrangement of weights inside one of the chimneys, was transported to the arms of his latest chum.

His sexual appetite was such that this lift must frequently have been going up and down like a yo-yo. Few women, it seems, could keep pace with his demands. His wife Maria, for instance, bore him ten children and, after complaining that she was either 'in bed, pregnant or brought to bed', was forced to retire from the fray on doctor's orders. His famous mistress, Madame de Pompadour, also knew when she was beaten and after gallantly attempting to fortify herself with aphrodisiacs and a diet of truffles, celery and vanilla, she, too, sued for peace. Yet there was an endless stream of willing substitutes, including four sisters from the same family and a succession of young girls, some of whom were supplied by none other than old thunder-thighs himself, Casanova.

Louis XVI (1754–1793). King of France and grandson of the above. He may not have been a political sophisticate but unlike his predecessors he had no mistresses, ate moderately, kept within his income, learned a manual trade, abolished both secret diplomacy and enforced labour, ended torture, halted the discrimination against Jews, studied science, stopped the opening of mail, freed the serfs, was bilingual, gave Protestants the freedom of worship, built hospitals and showed sympathy for the poor. The French responded by cutting off his head.

Ludwig I (1786–1868). King of Bavaria who slept on a most curious mattress. It was covered in velvet and stuffed with beards and moustaches kindly provided by the soldiers of his father's old Alsatian regiment.

Ludwig II (1845–1886). King of Bavaria and perhaps the closest to a truly Ruritanian monarch that history has to offer. In Ludwig, the idea of a ruler of a tin-pot state who lived swathed in luxury and cocooned from reality was made flesh. While his subjects tilled their soil and his ministers fretted over where the next pfennig was coming from, Ludwig sat on his sumptuous throne choosing a new suit of clothes or planning his next improvident enterprise. Yet what made him unique was not so much that he indulged his every whim, but that these whims were so absurd and out of scale with his tiny kingdom. He built outrageous fairy-tale castles with magic grottos, ordered coaches so heavily decorated that it looked as if they were draped in golden seaweed, dragged his court out in the middle of the night for mad sleigh rides through the Alpine snows, and dressed up in armour and imagined himself the lost hero of wild legends. All this and more was the stuff of Ludwig's world, for although the crown of Bavaria may have been on his head, his mind was perpetually in the land of make-believe.

Nothing typified his creation of this realm of fantasy more than the ludicrous winter gardens that he had built at the Residenz in Munich. Running along the entire west wing, it was an extravagant wonderland with trees, flowery bowers, a lake, waterfalls and castellated buildings – all encased in a vast glass roof with arches festooned with roses beyond count. The wildlife of these gardens was extraordinary. Parakeets flew among the chestnut and palm trees, gazelles grazed on the lush grass, peacocks strutted among the shrubberies and, perched on a golden swing, there was a great gaudy parrot who had been trained to greet the King with a cheery 'Good evening'. If the mood took him, Ludwig could always retreat inside his blue silk tent or one of the Turkish kiosks and contemplate the perfectly detailed Indian village that occupied one end of the gardens. To complete the exotic picture, the walls were painted with views of the Himalayas and there was even an artificial rainbow.

The centrepiece of this stunning creation was undoubtedly the lake whose waters were stained blue, spanned by a rustic wooden bridge and, just for good measure, scented with violets. At night, when the gardens were illuminated by thousands of lights hanging from the trees, Ludwig would come to the lakeside dressed in a silver suit of armour and step from its orchid-covered banks into a gilded boat. Here, as the boat was pulled by a mechanical swan, he would glide along in his paradise and be serenaded by the singers or instrumentalists who were concealed in nearby bushes.

Things, however, did not always go according to plan. One evening, for instance, the King and his companion, the composer Wagner, were so captivated by the siren-like voice emerging from one piece of foliage that they invited its owner to join them in the boat. So the ample figure of Fraulein Shefszky clambered aboard and the enraptured trio set off across the lake with the clockwork swan's feet going nineteen to the dozen. As they neared the opposite bank, the scene was idyllic: Wagner and the King were staring blissfully into space while the singer was bringing her final aria to a thundering conclusion. Then, as if carried away by the charm of the moment, Fraulein Shefszky made the fatal mistake of running her fingers through Ludwig's dark hair. The fastidious monarch was outraged and pushed the prima donna away with such force that the boat was upturned and all three were pitched into the blue-rinsed waters. Despite his armour, Ludwig was able to struggle onto the bank and he strode furiously away, leaving Wagner to fish out the gasping songstress with a boat-hook.

Such a ridiculous scene could never have been imagined by Ludwig's countrymen when he ascended the throne at the age of 18. They had no indication of the 'voices' which he had begun to hear in his youth and knew only that they had the most handsome and striking young sovereign in all Europe. He may have been vain (he had his hair curled every day by the court barber) but he promised to usher in a new age of glory for Bavaria. For a time he was indeed conscientious but gradually it became clear that Ludwig was a creature of obsessions and the first of these was with Richard Wagner and his music. Within five weeks of his accession, Ludwig had become the struggling composer's patron, paying off his debts, awarding him an annual salary of 4,000 guilder and installing him in a house near the castle. The King simply idolised the composer. They met every day, planned new productions and opera houses together and the King even went to the lengths of learning nearly all of Wagner's libretti by heart.

Such a cloying relationship could not last and when it ended, Ludwig began to devote all his efforts to building ever more outlandish castles, within whose walls he could make his strange fantasies come true. The first to be completed was Neuschwanstein, which was begun in 1869. This was the ultimate fairy-tale castle, festooned in turrets and built on a mountainside with a lake in the background. Inside its thick, ivory-white stone walls were marbled halls, panelled rooms and enough gold leaf on the fixtures to pay off the Bavarian national debt. The throne-room had gilt Romanesque columns and arches, white marble steps and a golden chandelier the size of a small room. Throughout the castle the woodcarvings were as sumptuous as Ludwig's subjects' money could buy and those in his bedroom alone kept 17 carvers working full-time for four and a half years – a statistic matched only by the ridiculous effort that went into his bedcoverings at Herrenchiemsee. It took no fewer than 40 women stitching flat out for seven years to make this rather fetching counterpane and one wonders if they would have put the same painstaking work into it if they had known that the King would occupy the castle only once. The men who lugged every piece of its mammoth walls onto Herrenchiemsee's island site would no doubt have felt the same.

However, for sheer architectural insanity, Linderhof must take the prize. From the outside this white marble baroque fantasy, with its 30 statues incorporated into the frontage, was indeed beautiful, but inside its fitments almost defied practical use. Rococo is, I believe, the correct terminology for its styling but here everything was so ostentatiously decorated that only the most careful scrutiny of an object could tell you its original purpose. With its carvings, gilt ornaments, tapestries and velvets, Linderhof was the kind of place where you expect to see ormolu drains. The dining-room, however, was remarkable not so much for its decor but its table – a large, heavy item which could be lowered through the floor and raised again with the plates loaded with food for the next course. Needless to say, in such a place, Ludwig could not have an ordinary throne; it had to be a richly upholstered one, shaped like a peacock,

George V – always a stickler for correct dress

George, Duke of Kent, one-time royal drug addict

(Right) *Princess Mary Adelaide*, mother of Queen Mary – an incorrigible greedy-guts and compulsively big spender

(Below) *Farouk I* – road hog, racketeer, glutton, womaniser and kleptomaniac (*Camera Press*)

Queen Victoria reigns b[...]
usual *John Brown*, [...]
minder, leads the way [...]
Mansell Collection)

Die Bildnus Ywan
Waßliervitz des jetzig-
en Großfürstenn Reuß,in
iß der Moßcow.

Des Großfürsten in Reußen ist
Ywan Wassilewitz
Die Moßcowiter wird genandt
Der jetzt mit gewaltiger Hand
Das Kriegsherren seiner Haubstad
Ein mechtig Heer gefüret hat/
Wider Poleßke unüberseln
Des mechtigen Königs zu Poln/ec.

Gedruckt zu Nürnberg/ durch
Hans Weygel Form-
schneyder.

Ivan the Terrible, sixte[...]
century psychopath, an[...]
staff with which he sle[...]
son (*The Mansell Collec[...]*)

Charles I – even before his head was cut off he was England's shortest monarch (*The Mansell Collection*)

Peter the Great, Czar of Russia and the most imaginative taxman in history (*The Mansell Collection*)

Ernest II, Duke of Saxe-Coburg-Gotha and Prince Albert's wicked older brother (*The Mansell Collection*)

Edward VII, whose insatiable appetities led to the
undoing of many a button

Edward VIII: his father told him, 'You dress like a cad, you act like a cad, you *are* a cad.'

flanked by two smaller five-foot-high birds and set in, of all things, a Turkish kiosk. Finally, his bedroom was a riot of gold leaf, which had been applied with such abandon that it might well have been emulsion paint. This, one might add, was the only bedroom. Never let it be said that Linderhof was anything other than the most opulent one-bedroomed residence in the world.

The grounds were, if anything, even more daft. In the formal French gardens jerked mechanical peacocks with bronze bodies and exuberant tails made of hundreds of pieces of coloured glass. Then, beyond the borders and trimmed lawns was Ludwig's grotto. One entered by means of an ingenious 'open sesame' rock and proceeded down a cave hung with stalactites (phoney, of course, and made of cast iron, covered in concrete and then painted). At the end of this was the main chamber containing a lake which was fed by a waterfall. In one of his typical 'improvements' upon nature, Ludwig had arranged things so that, at the touch of a switch, different coloured lights changed the hue of the water and the lake's surface was also rippled by artificial waves. One would never have guessed that the King had been forbidden toys as a child.

These, then (together with his nine other castles and residences), were the bizarre settings for Ludwig's equally improbable antics. Some of these, such as his habit of encasing himself in armour and impersonating Wagnerian characters, could be put down by his more sympathetic courtiers as a passing eccentricity. But when he began, in the late 1860s, to stand the court clock on its head and turn night into day, even the most loyal of Bavarians rumbled that their sovereign might have the odd slate loose. In 1865 he had ordered the installation of an artificial moon and stars on the ceiling of his bedroom at Hohenschrangen and soon afterwards he started his nocturnal rides. These were not wild gallops through the countryside but instead consisted of making incessant laps of the arena at the court riding school. He would arrive, announce that he intended to ride to, say, Innsbruck, calculate the distance and set off on his heroically aimless task. Round and round he would go, followed by a groom, changing horses at regular intervals, counting off the circuits and perhaps stopping for a picnic along the way. Finally, at about 3 am, he would declare that the required distance had been covered and retire in triumph to bed.

Sometimes, if Ludwig was staying up country, he might actually venture out of doors for his midnight ride. On these occasions he would climb into a huge fur coat, board his sleigh and, accompanied by liveried outriders, would be driven at breakneck speed through the Alpine snow. If that sounds unremarkable, then consider the sleigh – a monstrous gilded item which looked like a great mantelpiece on slides. Its seats were embroidered sapphire velvet, there were two vast golden lamps and above all this towered a tall mast, surmounted by a crown and up which the gilt figures of nine agile cherubs shinned.

What made these shenanigans even more alarming was that they were not the frantic efforts of an exhibitionist out to impress his fellows but the genuinely crazed impulses of a man who was, in fact, intensely shy. With few exceptions (such as the costume parties he gave for his staff), Ludwig loathed contact with people, especially if they were courtiers, and even ordered midnight performances of plays and operas in his own theatre so that he could view them alone. He regarded any court function as a particular ordeal and when he could be persuaded to turn up (which was less and less often as the years went by), he referred to his attendance as 'mounting the scaffold'. To bolster his courage before appearing, he would need to drink up to ten glasses of champagne and, at banquets, he not only ordered a huge bowl of flowers at his place so that he could hide from the guests but also instructed the band to play so loudly that all conversation was drowned. Increasingly, he preferred to dine totally alone, although he did once make an exception for a much-loved companion. This was his favourite grey mare Cosa Rava, who gobbled up the proffered soup, fish and roast and then showed her appreciation by smashing the dinner service into smithereens.

By this stage the crockery was not the only thing that was cracking up. Ludwig's court had been a world of make-believe on the never-never and, by the beginning of the 1880s, his debts had reached 7,500,000 marks. His ministers were also becoming harder pressed to make good the King's neglect of his duties. When Ludwig demanded 20 million marks to clear his debts and build yet more castles (he wanted, for instance, to rebuild Falkenstein with jewel-encrusted walls), the turning point was reached. The King decided that some desperate methods were called for and his ministers realised that only his removal from the throne would solve the problem. Neither side could now afford a mistake.

Ludwig's fund-raising plans were, to say the least, bold. Casting aside his pride, he made direct approaches for a loan to several fellow kings, the Sultan of the Ottoman Empire, the Shah of Persia, Emperor of Brazil and even the Duke of Westminster. These worthies refused and so it was on to Plan B – the recruitment of a gang of bandits who would rob banks in Stuttgart, Frankfurt, Berlin and Paris and, while they were about it, kidnap the Crown Prince and hold him in a cave in the mountains. When the requisite number of desperados failed to materialise, Ludwig had the bright idea of selling his entire kingdom and, with the proceeds, setting up shop elsewhere. Prussia and his uncle Prince Luitpold were offered first refusal and a privy councillor called von Loher was packed off on a voyage to look for a desirable property. Not surprisingly, it all came to naught.

Meanwhile his ministers had not exactly been idle and the plan they hatched had definite promise – they would appoint a commission to inquire into the King's mental health and use its evidence to declare him unfit to rule. It is at this point that our picture of the colourful Ludwig begins to show distinct signs of the retoucher's brush. Undeniably mad though Ludwig was, it is nevertheless difficult to swallow some of the more lurid depositions that were placed before the commission. It was said, for example, that the King would greet trees and hedges as if they were old friends, bowing and addressing them at length.

Then there was his alleged confusion of the seasons and insistence that picnics were organised in the depths of the Tyrolean winter. His servants, who were the bulk of the witnesses, also claimed that Ludwig's treatment of them had become abominable: he had forbidden them either to look at or speak to him and had given his orders to them by means of unintelligible signs. If they did not obey immediately, they said, he would spit in their faces and impose barbaric punishments. They also made much of Ludwig's known fixation about the courts of Louis XIV and Louis XV, saying that he not only dressed up as the Sun King but also ordered places set at his table for the dead kings and their ladies and held conversations with these shades.

We will never know now whether all this was a literal description of Ludwig's distressing symptoms or a lot of below-stairs hooey got up for the commission at the drop of a small consideration. Either way, it had the desired effect. In 1886 Dr Bernhard von Gudden, the presiding authority, declared Ludwig insane and the net closed in. There were still some loyal to the King, however, and when the first official deputation rolled up at the gates of Neuschwanstein to take him away, they were beaten back by local peasants armed with scythes and axes. For their next visit the posse were better prepared and they took Ludwig to Berg Castle, where his ultimate fate was to be decided. Von Gudden was there too and the next day he and Ludwig went for a walk in the grounds. When they failed to return, a search was mounted and there, in the picturesque lake, were found their bodies.

To this day no one knows what happened. Did Ludwig the lunatic determine that neither he nor his interlocutor should survive another day or did some unknown conspirators, having beefed up the case against Ludwig beyond reason, decide to destroy the evidence? All we know for sure is that the vain, spendthrift monarch, with his silly high-stepping walk and curious manias, is a great deal more beguiling at the distance of a century than he must have been at first hand. As is often the way with kings, their value lies less in the good they do their contemporaries than in the entertainment they provide for posterity.

> *'For a king, death is better than dethronement or exile.'*
>
> EMPRESS THEODORA.

M

'The first king was a successful soldier.'

VOLTAIRE, 1734.

Macbeth (d. 1057). King of Scotland and a much maligned monarch. Little is known about him but there is no evidence that he was the hen-pecked social climber portrayed by Shakespeare. He may have murdered Duncan (at Pitgaveny, near Elgin) but contemporary chronicles are conspicuously silent about the bard's other allegations. There is no mention of three elderly female advisors, mobile woodlands or even hard-to-shift stains. Moreover, his good lady wife was not the arriviste bitch-on-the-make that generations of theatre-goers have assumed her to be. Grouch, as she was called, was of royal blood, being a granddaughter of Kenneth III and was, by all accounts, a lavish patron of the Church. So too was her husband, who was also a good and strong enough ruler to survive on the Scottish throne for 17 years – which is more than 25 other occupants of that precarious hot seat can claim. Macbeth's reign was brought to a rude and sudden conclusion when he was slain by the future Malcolm III at Lumphanen near Aberdeen in 1057.

Mahomet III (1566–1603). Sultan of the Ottoman Empire who ensured that there would be no rivals for his throne by having all 19 of his brothers murdered on the night he succeeded. It was just hours after his father died that Mahomet summoned every one of the boys, the eldest of whom was 11 years old, to come and kiss his hands. When they filed into the throne room he said that they had nothing to fear but he thought they should all be circumcised. They were led into an ante-room for the operation to be performed but there waiting for them were deaf mutes with silken bowstrings. Each lad was then strangled. Just to make absolutely certain that no other claimants would emerge, Mahomet also had the seven of his father's harem who were pregnant tied up in weighted sacks and dropped into the Bosphorus.

Mahomet IV (1642–1693). Sultan of the Ottoman Empire and not one to give in too readily to feelings of sympathy for the victims of accidents. When 30 beaters died from exposure during one of his massive hunting parties, he viewed their bodies and then declared, 'These men would have doubtless rebelled against me. They have received their punishment in anticipation.'

Marie (1825–1889). Queen of Bavaria and an indefatigable old prude. She was so anxious to eliminate all indelicate references in literature that she once proposed that the word 'friendship' should be substituted for 'love' wherever it occurred in poetry. Queen Victoria's judgement on her was smack-on. 'Marie,' she once said, 'is not very bright and always a little cracked on religion.'

Princess Marie (1853–1920). Duchess of Edinburgh, daughter-in-law of Queen Victoria and footwear crank. She thought it was silly to have different shoes for left and right feet and so had leather boots that fitted either foot made to order in St Petersburg. This stout and dowdy woman was, in fact, a strange combination of the daring and the traditional, shocking society by smoking cigarettes in public yet also clinging so tightly to her old Russian religion that it was said that she never went anywhere without her own personal Orthodox priest and two chanters.

Marie Antoinette (1755–1793). Queen of France and, according to popular mythology, the deliverer of the most famous one-liner in history – 'Let them eat cake.' In fact, there is no evidence that she ever made the remark. The first printed reference to the phrase was in Jean-Jacques Rousseau's *Confessions*, which was written in the late 1770s when Marie Antoinette was but a child living in Austria. Not that the French ever let the truth get in the way of a good line when it came to their hated queen. She was said at one time or another to be both a lesbian and a nymphomaniac, to dabble in witchcraft and sleep between black sheets, to light her bedroom with 1,000 candles each night and keep a room at her house whose walls dripped with diamonds.

None of this was true but the wonder is that, with such a sitting target as Marie Antoinette, the pamphleteers should ever have felt the need to tamper with the truth at all, because for most of her life she was a haughty spendthrift whose frivolous ways did more for republicanism in France than all the revolutionary theorists put together. After all, the French may have had previous queens and royal mistresses who lived it up a bit but none of these were even fit to hold Marie's sequinned handbag when it came to ostentatious consumption. She dressed flashily, gambled wildly at cards, staged entertainments whose costs would have kept the French army for a month and found precious stones so irresistible that at one point she owed the court jeweller half a million francs.

It seemed that no desire of hers was too daft to be denied. When she and her circle of giddy friends had a wheeze to dress up and play peasants, the folly was immediately put into practice. Some land at her residence of Petit Trianon was commandeered and a miniature village was laid out beside a lake. It had cowsheds, dovecots and barns but there the connection between this plaything and true rural life ended. The buildings' cracks and signs of age were merely paint cleverly applied, the thatched farmhouse contained nothing more rustic than a billiard room and the milk churns were made of Sèvres porcelain. Here, on this filmset of a village, Marie

Antoinette and her chums dressed up in their chocolate-box shepherdesses' costumes and collected eggs, made butter and fed the animals until they were bored. As her mother, the Austrian Empress Marie Theresa once said, 'She is so occupied with her pleasures that she is almost incapable of thinking clearly on major matters.'

Nothing typified her showy silliness more than her hairstyles. With the hair combed upwards to about 18 inches above the forehead and the addition of plumes, they reached the heights of absurdity, towering to more than three feet above her head. As if this was not impractical enough, the summit of these coiffures was often decorated with small figures and objects that made up a hunting scene, a garden or a country vista, complete with windmill. So unwilling was Marie Antoinette to compromise on these creations that the flat-topped doorways to the boxes at the Versailles opera house had to be reshaped into semi-circular arches to allow Marie to pass without having to drop to her knees.

There were, admittedly, one or two mitigating circumstances for the frivolity that marked much of her life: she had been thrust alone into a foreign court when no more than a young girl and, because of her husband's physical condition, then had to endure seven years before her marriage was consummated. When it was, and children began to arrive, she did calm down a little and as the Revolution drew near she made an attempt to reform her character, spending more time with her husband and family and less on her silly pleasures. But by then it was too late and the Queen who had spent most of her reign behaving as if she had lost her head actually did so permanently.

Mary (1867–1953). Queen of England, consort of George V and an incomparable scrounger of her subjects' heirlooms. She was a passionate collector of objets d'art and royal knick-knacks and if she saw an item she wanted, she was not above using a little regal pressure to obtain it. Visits to the homes of friends or strangers alike were often little more than thinly-disguised window-shopping expeditions and if something caught her practised and beady eye, she was liable to slip into a familiar routine: she would stand in front of the item in question and say in a stage whisper, 'I am caressing it with my eyes.' If the prized object had not been pressed on her by the time she took her leave, then Mary would pause on the doorstep and ask, 'May I go back and say goodbye to that dear little clock/picture/vase etc.'

This rather leaden hint usually did the trick but if by some chance the old Queen left empty-handed, then her hostess would in due course receive a request to buy the coveted item, dropped, with something less than subtlety, into Her Majesty's letter of thanks. The object nearly always arrived by the return post. In time, some of Mary's more alert subjects learnt to pre-empt her visits with a precautionary stashing away of their more treasured possessions.

Mary, Princess Royal (1897–1965). Only daughter of King George V and Queen Mary, aunt of our present Queen and a highly superstitious creature. For example, if she saw a magpie she would bow deeply three times and the sign of a piebald horse would cause her to remain silent until the vision had been expunged by a dog coming into view. These practices must have been a considerable trial to a member of a royal family which led such a determinedly outdoor life.

Princess Mary Adelaide (1833–1897). Granddaughter of George III, mother of that paragon of respectability Queen Mary and yet, one is delighted to discover, an incorrigible greedy guts and compulsively big spender. Unlike her inhibited daughter, who was both trim and prim, 'Fat Mary', as she was called, was the very antithesis of restraint. She fed her face with enormous and perpetual gusto, spent far beyond her means (and those of her creditors, too) and generally lived life with her stays loosened. The people, sensing this and knowing of her unflagging work for charity, took her to their hearts and made her arguably the most popular royal of the Victorian era.

Her appearance made this public enthusiasm all the more charming, for Mary Adelaide did not remotely resemble the conventional idea of a princess. With her chubby face, over-generous bosom and legs like the trunks of mature oaks, she looked more like the owner of a pie shop who ate too many of her own wares. This impression was not so very far from the literal truth. As a child she constantly defeated her parents' attempts to confront her with a meal that was larger than her appetite and by the time she was 18 years of age, she weighed in at over 15 stone. Her entrance into society could therefore hardly help being a considerable one and her hostesses soon learnt that when Mary Adelaide's name was on the guest list, special provision had to be made. An extra chair would be needed, since the spread of the Princess's hips meant that she required at least two to sit down, and it was always wise to forewarn the kitchens of her presence. Initially her calls for copious second helpings of her favourite food caused problems but in time anticipating these demands became a relatively simple matter. A good rule of thumb was that if it was edible and could be put on a plate, then Mary Adelaide would declare it a favourite and want more.

Still, at least if she was sitting down and eating she was not dancing – an elementary observation, perhaps, but one that always meant much to her host and hostess. The sight of Mary Adelaide on the dance floor was yet another stressful experience for those who entertained her, for allied to her imposing girth was a surprising speed on her feet and this made her a positive menace when the orchestra struck up. In a particularly rollicking number, such as a gavotte or the Gay Gordons, she was like a hackney carriage careering out of control and it required all the agility of the other dancers to avoid a spectacular pile-up.

For many years she waddled cheerily through the social calendar, hoping that at the next venue she would find the husband that had so far eluded her. Then, when she was 32, and with her and her family on the verge of despair at her marriage prospects, she met Prince Francis of Teck. He liked her vivacity, she took a shine to his looks and they were married before second thoughts could set in. He was virtually penniless but, armed with her income of £10,000 a year, they set up home in Kensington Palace and began to live in the manner to which they thought their royal status entitled them. They entertained lavishly, richly redecorated their apartments, hired a vast staff and, much to Victoria's chagrin, clothed them all in identical livery to that of the Queen's servants. Soon Mary Adelaide's extravagance was outstripping not only their income but also the loans from wealthy friends. Angela Burdett-Coutts lent them no less than £50,000 with precious little expectation of ever seeing any of it back again and, when that was gone, the insolvent Princess began to live on tick. Soon she was putting the word around the local tradesmen that a forgiving attitude to her slate would entitle the business to display above their door the legend, 'Purveyors to her Royal Highness the Princess Mary Adelaide, Duchess of Teck'.

In those days such a motto was worth even more than a settled bill. But it was a trick she could play only once and eventually, with the Queen still refusing to increase Mary Adelaide's allowance, the reckoning arrived. It was decided that the spendthrift pair and their four children should go and live in Italy where extravagance came cheaper. So, in September 1883, their effects were put up for public auction and the shame-faced family, including the future Queen Mary, left Victoria Station to begin their exile. Mary Adelaide's good intentions lasted about as far as Clapham Junction. By the time they reached Italy, she had dropped not only her alias of the 'Countess of Hohenstein' but also any pretence of reforming. The Teck tribe and their hangers-on took over an entire floor of Paoli's, the grandest hotel in Florence, and, even when they moved out to a house in the country, showed few signs of curbing their expenses. By the spring of 1885 it was obvious that there was precious little point in them being abroad and so, on the promise of more discretion if not more economy, Mary Adelaide and Prince Francis (by now the victim of a stroke) returned. Needless to say, the Princess was soon in prodigious debt to practically every trader in Kensington High Street and it was this that gave rise to the most famous story about her.

One of her chief creditors was the Kensington grocer John

Barker, who founded the legendary department store. His largesse also extended to the local church and when he donated the cost of a new church hall, Mary Adelaide was obliged to perform the opening ceremony. Towards the end of her speech she turned to Barker and, with an utterly straight face, said, 'And now I must propose a special vote of thanks to Mr Barker, to whom we all owe so much.'

Not all of her – or rather other people's – money was now going on high living. Mary Adelaide was a relentless supporter of good causes, working almost every waking hour for them and giving freely from what she referred to, in her ironic moments, as her 'income'. She was a frenetically active patron of hospitals, orphanages, homes for widows, societies for girls whose parents were in gaol and also the London Needlework Guild, for whom she worked as hard as if she had been a paid employee. Her special passion, however, was reserved for opposing sweated labour and she did much to prompt the exposure of this practice. On her shopping trips she would also cross-examine tradesmen about the wages they paid their workers and, if she deemed them insufficient, then she would flounce out of the shop, vowing that her custom would not return until there had been a hefty pay increase.

It was gestures like this, her unceasing charity work and her beaming moon of a face that endeared her to the public. As Victoria ungraciously said of her once, 'The mob like fat people,' and when Mary Adelaide died in 1897 the East End wore black crepe for a week. Yet perhaps those who missed her most were the traders to whom she owed a total of £70,000.

Mathilde (19th Century). Archduchess of Hapsburg, she managed to set fire to herself shortly before her betrothal to King Umberto I of Italy. Mathilde was a secret smoker and one day, while her bath was being run, she decided to have a crafty fag. Sadly, she lit up not only her cigarette but also her gauze negligee and so incinerated herself.

Matilda (d. 1083). Wife of William the Conqueror and, at 4 ft 2 ins high, the only dwarf to be Queen of England.

Maximilian II (1811–1864). King of Bavaria and an incurable snob. He once asked the philosopher Professor Jolly, 'Have you any scientific proof that the high-born of this world will receive suitably deferential treatment in the next?'

Menelik II (1844–1913). Emperor of Ethiopia and devotee of an extreme form of Christian Science. Whenever he felt ill he would not bother with conventional medicines but would turn instead to the Bible. This was not for the religious or spiritual comfort it might bring but for the healing properties of the pages it was printed on. Whether it was an upset stomach or muscle strain he was suffering from, Menelik would simply tear out a few folios and eat them. He swore that this never failed.

So one day in December 1913, when he was battling to recover from a stroke and still feeling far from well, he decided that what he needed was a good stiff measure of his medicine. He had the entire Book of Kings ripped from the Old Testament and ate every page of it. Alas, it proved to be an overdose and he died shortly afterwards.

Princess Michael of Kent (b. 1945). Perhaps Britain's most dignified and talented royal. She was born Marie-Christine von Reibnitz in Prague, lived her early years in Australia and came to Britain in 1965. After a brief first marriage, she took her rightful place in the world's premier family by marrying Prince Michael of Kent in 1978. For some unaccountable reason, this most beautiful and stylish woman was soon the victim of unwarranted and scurrilous attacks in the press. They said that she was obsessed with money and rank, pushy and sometimes rude to other members of her family. A book even claimed that she was too haughty – just because she once ordered two female decorators down from a ladder so that they could curtsy to her.

The most serious calumny against her name came in 1985 when a tabloid newspaper alleged that the Princess had cast her eyes at a man who was not her husband. The object of her affections, according to the authors of this malicious report, was a Texas tycoon. The unlikelihood of a royal dignitary of

Princess Michael's stature stooping to such a liaison does not need emphasising here. It is as ludicrous as the idea that her book, *Crowned in a Far Country*, contained chunks that were directly cribbed from other books on royalty. What happened was simply that the Princess forgot to attribute to the original authors certain passages used in her book. It was the kind of natural oversight that could have been committed by any novice writer and was in no sense intentional. The fact that a legal settlement had to be struck with one author and the book reprinted with amendments only underlines how anxious the Princess always is to avoid giving offence. After all, as Princess Michael herself has pointed out, she has 'a better background than anyone else who has married into the royal family since the war, excepting Prince Philip.' As if anyone of such high breeding would do anything to embarrass her adoptive family.

Mrs Moore (19th Century). An American woman who was convinced that she was the true Queen Victoria. She gave herself the appropriate airs and graces, insisted on a proper deference from those around her and travelled in a carriage pulled by four greys, preceded by mounted trumpeters. Her daughter, Cary Amelia Nation, shared her mother's fantasy and informed anyone who would listen that she was related to the Duke of Argyll. In its more chronic phases, Cary's delusions prompted her to burst through the swing doors of Missouri saloons, brandishing an axe and yelling at the top of her voice, 'The Campbells are coming.'

Mpande (1798–1872). King of the Zulus, he became so fat with the passing years that in the end he was unable to walk and had to be conveyed from place to place in a wheelbarrow-like contraption pushed by two servants.

Murad IV (1612–1640). Sultan of the Ottoman Empire and psychopath. Some rulers in history are said to have been so cruel that they would order a man's execution if they did not like the look of his face. Murad, however, never needed as good a reason as that. He killed people just because they were there and if he could do it with his bare hands, then so much the better.

For the Sultan, life had few pleasures that could compete with sitting in a small kiosk set in the western wall of the seraglio, taking pot-shots at passers-by with his arquebus. Ancient royal prerogative allowed him to kill ten innocent people a day but it was a pretty poor shoot when his bag did not vastly exceed this figure. If he felt more active then he would take his chief executioner Kara Ali and go into the streets of his capital to look for victims. These safaris were a great success, for he never had to roam very far before he came across someone who inadvertently wandered into his path or was wearing some garment that offended him. Then he would turn to Kara Ali, root through the nails, gimlets and clubs that hung from the executioner's belt and select the tool he thought most suited to the job in hand. If he saw no weapon there that took his fancy, Murad could always ask his unpleasant caddie for a canister that contained powder for blinding.

There were, of course, the odd sunny mornings when Murad was so well-disposed towards his fellow men that he felt he thought he ought to have some kind of excuse before reaching for his eye-gouger. Not that the pretext had to be anything elaborate; he once beheaded his chief musician for playing a Persian tune and, on another occasion, drowned a party of women when he came across them in a meadow and objected to the unholy row they were making. Sometimes it would just be the suspicion of wrong-doing. When a Venetian called Zanetti built an extra storey on top of his house, the Sultan accused the Italian of doing so in order to peek at the ladies of his harem and had the man hanged.

If any of Murad's subjects had been momentarily tempted to protest at being used for target-practice or as gallows-fodder, one look at the Sultan would have instantly dispelled the idea. His intimidatingly large frame, brooding eyes and great, grasping paws did not exactly encourage dissent and he added to the effect by sporting a sinister beard and always clothing himself in black silk. Coupled with this stage-villain appearance was a reputation as a superb archer, javelin thrower, swordsman and shot. He was also believed to be well-nigh invincible as a wrestler, thanks mainly to fists that could exert a clam-like grip. It was said that if those thick fingers began measuring the circumference of your neck, then the only hope of their removal lay in mining them with the best Chinese gunpowder.

Yet the carnage he wreaked was on such a scale that only a small percentage of his victims had the honour of dying by their Sultan's swarthy hands. In 1637 alone he had 25,000 subjects executed, a total that stands as a magnificent testimony to the thoroughness of his judicial code. At times it must have seemed to the Turks that breathing was the only human activity not directly proscribed – and they could never be entirely sure of even that. Breathing tobacco fumes was certainly forbidden, especially if it was done in public and Murad liked to ensure that this particular law was being enforced by roaming the taverns incognito in search of smokers. If he caught one, he would throw off his disguise and have them executed on the spot. When he found one of his gardeners and his wife having a crafty puff, he ordered their legs amputated and the two miscreants wheeled through the streets until they bled to death. Nor were diplomats safe from his catch-all laws and when a French interpreter broke the embargo forbidding foreigners to associate with Turkish women, Murad sentenced the man to impalement.

So it went on, until in 1640, to the relief of all but his armourer and executioners, he died after a drinking bout at the age of only 28. Yet even then, as he lay breathing his last, he was in no mood to show a little of the traditional deathbed clemency and contrition. Summoning up his few remaining crumbs of strength, he demanded that his brother and successor Ibrahim should be murdered. Only when their mother told him that his order had been carried out did Murad, with his face wreathed in a maniacal, gloating smile, allow himself the luxury of sinking back onto his cushions and dying, a satisfied man. As it turned out, the mother had been lying and so Murad was succeeded by Ibrahim, probably the first man ever to survive one of his bloodthirsty brother's sentences of death.

Mutesa I (1837–1884). King of Buganda and an optimistic savage. When Christian missionaries told him that his baptism was dependent on him giving up all but one of his 7,000 wives, he replied, 'Give me Queen Victoria's daughter for my wife and I will put away all my wives.'

> *'The clearest mark of a true king is that he is one whom all good men can praise without compunction not only during his life but even afterwards.'*
>
> DIO CHRYSTOSTUM.

N

'Remember, to be a king, all you need to know is how to sign your name, read a manuscript and mount a horse.'

KING UMBERTO I of Italy.

Nasir ud-din (1831–1896). Shah of Persia and a most unwelcome royal visitor. On successive tours to Europe, he fouled his quarters, abused his hosts, insulted their women and generally made no effort to compromise his earthy native habits. Yet because his state was such an important part of the Middle East jigsaw, the rulers of Europe had to bite their tongues and tolerate him.

His debut on the Continent came in 1873 and the highlight of the trip was definitely his stay in Berlin as the guest of the German Emperor. First of all, he was preposterously late for everything – annoying enough for any hosts but positively maddening to the methodical Germans. Then, at a ballet at the Berlin Opera House, he scandalised the entire audience with his own performance of devastating vulgarity. Seated in the royal box, the Shah called for a glass of water, drained it in one gulp, handed the empty glass to the Princess Karl, cleared his throat with a loud flourish and then, as Prussian nobility in all their finery gazed up at him from the stalls, he expectorated on their heads. Not surprisingly, several ladies immediately took their leave.

That little demonstration was, however, nothing compared to what he and his retinue perpetrated back at the Emperor's castle. At night, as his hosts lay awake wondering what atrocities the Shah would commit the following day, strange and fearful noises came from the Persian quarters. The Germans hardly dared imagine their cause but when the Shah left, they found out. He and his followers had fouled everywhere. On the Turkish carpet – bought and installed especially for the state visitors – poultry had been ritually slaughtered and then roasted over braziers of glowing charcoal. The carpet was bloodstained and burnt all over. The rich silk hangings and satin upholstery of the apartments were torn and covered in grease and barely a fixture or fitting had survived intact.

On a smaller and less dramatic scale, this carnage was repeated wherever the Persians went. In Russia, Czar Alexander was particularly outraged by the Shah's antics, especially when, on his departure, he turned to his host and solemnly declared for all to hear, 'I have noticed the way in which you govern this great country. I am well satisfied with it; you may continue to rule here.' Fortunately in England he contented himself with merely failing to use the toilet facilities provided, organising a wrestling match between two of his retinue in the gardens of Buckingham Palace and eating his private meals off plates strewn around the floor. Victoria said she rather liked him and he, in turn, hailed her as 'my auspicious sister of sublime nature', which was probably the only time she was ever called that.

By the time the Shah returned to London in 1889, he had mellowed in some respects and the worst that was reported of his table manners was that at a banquet at Windsor Castle he repeatedly spat cherry stones on the carpet. He had, however, become with age if anything even more outspoken. When he was introduced to the Marchioness of Londonderry, for instance, he liked her so much that he promptly made an offer to buy her. The Prince of Wales was similarly taken aback when, at a crowded reception, the Shah gazed at the society matrons present, asked loudly if they were his wives and stated that if they were his, he would have them beheaded and find prettier ones.

It was also on this tour that the Shah visited an English

prison. While there, he was shown a gallows and, not unnaturally, wanted to see it in operation. The officials explained that since there was no one due to be hanged that morning, this was out of the question. The Shah's face fell, then brightened considerably as he had an idea. 'Take one of my retinue,' he said and, for the life of him, could not understand why this generous offer was not accepted. This unlovable man was assassinated as he entered a mosque near Tehran in 1896.

John Camden Neild (1780–1852). Eccentric businessman and notorious skinflint, he left his entire fortune of £½ million to Queen Victoria. It was a bizarre bequest for, since succeeding to his father's estates in 1814, Neild had apparently shown not the slightest flicker of interest in royalty. All his energies had instead been devoted to hanging on to and multiplying his wealth. In the process, he earned the reputation for being one of the most crabby old misers of the nineteenth century.

Neild may have inherited £¼ million but anyone who passed him on the road would never have known it. His dress was shabby and old-fashioned and it invariably consisted of a blue swallow-tailed coat with gilt buttons, brown trousers, short gaiters, worn stockings and shoes that were patched and down at heel. His appearance was not improved by his insistence that his clothes should never be brushed, as this would destroy the nap and make them wear out more quickly. Even in the foulest weather he spurned a greatcoat as a frivolous luxury and so those who came across this ramshackle figure would have immediately assumed that here was a man very much down on his luck.

This was precisely the impression he wanted to create, since it meant he would frequently be the object of pitying offers of charity. He refused none of this misplaced generosity and in time became a highly accomplished scrounger. He was particularly adept at begging lifts and would be prepared to travel in the dirtiest coal cart rather than pay a coach fare. He also had an aversion to finding his own keep and many were his tenants whose hearts must have sunk at the news that 'Mr Neild has come to stay for a few days.'

When Neild was not imposing himself on his long-suffering tenants, he resided at his large house in Cheyne Walk, Chelsea, where he slept on a bare board, or at his estates in North Marston, Buckinghamshire. There he monitored every item in his possession with amazing attention to detail. He kept a record of every tree that grew on the lands and would often walk a dozen miles or more to check that these and everything else he owned was intact. His fear of being rooked of the slightest groat also made him query the accounts and survey the performance of any tradesman who served him. This paranoia was especially marked when North Marston church was being repaired. Having been forced to agree that the mending of holes in the chancel roof could not be delayed any longer, Neild made sure that he got value for his money by sitting up on the roof all day to see that the workmen did not slack. He was not keen to see any money wasted on unnecessarily durable materials and he insisted that the hole in the lead-lined roof be patched up with strips of painted calico. 'That will last me my time,' he said.

Restoring this church was one of the responsibilities that Queen Victoria felt obliged to take on when she inherited Neild's bequest. The will may have said that his fortune was left to her, 'for her sole use and benefit', but the Queen thought it only fair to make some sort of reparation for her benefactor's extreme meanness. There was also, for example, the matter of Neild's housekeeper who had served him for 26 thankless years and a Mrs Neal who had saved his life and cared for him when he attempted suicide in 1828. Neither of these good women had been left a penny and Victoria thought it only right to make amends by settling an annuity upon them both. Still, with £½ million in the kitty, she could afford to be generous and there was still more than enough left over for her to buy and run Balmoral with the proceeds. Few who enjoy that Aberdeenshire residence can have any idea that its royal ownership owes so much to one of the meanest Englishmen who ever lived.

Norasingh (17th Century). Coxswain to King Surasak of Siam and an excessively correct royal servant.

One day, during the flooding season, he was navigating the royal barge down river when the craft struck the bank. Norasingh could hardly be blamed, for the current was racing very fast and the river was a winding one with the bank not clearly visible. But that was not how the coxswain saw it. He was so mortified by his momentary lapse in concentration that he leapt onto the bank, begged the King's forgiveness and demanded to be executed on the spot.

Technically he was right. According to the Palace Laws of 1450, a cox of the king's barge who allows the craft to hit the bank has to forfeit his life. The King, however, was fond of Norasingh and, since the accident was both trivial and unavoidable, he said that his life should be spared. Yet the cox was having none of this. He told the King that he had broken the law and proved an unworthy servant. He insisted that for the honour of his profession he should be punished according to the law. So, without further ado, he was executed. Such was the King's distress that he subsequently ordered the bend in the river to be removed by the building of a canal – a task that eventually required the labours of 30,000 conscripts.

Norton I (1819–1880). The first, last and only Emperor of the United States. Self-proclaimed he may have been but for some reason the people of San Francisco took a shine to this harmless nutcase and played along with his delusion of imperial majesty. They bowed and scraped, voted him funds and allowed him to lord it over them in his own inimitable way for over 20 years. When he died in 1880, they rounded off the joke by giving him a send-off that would not have disgraced a president. It was a considerable achievement for a man who was not only English but also, until he declared himself royal, nothing more than a failed commodity speculator.

Joshua Abraham Norton, to give his highness his full name, was born in London in 1819. Almost before he could walk, his family had emigrated to South Africa where his father, a ship's chandler, started a farm and helped found Grahamstown. When Norton Snr died in 1848, young Joshua sold up and went to Brazil but before a year was out he was on the move again. Gold had been discovered in California and, tempted by the tales of rich pickings, Norton abandoned his South American plans, joined a boatland of fellow opportunists and blew into San Francisco. For a while he did well. He opened a general store and, by provisioning the prospectors and their hangers-on, he made $250,000 inside four years. That, however, was not enough. What he hankered after was one big business coup that would, at a stroke, turn his comfortable prosperity into startling wealth. In 1853 he hatched his plan: he would corner the West Coast market in rice.

His scheme, like all commodity speculations, sounded wonderful in theory. All he had to do was to buy up every grain of rice he could get his hands on, watch the price soar, wait until the stuff was like gold-dust and then sell, ever so slowly, at a vast profit. In practice, however, success at such ventures depends on knowing precisely when to sell and Norton's sense of timing was awful. Having bought most of his rice stock at 5 cents a pound and seen its price rise inexorably to 50 cents a pound, the greedy Norton was still refusing to sell in the hope that the price would go even higher when, unknown to him, a fleet of ships docked in the bay. They were laden with rice and within a week the market was swamped and the price was at flat bottom. Norton was ruined.

The blow must have affected his brain as well as his bank balance; for, by the time he resurfaced in 1859, Norton had undergone an extraordinary transformation. In September of that year he thought it was high time that his fellow citizens knew about it. So, wearing the blue and gold uniform of an army colonel (the best cast-off he could find), he walked into the offices of the *San Francisco Bulletin*, demanded to see the editor and, when the man appeared, dumbfounded him with the words, 'Good morning, I am the Emperor of the United States.'

Unlike most people who make such pronouncements in newspaper offices, Norton was not immediately shown the door. Indeed, the editor was so delighted with his eccentric visitor that he said he would publish the Emperor's first proclamation to his subjects and, with his tongue firmly in his cheek, he duly did so in the very next issue. The people of San Francisco were as quick to see the joke as the editor of their newspaper. Soon they were pointing Norton out in the street, bowing to him and having wonderful fun addressing this down at heel bankrupt as 'Your Imperial Highness'. By the time he issued his next proclamation, a week later, the entire city was convulsed.

'Let it be known,' he began, obviously warming to his new role, 'that because of corruption in high places, the President is to be deposed, Congress abolished and henceforth I, Norton I, will rule in person.' When President Buchanan and the other Washington worthies paid not the slightest heed to this imperial edict, Norton ordered the Commander in Chief of the US Army to 'proceed with suitable force and clear the Halls of Congress.' In addition, all states were told to send delegates to San Francisco's Hall of Music to pay homage to their new ruler and decide on any necessary changes in the law. He even declared that, as the Mexicans were clearly incapable of managing their own affairs, he was assuming the title of 'Protector of Mexico' as well.

By now the high-spirited cult surrounding Norton was in full swing. Every morning the threadbare Emperor held court in his royal residence – two lodging-house rooms upon whose dowdy walls hung cheap prints of two fellow practitioners of his trade: Queen Victoria and Napoleon. Then, in the afternoon, he went on an imperial progress through the streets. Accompanied by his two moth-eaten dogs, he would present himself to his people, graciously acknowledge their bows and pass around the city, solemnly inspecting its drains and omnibus timetables. He took these duties seriously and each Sunday he made it his practice to visit a different church, lest habitual attendance at any one establishment arouse jealousy among the denominations.

He was now a bona fide celebrity and when, in 1862, his dog Lazarus died, 10,000 people turned up at the mongrel's funeral, making it the best-attended animal interment on record. The city's theatres also responded warmly, not only reserving seats for him but also, when he honoured them with his presence, making sure that the audience stood in respectful silence. Yet for all this deference shown him, he still had the appearance of what he unfortunately was: an engaging lunatic living in reduced circumstances. So one could hardly blame the over-zealous policeman who, oblivious of Norton's assumed identity as ruler of the United States, took one look at him one night and arrested him for vagrancy. As soon as the news broke, the entire city rose in indignation. The chief of police was despatched to the county jail to release him personally and a delegation was sent down to the Emperor's lodgings to crave forgiveness. Norton generously agreed to blot the incident from his memory.

Being mistaken for a tramp obviously hurt His Imperial Majesty's pride, for soon after his arrest he issued the following proclamation, 'Know ye that we, Norton the First, have diverse complaints from our liege subjects that our imperial wardrobe is a national disgrace.' What else could the city do but vote funds for a new uniform? This and the offers of free meals, free board and buckshee travel that were showered upon him must have awoken the long-lost commercial instincts of the man who once tried to corner the rice market. Soon he was levying a tax on the city – 20–25 cents for shopkeepers and up to $3 for banks – and most paid up with a smile on their face. There was, of course, no bureaucracy for chasing up defaulters but those who did not pay their dues were occasionally treated to the full force of Norton's imperial wrath. Once, when the Central Pacific Railroad refused him a free meal in a dining car and ceremoniously kicked him off the train, he stomped back to his lodgings and issued a decree announcing the abolition of the company. The railroad made an immediate and abject public apology and gave him a gold pass for life.

So he went on for the duration of his reign, proclaiming his commands and living a life of such grace and favour that one wonders if he was really mad or had simply found a way of getting his rice money back at long last. After all, how many American bankrupts manage to persuade a city to fund them for

20 years? Whatever the truth, the San Franciscans certainly gave him the benefit of the doubt and when he died in 1880 it took two days for 10,000 of them to file past his coffin. The *San Francisco Bulletin*, the paper that had started it all in 1859, wrote, 'The Emperor killed nobody, robbed nobody and deprived nobody of his country, which is more than can be said for most of the fellows in his trade.' More than 50 years after those words were written, a subscription was raised and above his grave in the Woodland Cemetery was placed a tombstone. On it was chiselled the simple inscription, 'Norton I, Emperor of the United States, Protector of Mexico 1819–1880'.

Nysa (d. 126 BC). Queen of Cappadocia, a kingdom of Eastern Asia Minor, who was so keen to rule in her own right that she personally murdered all of her five sons who stood between her and the throne.

> *'When a king is said to be a kind king, his reign is a failure.'*
>
> NAPOLEON.

O

'There are princes whom men compare with Alexander the Great and who are not worthy of being compared with his horse Bucephalus.'

QUEEN CHRISTINA OF SWEDEN.

Ogadei Khan (b. 1242). Emperor of the Mongols, son of Genghis Khan and an artful drinker. His consumption of alcohol was the subject of so much comment that, when he came to the throne, his first act was to promise that he would only drink half as many goblets of wine a day as he had done in the past. His second act was to order that his goblets should be doubled in size.

David O'Keefe (d. 1901). Irish-American immigrant and the only King of Yap. He found his kingdom, a group of islands in the West Pacific, south-west of Guam, when he was shipwrecked there. His original destination had been China but, having been washed up on the shores of Yap, he liked the place so much that he decided to settle there and acquired some land from the local chiefs. They, in turn, admired him so much that, in 1872, they hailed him as their king.

O'Keefe was not slow to recognise that even on a remote group of Pacific islands his new regal status provided endless opportunities for leading the life of Riley. Soon he was dispensing proclamations here and there, building a castle and travelling about his lands in state – or at least in the best bark canoe available. This founder of the royal house of O'Keefe even designed a royal emblem, which consisted of an American flag fluttering over the letters 'O.K.'. Meanwhile, his subjects were anxious to secure the succession to the throne and they pressed him to accept their offer of a queen. O'Keefe protested that he already had a wife back home in Savannah, Georgia but the islanders insisted and in the end he reluctantly agreed to take a dusky maiden called Dollyboy as his consort. He managed to overcome his reservations about this marriage sufficiently to produce seven heirs.

Yet King David did not altogether forget his original family back home in Georgia and for the next quarter of a century he scrupulously sent them money twice a year. Finally, after having ruled the islands for several decades, O'Keefe sent word that he was coming 'home' and in 1901 he and two of his Yapese sons boarded the *Santa Cruz* bound for the United States. Sadly it – and the King of Yap – was lost at sea.

Osman II (1603–1622). Teenage Sultan of the Ottoman Empire and archery enthusiast. One of his successors, Selim III, shot a world record that lasted for well over a century; Osman, for his part, always felt he got more fun out of the sport when he was using live targets, preferably human ones. Prisoners of war were his main source of supply but when they ran out he would use his own pages. After four years of this hooliganism, he was deposed and strangled by the royal guard.

> *'Kings most commonly, though strong in legions, are but weak in arguments.'*
>
> MILTON.

P

'The halls of kings are full of men but void of friends.'

SENECA, 64 AD.

Robert Pate (19th Century). A royal servant who gave Queen Victoria quite a turn in 1850 by suddenly, and without provocation, hitting her over the head with a walking cane. She was not seriously hurt but Pate was transported to Australia, where his attitude to royalty was more widely appreciated.

Bhupinder Singh, Maharajah of Patiala (1891–1938). Indian Prince and the original man who had everything. This was hardly surprising, since he appropriated no less than 60 per cent of his state's entire annual income of £1¼ million and spent every penny on himself. The result was that he wanted for nothing and, if he saw anything he fancied, then he would instantly buy it – or, more likely, several dozen of it. Shirts, for instance, were ordered by the gross and he managed to spend £31,000 a year on underpants alone, having special pairs run up at £200 a time and discarding them after they had been worn twice.

He had so much spare cash that he hardly knew what to do with it. His solution, when he found something that he liked, was simply to go on buying it regardless of need. Thus he acquired over 130 cars, including 27 Rolls-Royces. Many of them were never driven. His seven palaces also overflowed with tin trunks full of knick-knacks and jewellery – all bought on impulse, shipped back home and promptly forgotten. There was no telling what the staff of this human magpie would have to find room for next: crates of china, boxes and boxes of souvenirs or even, on one occasion, several lorryloads of sheet music. Apparently, just before he had set out on a trip to Austria, the conductor of his personal orchestra, Max Geiger, had given him a list of scores that he required. When the Maharajah arrived in Vienna's premier music shop, he discovered that he had lost the list so, just to be on the safe side, he bought up the entire stock for cash on the spot and had it sent home.

In time, Bhupinder's shopping sprees to Europe became the stuff of legend, not least for the style in which they were conducted. When he came to London in 1925, for instance, he took over all 35 suites on the fifth floor of the Savoy. This accommodation might be thought excessive, until one remembers that he brought with him not only 200 pieces of luggage but also a retinue of 50, including five personal secretaries. At the hotel, no creature comfort was denied this high-liver from the Indian plains. His rooms were filled with 3,000 roses ordered fresh every day, a silver bath was installed for him and he had exclusive use of a private lift decorated in scarlet and gold lacquer. Grub was important to the 20-stone Maharajah and he shifted 50 lb of it each day, regarding the speedy demolition of three whole chickens as little more than a tea-time snack. Menus were his favourite reading material and, if the Savoy could not supply what he wanted, then the order would go out that the dish must be found and hang the expense. Once, when he fancied quails, telegrams were sent all over Europe to unearth supplies. Only six could be located and they were in Egypt. But a special plane was chartered and the precious game duly wound up on the Maharajah's plate.

For three weeks Bhupinder used the Savoy as a launch pad for his daily raids on the shops of the West End. Aided by a fleet of 20 limousines, he carried his booty back to the hotel each night and by the time of his departure, the Savoy's fifth floor was bursting at the seams. Five truckloads of cricket gear, 100 new Savile Row suits and countless crates of purchases were eventually shipped home to Patiala.

The magnificence he lived in here made the world's most luxurious hotel look like a seedy boarding-house. His principal palace of Moti Bagh was constructed of pink sandstone and rose from the plains like a confection on a tablecloth. It covered 11 acres and behind its ¼-mile frontage lay bathrooms like ballrooms and numberless apartments filled with furniture made of the purest crystal. To cater for his every need at this and his half-dozen other palaces, there was a staff of nearly 4,000. Besides cohorts of the usual royal servants, they included a team of royal pilots for his private aircraft, gangs of motor mechanics, his own orchestra and conductor, a group of resident cricket professionals (Harold Larwood, no less, stayed one winter) and even a full-time court photographer.

Needless to say, there was also a harem which contained 350 of the flower of Indian womanhood, pampered beyond belief and, according to palace tittle-tattle, perpetually raring to go. Neither can this have been all talk, for Bhupinder fathered so many childen that they had to have their own palace, Lah Bagh. This residence was staffed to the lintels with dozens of British nannies, nurses and governesses but, despite this strong team of disciplinarians, the vast brood ran riot when the Maharajah was away. Using high-revving Land-Rovers to pull themselves up cliffs on ropes was apparently the least of their crimes. How reassuring it is to note that the children of the man who had everything were among the most unruly offspring one would ever wish to meet.

Paul I (1754–1801). Emperor of All the Russias who combined the fatal flaws of being both meddlesome and unhinged. It is no exaggeration to say that every minute of his four-year reign was devoted to half-baked attempts to regulate the last detail of his subjects' lives. In a torrent of orders and proclamations, he laid down the law on how they should dress, their manners, which books they should read, where they should travel and even how they should conduct their private parties. At its peak, this tidal wave of bumph was so great that every printing press in the capital had to work day and night just to keep pace. In the words of the Emperor's son, 'My father has declared war on common sense with the firm resolve of never concluding a truce.'

With even his nearest and dearest writing him off as a fruitcake, it is perhaps just as well that Paul did not ascend the Imperial throne until he was 42 years old. Before then, this son of Catherine the Great had spent his adulthood either going in cringing fear for his life or swaggering about as the resident martinet at his own personal barracks. Here, at Gatchina, he inflicted on his little private army a system of such senseless brutality and regimentation that it made the average Prussian garrison seem like a particularly informal gypsy camp. There was a lengthy drill three times a day, stiff uniforms that all but ruled out breathing and reams of pernickety regulations which specified such vital military matters as the precise distance between the end of the gauntlet and the elbow of the sleeve. The slightest deviation, of course, resulted in punishment to within an inch of the offender's life.

Unfortunately for his countrymen, Paul thought he could run his vast kingdom in the same way and on the very first day of his reign, in November 1796, he set about the great task of regulating Russia. Before the sun was up, he ordered that all army officers should adopt the harsh Gatchina uniform, even when on leave, and that Prussian army regulations should be applied throughout the royal household. Henceforth all government ministries would start work at six in the morning. He then turned his mind to licking the civilian population into shape and within two days a steady stream of new laws was pouring from his office.

His first major batch of decrees concerned the appearance of his subjects which, for some reason, annoyed him intensely. Everyone, he decided, had to powder their hair and brush it well away from the forehead. No one, not even the ladies at court, was absolved and backsliders were flung instantly into solitary confinement. Orders were also given to arrest anyone seen wearing pantaloons and a similar embargo was slapped on round hats, low collars, tail coats, trousers, boots and waistcoats. The only permissible wear was declared to be tricorne hats, stiffened high collars, tight tunics, breeches, gaiters and square-toed shoes. Just to make sure everyone's wardrobe could be correctly restocked, Paul instructed tailors, hatters and shoe-makers to apply to his officials for approved patterns.

This official civilian uniform not only flew in the face of tradition, it was also decidedly inadequate cover against the local winters and, not surprisingly, there was a fair measure of consumer resistance. Paul, however, was ready for the defaulters. In the capital alone, 300 police roamed the streets looking for the improperly dressed and they were empowered to seize any offending garment on the spot. This beady-eyed force was also responsible for ensuring that all the Emperor's laws regarding social occasions were observed. Every single aspect of how to give or how to attend a private dance, concert, wedding or funeral was laid down in the minutest detail and the effect on Russian social life was, of course, devastating. If, for example, you wanted to give a party, you had to report to the local police station, who would provide a uniformed officer to come and keep watch for any departure from the approved standards of 'loyalty, propriety and sobriety'.

It comes as no surprise to learn that Paul was also a great stickler for protocol. One ancient Russian custom, until Peter the Great abolished it, was that any citizen who encountered a member of the Imperial family should immediately stop his horse or coach, alight and prostrate himself on the ground, regardless of how deep the snow or how thick the mud. One of Paul's first acts was to revive this nonsense. Not content with that, he also produced rules for these acts of supplication, laying down exactly the depth of the bowing and precisely the extent of the scraping. His wrath at the slightest sign of disrespect was all-consuming and not just confined to humans. Once, when out riding in St Petersburg, his horse stumbled. The Emperor dismounted, condemned the animal to 50 lashes and stood by, counting each one as it was administered.

For his next trick, Paul decided that he would try and control his subjects' thoughts. The police moved into the bookshops and teams of censors battled to keep up with the Emperor's curious ideas of what was, and was not, acceptable reading material. The speeches of Cicero, for example, were proscribed because the ancient Roman had been a republican. In the spring of 1800 Paul went further, banning all imports of foreign books and music on the grounds of 'likely injurious consequences to the national morality'. It took him only a little longer to decide that Russian books were just as bad and he ordered all but two of the nation's printing works to close down.

By now, there were few Russians above the rank of peasant who had not at least toyed with the idea of emigrating. Unfortunately for them, this was about all they could do, since Paul's regulations made leave for foreign travel at first difficult to obtain and, ultimately, downright impossible. For some at court there was now only one alternative and, on 11 March 1801, they took it, murdering their lunatic of an Emperor before he could make their lives any more of misery than they were already.

Prince Paul (20th Century). Regent of Yugoslavia who was so determined to stamp out subversive works of art that in 1929 he even banned a Mickey Mouse cartoon for its allegedly anti-royalist sentiments. The offending item in the 'Mickey Mouse Cartoon Strip' dealt with a plot against a young king and a conspiracy to place an impostor on the throne. This story was judged to be a little too close to home, since at the time Prince Paul was ruling Yugoslavia during the minority of King Peter. So, rather than have Belgrade cinema-goers think that Walt Disney was producing a satire on the intricacies of Middle European politics, he refused the film a certificate.

Pedro I (1320–1369). King of Portugal who had a corpse disinterred, dressed in robes, placed on a throne and crowned as his queen. On the face of it, this behaviour would seem to be beyond rational explanation but, as will become clear, Pedro did have his reasons. Apart from anything else, the corpse in question was not just any old cadaver, dug up at random from the local burial ground; it was one that was rather special to Pedro and thereby hangs a particularly harrowing tale.

Even his best friends would never have described Pedro as the luckiest of men where women were concerned. One of his betrothed, Edward III's daughter Joan, was struck down by the Black Death on her way to marry him and although his next fiancée, Constance of Castile, did avoid plague and pestilence on the journey, she died a mere five years after their wedding, in 1345. He then took up with a certain Inez de Castro and at last seemed to have found true happiness. The one blot on the connubial horizon was Pedro's father, Alfonso XI.

Regrettably, as blots go, he was a hardened old professional, the bloody-minded veteran of many a family feud and, when Pedro announced his intention of making an honest woman of Inez, Alfonso put his mailed foot down. Noble she might be, he boomed, but no son of his was going to marry a girl who was illegitimate. Pedro, however, was determined not to have his plans founder on such a technicality and, undaunted, he obtained special dispensation from the Pope and married Inez in secret at Braganza on New Year's Day 1355.

Over the next few months Alfonso began to suspect that he had been hoodwinked and he was not best pleased. Kings are not accustomed to disobedience and this one was damned if he was going to tolerate it. When Pedro was out hunting one day, Alfonso went to Inez and confronted her with the fact that she was now his daughter-in-law. She begged for mercy but the bitter old King showed her none. As soon as he left, three courtiers broke into her villa at Quinta das Lagrinas and assassinated Inez and her three children. When the murders were discovered, Alfonso feigned anger and banished the guilty parties but no one, least of all the desolate Pedro, was fooled for a minute. He vowed that when he came to the throne he would extract revenge in the fullest possible measure. Within two years he was in a position to do so.

Almost his first act on ascending the throne in 1357 was to order the extradition of his wife's assassins. Only two could be found but they were brought back from Spain, tortured in the presence of their new King and then, finally, had their hearts ripped from their bodies. Two years later came the concluding twist in this sorry saga. Pedro ordered the body of his beloved Inez to be exhumed from its resting place in the cathedral at Coimbra and thence taken to Alcobaca. Here it was dressed in royal robes, placed on a throne, anointed and solemnly crowned. Pedro himself sat enthroned beside his 'Queen' as the nobility of Portugal stepped forward one by one to lift her dead hand and signify their loyalty with a kiss.

After this bizarre ceremony, Pedro had the newly-crowned corpse and throne sealed in a marble sarcophagus and placed opposite the one that awaited him on his death. There Inez remained until 1810 when Napoleon's invading troops forced open her tomb in search of souvenirs and cut the still-yellow hair from her skeleton. It was the final interference with her peace. The prince's wife who had been dug up twice, once to be crowned and once for a haircut, has not been disturbed since.

By way of a genealogical footnote, romantics may care to know that His Royal Highness the Prince of Wales is descended from Inez and Princess Diana from one of her assassins.

Pepi II (2300 BC–2199 BC). King of Egypt and holder of the world record for the longest occupation of a throne. He succeeded to his crown at the age of six in 2294 BC, lived to be a centenarian and thus reigned for over 94 years.

Peter the Great (1672–1725). Czar and Emperor of Russia who had an extraordinarily common touch. His position as the omnipotent ruler of a vast land gave him the opportunity to be treated like a god, especially as he was regarded in such awe by his subjects that most of them believed he ascended into heaven once a week for a consultation with his Maker. Instead, he spurned such mumbo-jumbo, revelled in manual labour, hated to be the object of deference, served as an ordinary fireman in St Petersburg and even enlisted in his own army as a private soldier.

Indeed, nothing perhaps illustrates his striking humility

more than his military career. Given the pick of all the fancy-breeched, behind-the-lines soft options, he chose instead to be a common artilleryman and, while he was on campaign, signed his letters 'Bombardier Peter'. This was no mere affectation. During the 14-week bombardment of Azor he worked ceaselessly, loading and firing siege mortars and sharing the discomforts of his fellows. He did allow himself to serve as a galley captain in his navy but that was only because of his undisputed expertise as a sailor and again he would accept no extra privileges. When there was a triumphal procession into Moscow after a great victory, he insisted on marching not at the head but along with all the other galley captains at the rear.

Few monarchs have despised pomp and ceremony as much as Peter did. He abolished the law that said all Russian men must prostrate themselves in his presence, ordered official functions to be kept to a minimum, maintained only a small staff, dressed simply and, although he owned a small carriage, would not use it if he could help it, preferring always to walk. In fact, he did his best to satirise ceremonial. When his old tutor Nikita Zotog, who was 84, married a buxom widow of 34 in 1715, Peter arranged a state wedding, the like of which one would never wish to see repeated. The guests were instructed to wear masks and, as they arrived, there to announce them were four of the most chronic stammerers that could be found in all Russia. Serving as stewards and sidesmen were a group of decrepit old men, especially chosen for their inability to walk or even stand without the most comprehensive of assistance. Needless to say, they also acted as waiters at the banquet afterwards.

The grand procession included not only Peter as a drummer and the happy couple on a sled drawn by bears but also featured a quartet of running footmen whose physical infirmities would be distressing to describe, let alone behold. Finally, to the complete despair of the blushing bride, the priest officiating at this chaotic function was, at 100 years old, in a state of advanced decay and minus both his sight and his memory. Mercifully, he retained a few vestiges of his hearing but his range was desperately restricted, thus affording his prompters, who were situated at the back of the cathedral, no end of comic possibilities.

Peter also adored manual labour, something for which, at 6 ft 7 ins tall and of impressive build, he was eminently qualified. He learnt, and didn't just dabble in, the trades of carpentry, stonemasonry, shipbuilding, typesetting and smithying and frequently spent lengthy spells putting these skills to practical use. He once, for example, worked for a month at the smithy of an ironmaster called Werner Muller and forged 720 lb of iron bars a day. When he finished his stint, he asked for his money and Muller greatly overpaid him. Peter rejected the excess, bought a pair of shoes out of his wages and showed them proudly to his court. 'Look,' he said, 'I have earned them by the sweat of my brow with a hammer and anvil.'

He loved these periods of working for the opportunities they gave him to be himself rather than the Czar of All the Russias, and for the same reason he hugely enjoyed paying unannounced visits to his subjects. Many were the country churchgoers who were astonished to see Peter stride up their aisle, find a place in the choir stalls and join in the singing in a booming voice. So it was typical that when he decided to tour Europe to see at first hand the advances being made in the West, he should declare his intention of travelling incognito. Despite the protests of his courtiers, he insisted and it was as plain Peter Mikhailov that he went. Members of his party were forbidden on pain of death to call him anything else. With his great height, the alias was hardly likely to fool anyone but the pretence was maintained as he worked in Dutch shipyards, toured London and studied every piece of technology he could find.

It was on this trip that he acquired his lifelong interest in anatomy and from then on his case of surgical instruments was an essential piece of his luggage. He instructed that he was to be told whenever any operations were imminent at a local hospital and, if they were sufficiently interesting, he would scuttle off and insist on being allowed to have his turn at the slab. His eagerness to experiment became so notorious that his servants kept their illnesses secret from him, lest their Czar should turn up at their bedsides, scalpel in hand.

When he returned from his European tour in April 1698 he was determined to modernise his backward land. He chose as his starting point the thick beards that adorned every Russian chin and on the day he re-entered Moscow he produced a long razor and began cutting off the luxuriant growths on the nobles' faces. Despite their strenuous objections, he was adamant that all at court should be clean-shaven and those who refused were visited by Peter's court jester armed with a cut-throat razor. Peter then decreed that all Russians, except peasants and the clergy, should remove their beards and his officials were permitted to shave on the spot any man who defied the law. His only concession was that those who wanted to keep their beards on religious grounds could do so on payment of a tax. For this they were given to wear around their necks a bronze medal bearing a picture of a beard and inscribed with the words 'Tax Paid'. Peter later extended the ban to moustaches and eventually got so carried away that he had his head shaved and ordered a wig to be made with the hair that had just been removed.

This beard tax was just one example of the highly inventive taxes which Peter imposed. He slapped duty on births, marriages, funerals, horse collars, hats, beds, baths, beehives, kitchen chimneys, firewood and even drinking water. These, and the state monopolies he held on the manufacture of everything from alcohol to chessmen and tobacco to coffins, were a large part of the reason why his extreme humility did not earn him the universal love that it might have done. There was also, of course, the little matter of his despatch of both his half-sister and his wife to a convent, his trial and execution of his son and his habit of torturing some criminals personally. Nevertheless, he modernised his country, founded its navy, built St Petersburg, overhauled the civil service, instituted humanitarian reforms, waged war on corruption and sponsored education. Strange, then, that the man who shouldered all this responsibility should carry through life a phobic fear of something as insignificant as cockroaches. He would run gibbering from a room if he so much as saw one and, when visiting, would never enter a building until he had been assured that his room had been thoroughly cleaned and none of the dreaded insects were present.

Yet no one could accuse him of a lack of bravery, least of all in the manner of his death. While out sailing during the winter of 1724, he saw a ship foundering and, without a second's thought, the monarch who had never hesitated to cast aside conventional ideas about royal dignity, leapt into the water and joined the rescue. He caught a chill, a fever developed and he died aged 53.

Prince Philip (b. 1921). Duke of Edinburgh and, by royal appointment, purveyor of embarrassing moments to Her Majesty the Queen. Whatever achievements he has managed or good causes espoused, Philip remains fixed in the public mind not for these but for the periodic hoo-haas that have erupted over some of his public statements. Equipped, according to his critics, with lips that move quicker than his brain, he has been accused of offending, at one time or another, virtually every sensitive soul on earth – from British businessmen to Canadian big-wigs, Brazilian admirals to the entire Chinese nation. No other member of his family has had to have their words so consistently clarified, explained, forgiven or denied.

His image as a sort of anti-ambassador, a globe-trotting trampler on delicate sensibilities, might appear to some to be an exaggeration but those who travel with him know that however long he behaves, sooner or later the royal mouth will open and out of it will emerge words that they will regret, even if he doesn't. Take his visit to China in October 1986, for instance. He had kept himself in check for some time and then, at a private reception in Peking, he said to an English student called Simon Kirby, 'If you stay here much longer, you are going to go back with slitty eyes.'

It was the kind of thin, rather tasteless joke that hardly deserved an audience of one, let alone the world-wide exposure it was shortly to receive. Young Kirby duly reported Philip's comment to a journalist and in no time at all the British press was convulsed with the story that the Queen's consort had, in just 15 words, gravely insulted one quarter of the world's population. Fortunately for Philip and his wife, who still had several days of their trip left, the Chinese people did not rise in immediate protest but remained commendably inscrutable. The royal party, however, were left squirming and uttering limp explanations for some time afterwards. Once again, the Prince's idea of comedy had proved considerably less funny than he thought it was.

Even when he has a good line, he invariably delivers it to the wrong crowd. During his tour of Canada, for example, he was due to open a new annexe to the city hall in Vancouver – typical of the wearying chores which fill so much of his diary at home and abroad. When he came to cut the ribbon, he momentarily forgot the name of the new wing and so, thinking his audience would appreciate a little satire, he said, 'I declare this thing open – whatever it is.' Spoken by a comic in a revue sketch, the line might have got a laugh but addressed to a gathering of city worthies by the head of the Commonwealth's husband, it went down like an Irish joke at a Sinn Fein rally. The ritual furore ensued.

There are times, of course, when the opportunity to offend entire communities is not open to him and Philip has to content himself with more personal targets for his joshing. Once, when talking to a Brazilian admiral, he thought it would be amusing to ask this representative of one of the world's lesser-known navies if he had won his spectacular array of medals by fighting on the artificial lake of his country's capital Brasilia. The admiral's answer was swift and decidedly below the belt, 'At least I did not get them for marrying my wife.'

Nor is ironical humour Philip's strong suit. When in Paraguay, he said to General Alfredo Stroessner, the local dictator and mine host to several former Nazis, 'It is a pleasant change to be in a country that is not ruled by its people.' The remark, which presumably raised a chuckle from the attendant diplomats, looked rather less rib-tickling when reported in Britain. Palace aides hurriedly explained that the Prince was, of course, thinking of meddlers back home like the Lord's Day Observance Society. Of course.

Equally awkward to explain away were the remarks he made during an interview on the Jimmy Young programme on BBC Radio 2 in 1981. 'A few years ago,' he said, referring to unemployment, 'everybody was saying, "We must have more leisure, everybody's working too much. . . . " Now that everybody's got more leisure, they're complaining. People don't seem to be able to make up their minds what they want, do they?'

It is remarks like this which have made him a folk hero in saloon bars up and down the country – the straight-talking, ex-naval officer who calls a spade a spade and a chink a chink. But the beery cheers might be less vociferous if the people making them listened to all that the Prince was saying. For every rash remark about the unemployed, the record can produce several quotes from Philip urging businessmen to shake themselves from their lethargy, adopt new ideas or otherwise 'pull their fingers out'. His attitude to social security 'scroungers' – 'They are no more evil than industrialists using high-powered accountants to avoid taxes' – is splendidly even-handed and places him, on this issue, considerably to the left of the Thatcher government.

Indeed, attempts to classify him in any neat category will always founder on the facts. He happily shoots pheasants (he and his friends killed 6,500 at Sandringham in the winter of 1979/80) yet he is President of the World Wildlife Fund and resigned from the New York Explorers Club in 1984 when he heard that lion's meat and hippo chops were served at its annual banquet. He has called for Britain to concentrate less heavily on the 'unsuccessful and unfortunate' and yet recently presided over an inquiry into housing which advocated an end to mortgage tax relief and proposed other radical measures.

Only the most severe critics would deny him the right to hold and express such beliefs and in doing so he is only carrying out his duties as self-appointed official stirrer-up of national debate. Take that away from him and all you would have left would be his jokes.

Philip III (1578–1621). King of Spain and a victim of the strict etiquette of his court. At this time, the rules which governed the running of the Spanish royal household were renowned throughout Europe for their absurd rigidity. The Queen, for example, was forbidden to dance, eat or laugh in public and the procedure for every facet of court life was minutely prescribed in the official manual of correct behaviour. This volume laid down everything, from the number of steps and the depth of the bows which each person was to make on entering the royal presence, to the type of chair or bench each rank of courtier was entitled to sit on. Even the width of cloak each person should wear was stipulated. The manual also set out, in strictly non-negotiable terms, precisely who did what job and woe betide anyone who even thought of crossing these immovable demarcation lines.

So it was, in this joyless and suffocating atmosphere, that Philip sat down by the palace fireside one evening. Unfortunately, the courtier whose task it was to fill the royal grate had gone a bit mad with the fuel and the roaring fire soon made the King feel distinctly uncomfortable. But being Spain, the problem was not so much what to do but who could do it? It would have been unthinkable for a king of Spain to get up and tend his own fire or move his own chair. Equally, the domestics and courtiers who, even as Philip sat there roasting, were lined up in order of precedence outside his room, did not include those who had authority to respond to his calls for help. Finally, much to relief of the over-heated monarch, the Marquis de Potat appeared and the King ordered him to damp the fire. That, however, said the Marquis, was awkward because court etiquette did not allow him to perform such a function. He suggested that it sounded like a job for the Duke D'Ussada and, after due consideration, felt it within his powers to summon this gentleman.

Now all, no doubt, would still have been well had the Duke been immediately available. But he was not; he was out hunting. So, while the court rested happy that they had played it by the book and the matter was being attended to, their King fainted away in front of the fierce flames. By the time he was rescued, Philip's blood had been heated to such a degree that a fever set in and he was carried off in the 24th year of his reign.

> *'Kings are naturally lovers of low company.'*
>
> EDMUND BURKE, 1780.

R

'I am beginning more and more to see that the upholding of the monarchy is a form of idolatry.'

MACKENZIE KING.

Maharajah Mulhar Rao, Gaekwar of Baroda (19th Century). Indian Prince whose novel method of executing opponents set new standards in the practice of legalised sadism. Those condemned to die in his kingdom were strapped to the hind leg of an elephant and the beast was then given a sharp prod to ensure that it set off at a smart pace, dragging the victim behind. If that did not do the trick and the poor wretch was merely concussed, then he was revived with a glass of water, his head placed on a large stone and the elephant was encouraged to step on it. The inventor of this disgusting ritual was finally deposed by the British after he had stood trial for the attempted murder of a colonial official.

Richard I (1157–1199). King of England and warmonger whose image as a 'good king' has successfully defied the facts for nearly 800 years. He was in reality an absentee monarch who spent no more than ten months of a ten-year reign in England, left the country to the vagaries of his brother John and failed to produce an heir or even, it is said, consummate his marriage. Indeed, his sexual proclivities meant that Robin Hood and his chums were not the only young men in tights who followed their king with expectations. In a less martial age than his own,

Richard the Lionheart would probably have been known as Richard the Limp Wrist.

Ivan Rimsky-Korsakov (18th Century). Grandfather of the famous Russian composer and a less than faithful royal lover. It was the practice of Catherine the Great, before she actually took a man to her bed, to have him thoroughly vetted by both her physician and principal lady-in-waiting. Dr Rogerson would give the candidate a meticulous going-over for any signs of venereal disease and, if all was well, he would then be directed to Countess Bruce for a more intimate assessment. Those who won her stamp of approval would then be passed ready for active service in the royal bed. They would be accorded the status of favourite, given an apartment connected to the Empress's by private staircase and, when they had served their time, handsomely pensioned off.

That, then, was the short but profitable career opening up for young Ivan in 1777, thanks to the positively glowing recommendation from Countess Bruce. She gave him a five-star rating and Catherine found that this was, if anything, an understatement. 'He is a masterpiece of creation,' she said of this young sergeant in her Household Guards, 'he sends out warmth like the sun, he is radiant.' Indeed he was; radiating here, radiating there, but chiefly, I am afraid, radiating back in the direction of Countess Bruce. He had such fond memories of her delightfully unscientific investigations that for two years he kept returning to her for further tests and she, for her part, was repeatedly eager to confirm her earlier judgement of him. Inevitably, when Catherine got to hear of the couple's thoroughness, the game was up. The Countess departed in disgrace and was replaced by a gimlet-eyed old procuress named Madame Protosova, while the banished Ivan was succeeded by Alexander Lanskey – the very last graduate of the Countess Bruce school of charm and virility.

Robert III (1337–1406). King of Scotland who was totally unfit to rule. He was shy and nervous and had been robbed by a horse's kick of the physical and mental vigour required by his calling. He was, however, refreshingly honest and, when he died, it was found that he had left this engaging epitaph: 'Here lies the worst of kings and the most miserable of men.'

> '*A modern king has become a vermiform appendix – useless when quiet, when obtrusive in danger of removal.*'
>
> AUSTIN O'MALLEY, 1932.

S

'Kings are not born, they are made by universal hallucination.'

GEORGE BERNARD SHAW.

Prince Christian of Schleswig-Holstein (1831–1917). Husband of Princess Helena, son-in-law of Queen Victoria and a rather upsetting dinner companion.

His anti-social behaviour began after he lost an eye on a Sandringham pheasant shoot when his brother-in-law, the Duke of Connaught, aimed at a low-flying bird, missed and hit Christian instead. Thereafter, the Prince always wore a glass eye. He was not, however, content with just the one and insisted on ordering a full range of different-coloured eyes, including a bloodshot one for when he had a cold. These were arranged on a special tray, from which, according to his mood and wardrobe, he would make his daily selection. He was so proud of these false eyes that he frequently showed them off at the dinner table, much to the consternation of other guests. As if being asked to admire these beady specimens set out on their tray was not bad enough, Christian also subjected his fellow diners to the sight of him changing eyes between courses – a spectacle which ruined many a hearty appetite.

Selim I (1524–1574). Sultan of the Ottoman Empire who was known for very good reason as Selim the Sot. With his ruddy face and vast stomach, he was the very picture of the dedicated dipsomaniac and was almost perpetually drunk. Unlike most alcoholics, however, he was in a position to be fussy about what he poured down his throat and for Selim nothing could beat a good casket of Cyprus wine; unless, of course, it was several caskets of the stuff. Imagine, therefore, his horror when he discovered that his stocks of this nectar were getting dangerously low and that the prospects of immediately replenishing them, with Cyprus in Venetian hands, were decidedly remote. Selim's solution was simple: invade the island, conquer it and thus ensure his supplies of the precious wine forever. So off, after only the most perfunctory of protests, went the Turkish army on their drunken ruler's errand.

Never was a thirst more expensively slaked. After a brutal siege of Cyprus, the Turks sacked Nicosia, massacred 30,000 islanders and then had to batter the main fortress of Famagusta for two years before it would surrender. Selim had at last got his wine. But then so, in a curious way, did the wine get him. One day, after downing a bottle of it in a single swig, he staggered off for a bath, slipped on the marble floor, broke his skull and died.

Shah Jehan (1592–1666). Moghul Emperor and the man who built the Taj Mahal. As one could tell from this structure, he was never one to be cowed by a fear of being thought ostentatious. His throne, for instance, was of solid gold with its canopy supported by 12 pillars of emeralds. Above was a golden tree dripping with fruit made of diamonds and rubies and, flanking this, were two gold peacocks, their spread tails shimmering with emeralds and sapphires.

To house fixtures and fittings like these, he built an increasingly fanciful series of palaces, each more imposing than the last. So when his favourite wife Mumtaz Mahal died in 1639, he was in no mood to have a simple headstone put up and leave it at that. Instead, he built her a mausoleum which became known as the Taj Mahal – funereal masonry in the grandest of manners and, with its prominent dome, a fitting monument to the wife who bore him 14 children. For the next 20 years no fewer than 20,000 men worked day in and day out to complete the building. Its brick scaffolding alone cost £9 million and the structure itself, complete with mosaics and jewelled decorations, cost at least as much again. The result was the white marbled wonder of the world, in front of which no visitor to Agra now dares go unphotographed.

Shah himself had little time to admire his masterpiece. Not long after the finishing touches were added, he was deposed by his sons and imprisoned in the nearby Red Fort. Here he remained until his death seven years later. In due course, he was laid beside his wife in her splenderous resting place.

Shaka (d. 1828). King of the Zulus, he had such a fastidious sense of dignity that even the slightest and most accidental slip of decorum was punished severely. Under his rule it was a capital offence to show the faintest sign of amusement at a ceremonial gathering and often even an ill-suppressed cough, sneeze or fart was enough for the King's finger to be raised and the executioners to close in on the perpetrator. His favoured way of despatching these unfortunates was impaling, a method for which sadistic hardly seems an adequate description, since it involved forcing the victim to sit upright on a vertical pole until he expired from his internal injuries.

When entertaining, Shaka would frequently order a few such killings to impress his visitors and he became so fond of these gruesome spectacles that he once sentenced 60 young boys to death before breakfast. It has been estimated that this unlovable man, who began each day by having his naked body publicly greased with a mixture of red ochre and sheep fat, was responsible, through his executions and military manoeuvres, for the death of over two million people. It was, perhaps, just as well that he reigned no longer than 11 years.

Shan-yin (b. 456). Sung dynasty Princess of China and Oriental good-time girl. When her brother Ts'am Wu came to the throne in 473, this saucy little minx went to him and complained that, while he had over 3,000 concubines with which to pleasure himself, she had only one lover. The King thought she had a point and the next day sent to her residence 30 eager young men

– one for every day of the Chinese month. The 17-year-old Princess was delighted and, after sorting out a timetable with the lads, kept herself amused for months. In time, however, she grew bored with having only one stud at a time. So she ordered a vast bed, told all the boys to clamber aboard and spent her nights rolling among them.

Richard Gibson (1615–1690) and Anne Shepherd (1619–1709). Celebrated portrait painters and court dwarves to Charles I. This pair were made a great fuss of in the royal household and, when they married, Charles (who, at a height of only 4 ft 10 ins, had a natural sympathy for the small-statured) consented to give Anne away. Gibson, who stood about a yard high, proved to be an adaptable little man and retained his position come what might – the fall of Charles, the days of Cromwell and then the Restoration. He painted mainly, as one would expect, in miniature and taught the rudiments of his craft to both the future Queen Mary II and Princess Anna. He and his wife were survived by five children, all of whom were of normal height.

Shkurine (18th Century). A good and faithful servant. In 1762 his royal mistress, the Empress Catherine, was expecting a baby by her lover Count Grigori Orlov. She had so far managed to conceal from her husband Peter III not only this liaison but also, with the aid of voluminous hooped skirts, the very fact that she was pregnant. Her labour and confinement were, however, another matter. How could she possibly hope to keep this a secret, even from a half-witted innocent like Peter?

Her valet, the loyal Shkurine, had the answer. He knew that Peter could never resist watching a good blaze and so, as soon as Catherine went into labour, he lured Peter away by actually setting fire to his own humble home. The resulting conflagration was so thrillingly enjoyable that Peter was kept safely entertained until Catherine, attended by a well-bribed midwife, was delivered of a son. Immediately after the birth the baby was smuggled out of the Winter Palace and into the care of Shkurine's wife. He was swaddled in beaver skin – bobrinsky in

Russian – and the romantically inclined Catherine named him Alexei Gregorovitch Bobrinsky.

Little 'Beaverskin' stayed with the Shkurines in their rebuilt home until he was a toddler. Then, with her husband dead and Catherine the Empress in her own right, his mother reclaimed him and installed him in his own suite in the children's quarter of the palace. She took intense interest in him, supervised his education, spoilt him terribly and, finally, when he was five, made him a count. Officially his real identity remained a closely guarded secret and it was one that the Shkurines, having sacrificed so much for the boy's birth, loyally took with them to the grave.

Stanislaus I (1677–1766). King of Poland and bon viveur. Such was his taste for the good things of life at the expense of his people that they deposed him in 1709 after a reign of just five heady years. Thus freed from any responsibility whatsoever, he was able to devote the remaining 57 years of his life to stylish high living. No king ever had a more softly cushioned exile.

He settled in Lorraine and soon collected about himself a staff so monumental that it would not have disgraced a medieval emperor. It consisted of no fewer than 510 persons, a clear indication that Stanislaus had no intention of having even the smallest of his needs uncatered for. Included among this vast throng of factotums were 16 gentlemen of the bedchamber, four private secretaries, 12 personal valets, over 40 footmen, 31 porters, 10 masters of the ex-king's horse, 41 gardeners and 63 musicians.

Fine buildings and rich food were his two great passions and he made sure that there were plenty of little helpmeets on hand to assist him pursue these interests. His own personal staff of architects numbered no fewer than 17 and, working with them, he virtually rebuilt the city of Nancy in the Italianate style. This was not to every local's taste and one old pewterer was so outraged at some of Stanislaus's 'vandalism' that he walled up his windows rather than look out on the offensive new buildings.

Yet the exile's thoughts were never far away from his

stomach and the staff hired to keep this regularly and well filled were his special pride and joy. There were 24 cooks, four confectioners, seven table-deckers, five cellar and pantrymen and even seven men whose job was merely to superintend the roasts – all of whom were presided over by eight stewards and three maîtres d'hôtel. Like many active gourmands, Stanislaus was no mean hand in the kitchen himself and he fermented his own version of Tokay wine and also invented several new dishes, notably sugared vegetables. Some of his culinary methods were, however, a little extreme. His special recipe for goose, for instance, required the bird to be plucked alive and then whipped to death before being cooked. Ironically, this appalling procedure bore an uncanny resemblance to his own death when, at the age of 89, he found his nightshirt alight and, in trying to beat out the flames, he hit himself so hard that he fell unconscious into the fire and was roasted.

Lord Stanley (1826–1893). English aristocrat who was heir to such fabulously wealthy estates in Lancashire that he could afford disdainfully to reject an offer of the Greek throne. This astonishing but totally sincere invitation to rule Greece was extended to him by the people of that country after they had deposed the demented Otto I in 1865. When he heard about it, Disraeli (who later appointed Stanley Foreign Secretary) commented, 'Had I his youth, I would not hesitate, even with the Earldom of Derby in the distance. It is a dazzling adventure for the house of Stanley but they are not an adventurous race and I fancy they will prefer Knowsley to the Parthenon and Lancashire to the Attic plains.' He was, as usual, correct.

Sunanda (1860–1881). Queen of Siam and a martyr to the reverential taboos surrounding royalty in that land. One day in 1881 she was travelling to the palace of Bang-pa-in in a boat towed by a launch when the craft overturned and she was thrown into the water. In any other country rescuing the queen from a ducking in a canal would present no particular problem. One of the many watermen on hand would have dived in, helped the spluttering monarch to the bank and humbly accepted his subsequent reward. The queen might lose a little dignity but her life would be saved.

Siamese protocol, however, took a rather different view of the manhandling of royal personages. Dignity was all and it was simply forbidden, on pain of death, to touch any part of any royal body whatsoever, however good the excuse. Indeed, the laws of Siam laid down a detailed etiquette in the event of a boating accident. According to Quaritch Wales's translation of these rules in his *Siamese State Ceremonies*, the procedure was this:

'If the royal barge founders, the boatmen must swim away; if they remain near they are to be executed. If the boat founders and the royal person falls into the water and is about to drown, let the boatman stretch out the signal-spear and throw the coconuts (a string of which were kept especially for this purpose) so that He may grasp them if He can. If He cannot, they may let Him grasp the signal-spear. If they lay hold of Him to rescue Him they are to be executed. He who throws the coconuts is to be rewarded with 40 ticals of silver and one gold basin. If the barge sinks and someone else sees the coconuts thrown and goes to save the royal person, the punishment is double and his family is to be killed. If the barge founders and someone throws the coconuts so that they float towards the shore (ie away from the royal person) his throat is to be cut and his house confiscated.'

Thus it was when Sunanda fell overboard, her life hung by a mere string of coconuts. Being pregnant at the time and so not at her most agile, she missed this flimsy buoyancy support when it was thrown to her and began to go under. Some peasants were watching from the bank and one of them made a move to go to the rescue of his sinking Queen. As he was poised in his dive, a voice rang out. It belonged to a court official and reminded the would-be hero of the laws forbidding such an attempt. The peasant stayed where he was and the Queen drowned, aged just 21.

Augustus, Duke of Sussex (1773–1843). Son of George III,

Queen Victoria's favourite uncle and a man of unusual tastes. He accumulated all manner of curios, collected coach whips, had a negro page whom he called Mr Blackman and owned more Bibles than any other man in the world, keeping over 5,000 of them in a special room in his library in Kensington Palace. The Duke was also the first member of the British royal family to leave his body to medical research. In an unusually democratic codicil to his will, he additionally requested that when the boffins had finished rummaging around in his remains, they should have them interred not at Windsor but in a public cemetery at Kensal Green.

Carmen Sylva (1843–1916). This was the pen name under which the magnificently ridiculous Queen Elizabeth of Romania wrote some of the most lamentable poems and fairy tales ever committed to paper. Today these florid works are mercifully out of print but Elizabeth's courtiers found them less easy to avoid. The ladies-in-waiting and hangers-on who attended her daily salons had to sit and listen for hours on end while the Queen declaimed her latest masterpiece.

This circle, which included for a time Sarah Bernhardt, were also expected to provide a captive audience for Elizabeth's artistic protégés. These were a seemingly unending line of budding musicians, painters and authors, all of whom were spectacularly untalented in their chosen fields – a fact which always rather eluded Elizabeth. Once, for instance, she produced before her soirée an elderly French painter and declared him to be a musical genius. He knew, she told them, not only every major opera by heart but had a voice so incredibly versatile that he could also sign in turn the parts of tenor, baritone and bass. Regrettably, this claim was never put to serious test, for he also involuntarily changed key after every few notes and this, combined with his earnest hand-on-heart pose, forced most of his audience to make a giggling bolt for the door. In the end only the enraptured Elizabeth remained.

These curious artistic fixations and her insistence on being addressed by her nom de plume rather than her royal title were not her only eccentricities. There was, for example, her habit of standing on the terrace of her home overlooking Constanza harbour and yelling out blessings to departing ships through a loud-hailer. Besides being a danger to shipping, this strange, restless individual also considerably alarmed one of her maids of honour, Helene Vacarescu, by telling the girl that she was the reincarnation of her daughter Marie, who had died in infancy many years before. Like most of her fancies, this one was soon forgotten.

Elizabeth was, however, a deeply charitable woman and she produced many schemes for the relief of suffering among her less fortunate subjects. Some of these were less practical than others, like her idea for building a totally white city for the blind. Ironically, her own eyes began to deteriorate in later life. She became severely short-sighted and on boating trips down the Danube she would wave a large white table napkin at the cows standing in riverside fields, earnestly believing them to be loyal peasants who had come out to greet her. 'She was,' in the words of her successor Queen Marie, 'both splendid and absurd.'

'The pleased incredulity with which the public reacts
to the elementary demonstrations on the part of
royalty that they are, after all, like other people
is matched by the public's firm refusal to accept them as such.'

EDWARD, DUKE OF WINDSOR, 1966.

T

'*The probability is, I suppose, that the monarchy
has become a kind of ersatz religion.*'

MALCOLM MUGGERIDGE, 1955.

Prince Francis of Teck (1870–1910). The brother of Queen Mary
and, until his reformation in later life, very definitely the black
sheep of the Victorian royal family. His wayward career got off
to an early start when the short-trousered miscreant was forced
to leave Dr Morton's school in Farnborough under something
of a cloud. Little Francis was then sent to Wellington College in
the fond hope that the school's military-style curriculum would
instil a sense of discipline into the lad. Regrettably, the bold
experiment was a failure and he was expelled for throwing his
housemaster over a hedge for a bet. The next stop was
Cheltenham where there was further, if less violent, trouble
over gambling. It was with some relief that the English public
school system eventually passed him over to Sandhurst to begin
his military training.

Like many an upper-class hooligan, Frank found that life in
the British army suited his talents admirably. After spells with
the 9th Lancers and 90th Rifles, he settled down with the 1st
Royal Dragoons where his affability and horsemanship made
him popular with officers and men alike. Money, however, was
a continual problem. Like his mother, Princess Mary Adelaide,
he never believed in living within one's means and his stud of
horses, fine clothes and gambling began soaking up every penny
he could lay his hands on and much more besides. Soon Frank

was living almost entirely on tick. For a time he muddled through, regarding bills from his tailor and bootmaker as little more than the opening bids in a protracted and delicate negotiation. Bookmakers, however, were less patient and when, in the summer of 1895, he found himself in hock to a professional gambler to the tune of £1,000, he decided to risk all in one glorious plunge at the races.

This was a mistake. After all, a man whose grandmother was trampled to death by a galloping troop at a cavalry review should have known better than to expect any favours from a horse. Yet such was his desperation that, when he arrived at The Curragh racecourse near Dublin on 26 June, his one obsessive thought was to recover his debt and his eye was caught by the card for the Stewards' Plate for two-year-olds. The race was a sprint of five furlongs, only four runners were declared and there among them was Bellerin – at 10–1 on, the closest thing to a sure-fire winner that Frank had ever seen. With only the coin in his pocket to his name, he promptly wrote out a promissory note for £10,000 (nearly £100,000 in 1987 currency) and put the lot on Bellerin. Sure enough, it was beaten by a short head by Winkfield's Pride and a dazed Frank left the course owing a total of £11,000.

There was nothing for it but to confess everything and face the consequences, the recriminations and all the told-you-so's from his family. They did not disappoint him, turning in a virtuoso performance of collective hair-tearing, head-shaking and finger-wagging. However, when all the moralising had subsided, they did at least have the good grace to see him right. His sister Mary, then Duchess of York, organised the royal whip-round and when the debt was cleared, Frank was packed off to Victorian England's answer to all such embarrassing problems – India.

The experience must have had its chastening effect, for over the next few years he served with some distinction in the Egyptian army, where he won the DSO, and in South Africa. By 1901, when his sister was Princess of Wales, he was, publicly at least, a respected and proud-looking army officer.

Not, however, that she was speaking to him by then. The gambling debts she was prepared to forgive and forget but when he gave their late mother's emeralds to his aging married mistress, Mary cut him dead.

Frank duly left the army at the end of the second Boer War and for the next few years he and Mary remained estranged. Yet gradually it became apparent that he was, in part at least, a changed character. He still overspent and haunted his London clubs but now he devoted more and more time to his charity work for a boys' club and the Middlesex Hospital. He was also an enthusiastic chairman of the Royal Automobile Club and president of that vital organisation for pioneer motorists, the Roads Improvement Association. By the time Mary was crowned Queen in 1910, she had become reconciled to her brother. Sadly, he now had only a few months to live and he died in the October of her coronation year. At his Windsor funeral she broke down and cried, the only public tears she was ever to shed. However, her distress was not so great that she overlooked the issue that had rankled with her all these years. Within months of Frank's death, Mary had recovered all her mother's jewels from his former mistress.

Theodore I (1696–1756). Self-styled King of Corsica whose career as a monarch came to a sorry and farcical conclusion in a London debtors' prison. In the end, only the generosity of a passing philanthropist kept him from a pauper's grave.

He was born Theodore von Neuhoff, the son of a gentleman, in Metz, Germany in 1696. After a brief spell in the French army he left and became one of the itinerant assortment of adventurers who then roamed Europe armed with a little cash and some big ideas. In Theodore's case the ideas were both female and expensive and when the money ran out, he found himself in a Dutch prison for debts. Thereafter followed a series of squalid escapades. He worked for a corrupt Swedish diplomat (learning a few handy tricks in the process); married a lady-of-the-bedchamber to the Queen of Spain, did a flit shortly afterwards with her jewellery and then turned up in Paris, only to flee that city after stealing from his sister. He next surfaced in Amsterdam, conned a loan for a non-existent trading venture and, by 1736, had somehow wound up in Corsica where he soon found himself embroiled with the leaders of a group of native insurgents trying to overthrow the occupying Genoese. They were largely successful and Theodore, ever the plausible rogue, impressed them with his aristocratic mien and promises of arms.

The rebels now faced the problem of how to govern Corsica and, to the horror of the more level-headed among them, Theodore was offered the crown of the newly independent state. Worse, he accepted and began to play the part with undisguised relish, issuing coins, founding orders of knighthood and generally having a whale of a time at the expense of his new subjects. They, however, were quick to spot their mistake and within a few months they deposed him.

His return to Europe was not a success. In virtually all of his old haunts he was recognised by his creditors and for the next twelve years His ex-Royal Highness must have seen the inside of fully half a dozen continental prisons. It was a sort of old lag's Grand Tour, punctuated only by two calamitous bids to recapture his former kingdom. By 1749 he was in London, still calling himself the King of Corsica, still spending other people's money and, naturally, still unable to pay a penny of it back. Within three months he was in the King's Bench Prison and this time it was for keeps.

Prison is not the best place to display one's regal state but His Majesty did his best, sitting under a tatty canopy and receiving visitors with exaggerated ceremony. So earnest were his attempts to maintain appearances that the London literati adopted him and began trying to raise money for his release. David Garrick gave a benefit performance of a play for Theodore and Horace Walpole tried to raise a subscription for him by placing an appeal in *The World*. Unfortunately, as Walpole reported, 'His Majesty's character is so bad that it only raised £50.' Theodore promptly proved the point by being so upset at the sum that he threatened *The World*'s printer with an action for misuse of his name. Nevertheless, he took the cash and, with the aid of this and by putting down the island of Corsica as one of his assets, he obtained his release.

His ex-Highness survived his liberation by a mere four days and was just about to be unceremoniously tipped into a pauper's grave when along came one John Wright, a Compton Street oil dealer, who paid for a more dignified interment at St Anna's, Soho. All that was left for Theodore's son Frederick to inherit was his father's compulsive insolvency. He duly did, and finally, facing ruin, he felt obliged to take himself into the porch of Westminster Abbey and blow his brains out. Thus ended the short-lived royal house of von Neuhoff.

Mr Thompson (19th Century). A disrespectful angler, if a Victorian book of curios is to be believed. The volume, *Historical Ninepins* by John Timbs, reports, 'There is a disgusting story of a Mr Thompson of Worcester who baited his angling hook with part of the corrupted form of King John and carried the fish that he caught with it in triumph through the streets.' Sadly, Mr Timbs does not record how Mr Thompson came by his morsel of the old king's cadaver. All that can be said by way of circumstantial evidence is that King John's remains were interred in Worcester Cathedral and may well have been disturbed by renovation work at some stage.

Maharajah of Tikari (20th Century). Indian Prince who showed his loyalty to the British crown during the First World War by enlisting as an ordinary despatch rider. He was not, however, quite like any other Tommy. He was sufficiently wealthy to present Field Marshal Haig with an entire squadron of tanks later in the war and he was also single-handedly responsible for the Germans protesting to the Allies about a breach of the Geneva Red Cross Convention.

Their complaint was that the British were using illegal ammunition on a certain part of the front. The Allied high command were appalled and immediately sent a senior officer down to the offending area to investigate. When he reached the line, he found a group of staff officers clustered round the despatch-riding Maharajah who was taking pot-shots at the German defences with his Westley-Richards 476 high velocity, double-barrelled tiger gun. He was politely asked to desist, the Germans were informed that the incidents would not be repeated and the Maharajah of Tikari reverted to the anonymity of his motor-cycle duties.

> *'It has been said, not truly, but with an approximation of truth, that in 1802 every hereditary monarch was insane.'*
>
> WALTER BAGEHOT.

U

*'The vices of kings cannot remain hid, for the
splendour of their lofty station permits
naught to be concealed.'*

CLAUDIAN, 398 AD.

Umberto I (1844–1900). King of Italy who was saved from
assassination by the lack of 50 lire. An Italian anarchist called
Luigi Luccheni had intended to kill the King but he could not
raise the extra 50 lire he needed for the fare to Rome. So he
went to Lausanne and stabbed the Empress Elizabeth of
Austria instead. At his subsequent trial in 1898 he told of his
precarious finances and admitted that the only grievance he had
against Elizabeth was that she wore a crown. However,
Umberto could not count on would-be assassins always being so
penniless. Eventually, in 1900, one came along who was
properly prepared and shot the King after he had presented
some prizes at a gymnasium display in Monza. Umberto left to
his son, Victor Emmanuel, not only his precarious crown but
also this immortal advice: 'Remember, to be a king, all you
need to know is how to sign your name, read a manuscript and
mount a horse.'

Umberto II (1904–1983). King of Italy for just 34 days whose
chief claim to fame was that he produced children by remote
control. As heir to the throne he had romped on the ski slopes
and beaches of Europe, living the life of a sensual playboy. His
father, however, wanted him to settle down and in 1930 he
ordered his wayward son to marry Princess Marie-Jose of Bel-

gium. Umberto was not happy but, despite sulkily declaring, 'I wish I were a fireman so that I could marry whom I please,' he did as he was told. Not surprisingly, this public relations affair rapidly became a cold farce in private and Umberto was soon on the rove, casting his leery eye in the direction of some of Hollywood's more exotic lovelies. There were rumours of liaisons with the warbling Jeanette MacDonald and the sultry Delores del Rio. Furthermore, he found his wife so unenticing that he could not even bring himself to share her bed and his first two children were born by means of artificial insemination.

After his father abdicated in 1946, Umberto came to the throne. In the years ahead he was to be known as 'The May King' because his reign lasted only marginally longer than the month of that name. A few weeks after his accession, with the Italians determined to find a scapegoat for Mussolini's regime and their defeat in the war, there was a referendum on the subject of the monarchy. It was conducted with about as much moral scruple as one would expect from the land of Machiavelli and after everyone had cast their vote (or, in some cases, votes), Umberto found himself on the wrong end of a 12 million to 10 million decision. Among those voting republican was his wife, Queen Marie-Jose, who was even alleged to have spent the election campaign busily tearing down monarchist posters. There must, however, have been something of a reconciliation between them, for he soon joined her in exile in Portugal where he remained to the end of his days, tending his coin collection and pining for his beloved 'Italia'.

> *'Kings judge the world, but the wise judge kings.'*
> SALOMON IBN GABIROL, 1050.

V

*'All the kings of the earth, before God, are as grasshoppers;
they are nothing, and less than nothing; both their love
and their hatred is to be despised.'*

JONATHAN EDWARDS, 1741.

Vatel (1622–1671). A temperamental French chef who some-what over-reacted to a little local difficulty in the royal kitchens. When it looked as if the lobster sauce for Louis XIV's turbot might run short, M. Vatel was so distraught that he withdrew to his quarters and killed himself. Far from regarding this as the act of an overwrought lunatic, chefs have ever since revered Vatel's sense of honour as an example to their profession. The *Almanach des Gourmands* wrote of his suicide with undisguised glee, 'So noble a death ensures you, venerable shade, the most glorious immortality. You have proved that the fanaticism of honour can exist in the kitchen as well as in the camp and that the spit and the saucepan have also their Catos and Deciuses.'

The event that inspired this rococo prose took place at Prince Conde's residence of Chantilly in 1671. Vatel was in the employ of the Prince and was renowned for the almost unattainably high standards that he set himself. As soon as he was told of the King's visit, he began to work himself into something of a froth over the arrangements. However, when his majesty and his retinue arrived late on the Thursday afternoon, the cold collation served them was beyond reproach and the supper that evening was declared to be a veritable triumph. The only slight hitch was that several groups had turned up unexpectedly and the roast had not quite stretched to their tables.

To Vatel this was a tragedy of quite appalling proportions. Everyone else present may have seen it as a minor blemish on an otherwise magnificent occasion but, to the proud and excitable chef, it was a vast, ugly and indelible stain on his reputation. 'I am dishonoured,' he said several times, 'this is a disgrace that I cannot endure.' And despite the kindly reassurances offered to him by the Prince, he was inconsolable.

The next morning he rose at 4 am, determined to oversee every detail personally. He was still fretting about the events of the night before and as each of the new day's little crises came and went, he grew ever more agitated. By the time he went down to see in the delivery of the lobsters, he was in a state of high anxiety, with his self-control deteriorating with every passing minute. So the news that only two hampers of lobsters had arrived, thereby leaving him hopelessly short for the King's sauce, was all that was needed to tip the balance of his mind. With a despairing cry of 'I shall never survive this disgrace,' he went upstairs to his room, placed his sword against the door, stabbed himself to the heart and fell dead with the third blow. He was found by a messenger who had come to tell him that reinforcements of lobster were on their way.

Vickramabahu II (d. 1196). King of ancient Sri Lanka who barely had time to get used to the idea. Shortly after his coronation at Ponnaruvva in 1196, he was struck down by an assassin and died within the hour.

Victoria (1819–1901). Queen of England whose reaction to her husband's premature death was so extreme and prolonged that it brought her sanity seriously into question. From that day in December 1861 when Albert breathed his last, the 42-year-old Victoria became what can only be described as a mournomaniac. Initially merely prostrate with hysteria, she was soon wallowing in grief and insisting on the most absurd marks of respect for 'His memory', most of which she upheld for the next 40 years. She wore black for the rest of her life, death alone releasing her from official mourning; his room became a sacred shrine; she treated his clothes and effects like the relics of a saint; at her behest memorials to him sprouted up in every conceivable part of the kingdom and, most damaging of all, she plunged into purdah, refusing to appear in public for years afterwards.

It was this self-indulgent seclusion that earned her the nickname 'The Widow of Windsor' and prompted doubts not only about her mental health but also, for a time, even the continued existence of the monarchy. Indeed, the conventional picture of her as 'our beloved Queen' is true only of the last two decades of her 63-year reign. She may by then have become prized for her longevity and revered as a symbol of the Empire but, for a dangerous period before that, her behaviour fuelled what was the most widespread outbreak of republicanism since the days of Oliver Cromwell. Only the Queen's agreement to show her subjects something of her moping face and the Prince of Wales's timely illness and cliff-hanging recovery stemmed the anti-royalist tide.

If the realisation that things ever reached such a pretty pass comes as a shock, it must be remembered that for all but the last 15 or so years of the century, criticism of royalty was both open and unrestrained. Personal comments about the sovereign that would now threaten a breach of the peace were then but the common currency of drawing-rooms and public prints. The periodical *Town*, for instance, would never have thought itself particularly outlandish for using these words to describe the Queen on her accession: 'Her Majesty is short and not well proportioned; her bust is somewhat fine, her mouth is imbecile in expression; her teeth are irregular but sound; her feet are not small and her hands are not white.' Royalty then may have wielded power but it did not command universal awe.

This situation was not improved when in 1841 the part-German Victoria married the wholly-Teutonic Albert. The smart end of the Establishment saw him as little more than a comic foreigner and for several years there was stern resistance to any suggestion that this intelligent and accomplished Prince should play a full role in government. The Queen's resentment of this heightened her already intense passion for Albert and over the next decade or so, as she bore him child after child, she became almost entirely dependent on him. He was not only her adored husband but also, to an extent she never quite realised, the father whom she had never known. By now his obvious gifts had triumphed over prejudice and he was distinguishing himself as an unofficial 'deputy monarch' – advising her, consulting with her ministers and hurling himself into project after project, most notably the Great Exhibition. Thus the Prince Consort was not only the centre of Victoria's emotional life but also the very core of her working one.

Then, quite suddenly in 1861, when she was but 42 years old, typhoid fever ripped him from her. That she was immediately convulsed with grief is understandable; so, too, was her desire to see him commemorated in some way. Yet what was astonishing, to her sentiment-soaked contemporaries as well as to more hardened generations such as our own, was the exaggerated form this mourning took. From the moment Albert died until her own death 40 years later, no one was allowed to forget that she was a widow. She always wore black, instructed her family to name all heirs to the throne Albert, spent many an hour gazing at the pictures and busts of the Prince that cluttered her homes (Osborne, in particular, looked like a well-stocked funeral parlour) and every night in bed she clutched his nightshirt to her chest and stared at the picture of him that lay on her pillow.

His rooms became shrines. On her orders everything was to stay exactly as he had left it and even the glass from which he had taken his last swig of medicine remained by the bedside. There was also, in a mawkish way, a bizarre pretence maintained that he was still alive. Each morning at Windsor hot water was brought into Albert's apartments, his chamber pot was taken away to be scoured with all the others in the household, the bed was made up with fresh linen, clean towels were laid out, his watch wound and inkwells filled. In the evening his dinner suit would be put out and, finally, at a suitable hour, a clean nightshirt would be placed upon the bed. Then, every night when she was in residence, the Queen would creep into this sanctum and kneel by the bed where he died. She even had her portrait painted in this pose.

It might seem fanciful to depict Victoria behaving as if Albert was a figure of enormous religious significance, until one realises that this was precisely how she saw him. When she wrote about the Prince in her letters and journals, she referred to 'Him' (as opposed to the more mortal lower-case version) and deemed that the anniversary of his death should be regarded as a holy day devoted to the solemn contemplation of his virtues. She also demanded that all her writing paper should be black-edged and she was most particular about it, once sending back some papers she had to sign because the black border was insufficiently broad. Nothing, in fact, infuriated her more than the slightest sign of disrespect to dear Albert's memory. On one occasion Lady Beaconsfield said to the Queen, 'Your son must be a great comfort to you, ma'am.' To which Victoria replied, 'Comfort! Why, I caught him smoking a fortnight after his father died.' The wonder is that her insistence on the Windsor staff wearing black armbands lasted only eight years.

As well as creating a claustrophobic air of veneration inside her residences, Victoria also seemed to want a memento of Albert to adorn every street corner. She had the Royal Mausoleum built for his interment at Frogmore (upon which 100 workmen toiled virtually day and night so it could be ready for the first anniversary of his death), raised the Albert Memorial Chapel at Windsor, Albert Memorials in London and Manchester and egged on countless corporations to erect a statue of her husband in their market squares and town halls. The scale and grandeur of this masonry mattered a great deal to her and when she presented a statue of Albert to the tenants at Balmoral, she was so peeved at its puny size that she ordered it to be removed and replaced with a truly monumental version. Nowhere, it seemed, was safe from her commemorative urges and she even had the spot where the Prince shot his last stag solemnly marked.

Albert would have strongly disapproved of all this. He had said once that if he died before her, she was to raise not even a 'single marble image' to his name. But regardless of these instructions, the statues sprang up and her homes filled with every kind of morbid keepsake. There were pictures of him (hand-coloured photographs of his corpse hung over his bed at every residence), casts of his face and hands (these treasures were kept by her bedside) and busts beyond number (one sculptured likeness of 'Him' was placed in his bed in the Blue Room at Windsor on the anniversary of his death).

All this could have been dismissed as the harmless, if eccentric, consolations of widowhood, were it not for the fact that Victoria also withdrew into almost complete seclusion when Albert died. At first, her court imagined that once her near-hysterical grief had been controlled, she would emerge from the confines of her rooms to assume her visible role as sovereign. But she did not. Ranting and weeping gave way to sullen moodiness and still she remained behind the walls of her homes, incarcerated by her own emotions. Month after month passed and even when she finally adjusted herself to the mourning-drenched normality that she assumed for the rest of her life, Victoria stayed unseen by her people. Even the shipment of this squat little parcel of sorrow meant that the railway stations she used had to be cleared of other passengers. Only when the second anniversary of her husband's death loomed, in October 1863, did she deign to show herself to her public – and then it was the briefest of appearances, her dumpy figure swathed in black and hooded against prying eyes. The occasion, of course, was the unveiling of a statue of Albert.

Her attendance at the wedding of the Prince of Wales and Princess Alexandra was, if anything, even more absurd. She arrived late at St George's Chapel, took her place behind a grille in an isolated stall and left as soon as the ceremony was over. While the other guests were tucking into the wedding breakfast, Victoria was dining alone before scuttling off to the Royal Mausoleum at nearby Frogmore where she sat and stared at 'His' tomb. Her attitude to the whole occasion was captured by the one wedding photograph in which she features. There, beside the nervous bride and groom, sits a disconsolate

Victoria, her mournful gaze fixed on a bust of Albert.

As far as opening Parliament was concerned, that was naturally out of the question. Despite constant exhortations from ministers and a chorus of criticism from the press (even *The Times* warned her of 'the dangers of indulging in the luxury of sorrow'), she refused to countenance such an act. She was prepared to work on her papers and meet her ministers in private but she was, she insisted, in no state to stand up to public ordeals. When *The Times* reported in 1864 that she was about to break her 'protracted seclusion', she demanded that the paper publish a retraction. 'This idea cannot be too explicitly contradicted,' stormed the Widow of Windsor, fully three years after her husband's death.

This was the year when public criticism of her was most sharp. In the March *The Manchester Examiner* reported that a large placard was hung on the gates of Buckingham Palace. It read, 'These commanding premises to be let or sold, as a consequence of the late occupant declining business.' It was taken down but a few days later it reappeared. Despite her agreement actually to open Parliament in the following year and the granting of a few other tentative public appearances as the decade proceeded, the damage, as far as the people were concerned, was done. Republicanism had taken root and it was not just the work of a few disaffected rabble-rousers. Men like Sir Charles Dilke espoused the cause and by the early 1870s there were more than 50 vigorous republican clubs in the provinces.

Just when the idea of abolishing the monarchy seemed poised for a political breakthrough, the Prince of Wales succumbed to typhoid. For some days he hovered between life and death and then, when news of his survival was announced, there broke an absolute torrent of public sentiment. Republicanism was virtually washed away and although even as late as the 1886 Liberal party dinner many ignored the loyal toast and responded instead with some hissing, the continued existence of the monarchy was thereafter never seriously in doubt.

As the 1870s wore on, Victoria (prompted by Disraeli and her manservant John Brown) began to appear in public more and more. She still refused to visit the theatre or concert hall and she never gave or attended a court ball but her subjects did at last come to see the by now venerable little black presence trundling past in her carriage. The Queen even recovered some of her former spirit and when a clergyman suggested to her that she should fill the emotional vacuum in her life by regarding herself as a 'bride of Christ', she replied, 'That is what I call twaddle.'

Yet although she learnt in time to put some sort of face on in public, she never ceased to feel a keen sense of loss. Her comforts were her burgeoning family, the devoted Brown, her relics and mementoes of Albert and, one could believe, her late-flowering relationship with her people. There was also, although few knew it at the time, her spiritualism. When Disraeli said on his deathbed in 1881 that he did not want to see the Queen because 'she would only want me to take a message to Albert', he was joking. But by then she was already attending seances organised by Robert James Lees in an attempt to contact her husband. Brown is also believed to have acted as a medium for her. Whether she was successful or not we will never know, for her family destroyed large parts of her journals on her death. What we do know is that her husband's name was on her lips when she died. 'Oh that peace may come, Bertie!' gasped the 81-year-old Queen. No more appropriate last words can be imagined for a woman whose married and widowed lives were so dominated by one man.

Vlad (d. 1476). Prince of Wallachia (part of modern Romania) whose bloodthirsty reign of terror earned him the nickname of Vlad the Impaler and made him the prototype for Dracula. What gave him his dreadful reputation was not so much that he impaled people (plenty of other rulers have done that) or even that he claimed such a large number of victims. What made Vlad special was the lip-smacking relish and attention to detail that he brought to the task. Not for him the stakes sharpened to speed the efficient despatch of the condemned; Vlad preferred the wood rounded and oiled at the end so that the whole ghastly business took as long as possible.

He was so fond of the spectacle that he frequently laid on a few impalements for the entertainment of his dinner guests. It was wise to feign enjoyment on these occasions, lest one find oneself suddenly part of the floor show. One sensitive soul, who recoiled and turned away holding his nose, annoyed Vlad so much that he was seized and ordered to be impaled on an especially long pole. These unpredictable moods were something of a trial for house guests. A group of emissaries from the Ottoman Empire once upset him no end by failing to remove their turbans in his presence. When he demanded to know why, he was told that it was part of their religion to keep them on at all times. 'Very well then,' Vlad replied, 'I'll make sure they do,' and he ordered the Turks' headgear to be nailed to their heads.

He spent most of his life fighting the Ottomans and it was Turkish chroniclers who were responsible for most of the more far-fetched tales that were spread about his cruelty. He was said to have impaled some Saxon merchants because they dared to charge him full price, to have ordered 400 young apprentices to be burned alive, tortured animals, impaled women and children and slaughtered nearly ten per cent of his country's population of half a million. Such propaganda – if that is merely what it was – certainly had its benefits for Vlad. When Sultan Mehmet the Conqueror came visiting in 1462, his army got to within a mile of the open gates of Vlad's capital and then discovered truly appalling scenes of carnage. Thousands of bodies were piled up in rotting heaps on either side of the narrow gorge that led to the city. Mehmet did not hang around to find out if this was Vlad's work; he withdrew immediately. Vlad himself went on butchering until 1476 when he was killed in battle against the Turks – slain, it is said, by his own men.

Abraham Van der Voort (d. 1640). The keeper of Charles I's collection of pictures and a terrible worry-guts. One day in 1640 the King asked to see a painting called 'The Good Shepherd' by Richard Gibson. To his horror, Van der Voort could not find it.

He panicked and, rather than tell the King he had failed in his duties, hanged himself. The painting was found shortly afterwards.

Caelius Votepacus (5th Century). A King of northern England at the time of the Roman departure from Britain, also known as King Coel or, more commonly, Old King Cole. Our present Prince William will no doubt be delighted to know that this merry old soul is one of his distant ancestors.

> *'Divine right of kings means the divine right of anyone who can get uppermost.'*
>
> HERBERT SPENSER, 1851.

W

*'Kings are in the moral order what
monsters are in the natural.'*

HENRI GREGOIRE, 1792.

Wamba (7th Century). Visigoth ruler of Spain and a most unfortunate King. His troubles began in 680 when he became seriously ill and fell into a coma. The finest physicians of the time were called in and they applied their most advanced remedies – buckets of cold water, clanging cymbals in the patient's ear and jumping up and down and whooping at the tops of their voices. Yet it was all to no avail; Wamba remained sparko.

Not unnaturally, his attendants concluded that the King's life was drawing to a close and, following the custom of the day, they dressed him in a monk's habit and cut his hair to the tonsure so that he could be received into the Church before he died. Even all this messing about with him failed to raise a flicker of response from the unconscious Wamba, so a noble called Erwig decided that, as the King was on his last legs anyway, he might as well seize the throne now and have done with it. He duly took possession of the royal treasury and had himself crowned.

And so, in this time-honoured fashion, might the story have ended, had not the previously insensible Wamba now begun to show distinct signs of a complete recovery. Here, indeed, was a ticklish problem for the courtiers. Someone now had to tell the old monarch that, even though he was not aware of it, while he had been in a coma he had become a monk and so was no longer eligible to be their king. Eventually, some of the clergy plucked up courage and somehow found the words to break the news to the stunned Wamba. To his credit, he took his demotion philosophically and, after wishing Erwig well, retired to a monastery where he lived to a ripe old age.

Wenceslas (1361–1419). King of Bohemia, Holy Roman Emperor and dog-lover. He was so attached to his hunting hounds that he even took them to bed with him. As can be imaganed, his wife Johanna was not best pleased and one night her worst fears were confirmed when a particularly vicious member of the pack savaged her to death. Wenceslas seemed genuinely surprised at this turn of events and he took to drink, becoming a thoroughgoing public nuisance. He prowled the streets with his cronies at night, breaking into houses, molesting his female subjects and generally venting his feelings in a riot of cruelty. No one was safe and a royal cook whose roast did not come up to scratch was himself ordered to be roasted on the spit. All in all, then, Wenceslas was the very antithesis of his namesake who performed such sterling good works on the feast of Stephen and he was deposed in 1400.

William II (1057–1100). The only adult King of England to remain a bachelor. This, in an age when the first duty of a king was to provide an heir, was strange, although not nearly so strange as some of the company William kept. He and his young chums were known to ride out in flamboyant fancy dress and that medieval master of nudge-and-wink, William of Malmesbury, wrote of his court, 'The model for young men was to rival women in delicacy of person, to mince their gait, to walk with loose gesture and half-naked.' These carryings-on, of course, may well have been the reason why King William had a permanently red face and thus the nickname of Rufus. Anyhow, just as even the least sophisticated of his subjects were starting to think that it was funny their king had never married, he was mistaken for a deer in the New Forest and killed by an arrow.

William IV (1765–1837). King of England and, for much of his life, such a foul-mouthed roustabout that no fewer than 12 women declined his proposal of marriage. He was, admittedly, hardly in the first flush of youth when he made most of these approaches but the allure of royalty and the prospect of a crown, however remote, ought to have tempted one of them before number 13 finally accepted him. That they did not was a ringing tribute to his spectacular lack of couth.

He joined the Royal Navy at the age of 13 and whatever superficial polish he may have acquired in the royal nursery was very soon removed by the abrasive ways of the Senior Service. In no time at all even his fellow officers were cringing at his quarterdeck language and wild antics when in port. At the age of 16 William was arrested for taking part in a drunken brawl in Gibraltar and it seems that if he was not drinking or fighting, then he was sampling the cheap delights of colonial prostitutes. Few of them appear to have offered what would now be construed as a good time. From America, for instance, he wrote to his elder brother, 'Last night I retired into the arms of a chaste(!) Irish whore whose breath was impregnated with gin and tobacco.'

His reputation tended to precede him and when he and a brother toured Europe in 1784 under a nominal incognito (as Lord Fielding and Count Hoya), they had a rare old time. Prague was probably the high spot where, at a masquerade, Prince William is said to have ended up with 47 cards slipped into his hand by different ladies seeking assignations. His pleasure at this tally was only slightly muted by the knowledge that a local bishop had 53 such billets-doux pressed upon him. Hanover, however, was a less happy haunt and he was particularly scathing about the city's brothels, establishments of which he was by now a seasoned connoisseur. In a letter home to his brother, the Prince of Wales, he wrote, 'Oh for England

and the pretty girls of Westminster, at least to such as would not clap or pox me every time I fucked.' This and similar examples of the future king's English have brought many a blush to winsome researchers innocently rooting around in the Royal Archive.

With a lifestyle such as William's, the 'pox', as he called it, was a constant threat and by his mid-twenties he had already suffered several bouts of venereal disease. Only his departure from the navy at the age of 24 and his subsequent establishment in bachelor apartments in St James's Palace seem to have fended off further outbreaks of the disease. Not that this was due to any reform on his part (he still drank, gambled and whored as much as before), it was just that by now he had the sense to avoid the real rough end of the trade. It was perhaps a comment on his former low-life that a fling with one Polly Finch constituted a decided step-up in class.

So it was hardly surprising that when he did set up home in 1791 it was not in marriage to some continental princess or duke's daughter but in cohabitation with an overweight actress called Miss Dorothy Bland, known as Mrs Jordan to give her three illegitimate children some cover. This pair of fun-lovers lived together for the next 20 years and she, fortified by her favourite tipple of calf's-foot jelly dissolved in warm sherry, produced 10 children in just 13 years, each child conveniently alternating in sex until they had five of each. This vast brood was an added burden on William's meagre allowance as Duke of Clarence and had it not been for Mrs Jordan's inter-natal stage earnings, their debts would have overwhelmed them completely. Home, for instance, was nothing more grand than Bushey House, a grace and favour residence he obtained in return for acting as ranger of the local park.

In 1811 the pair split up and, while she made an ill-starred comeback on the stage (which was to lead to her impoverished death in France five years later), he set about putting his fortune on a solid footing with a proper marrige. He had, at the time he was strewing wild oats all over Europe and the Colonies thirty years before, already made several rash and unsuccessful proposals of marriage – none of which seemed to involve the young ladies concerned in too much agonising before they refused. Now, as he neared his fifties, he was an even less enticing prospect. His language and manners were as rough and ready as ever and he also had a curious bullet-shaped head, which looked as if a pioneer brain surgeon had experimented on him, lost interest and made a rather hurried job of putting everything back together again. Added to which, there were his ten illegitimate children.

Thus, even the most determined gold-digger might have hesitated before making a match with him and in the next few years his proposals were spurned by seven women, among them the Dowager Lady Devonshire, Miss Margaret Mercer Elphinstone, the youngest daughter of the King of Denmark and the Duchess of Olderburg. The death in childbirth of the Prince of Wales's daughter, Princess Charlotte, had added constitutional urgency to this search, for suddenly there was no heir of the next generation and William and his aging brothers were now involved in a race to marry and provide a legitimate offspring to carry on the line. Under this unseemly pressure, William at last found a woman who was prepared to overlook his uncouth ways. His bride was Princess Adelaide of Saxe-Meiningen and they married in 1818. She was, at 26, half his age, far from beautiful and religious in a morbid kind of way but they were nevertheless happy. None of their children survived infancy but Adelaide warmly accepted his existing family and, under her evangelical influence, William began to cut down on his drinking and even, on occasions, moderate his language.

There were, however, limits to the transformation that could be worked and when William succeeded to the throne in 1830 he was still rather a rough diamond. Women in his presence had to have their ears periodically covered in protection against the stream of sailor's cusses that he would let slip and he also had an unbreakable habit, when out driving, of spitting loudly and copiously through his carriage windows. Equally unrestrained was his pleasure when he became king and, on the day he succeeded, he celebrated by racing around London in an open carriage, grinning broadly and constantly doffing his hat and bowing his head to any who would acknowledge him. An impromptu walkabout, however, nearly ended in disaster when he was mobbed in St James's Street. Only prompt action by the members of White's, outside whose premises the fracas occurred, prevented him from being totally engulfed by the crowds.

After the sophisticated and reclusive George IV, William was like a breath of fresh air straight off the common. Never one for pomp and ceremony, he rapidly reduced much of his predecessor's expenditure. He dismissed George's large German band and French cooks, sold three of the five royal yachts, reduced the stud by half, pruned the Windsor Castle staff, donated the entire contents of George's menagerie to the London Zoo and made over much of his brother's art treasures to the nation. He also said that he did not want the fuss and expense of a coronation and declared that a simple crowning and oath-taking in Parliament would do for him. Much against his better judgement, he was persuaded to change his mind but he did all he could to keep the ceremony simple and the eventual cost was £30,000 – a mere eighth of his predecessor's.

The high popularity this brought him did not survive his fumbling of the Reform Bill crisis and its aftermath. Although by no means an implacable opponent of reform, he wavered and stalled sufficiently often to give that impression. As his seven-year reign wore on, the old King was also harried and distracted by the paranoid behaviour and accusations of Princess Victoria's mother, the Duchess of Kent. Increasingly, his most urgent ambition became to live long enough to see Victoria's 18th birthday and so deny her harridan of a mother the opportunity of acting as regent. He realised this wish with a month to spare.

Today William is best remembered for being Sailor Billy, the coarse-grained predecessor of Queen Victoria. Yet true students of the British royal family treasure him for other reasons: not only was he the last king of England to contract VD but he was also the last to sire publicly acknowledged bastards. Thus (so far as we know) two proud old royal traditions died with him.

'Kings are for nations in their swaddling clothes.'
VICTOR HUGO, 1848.

Y

The Hon. Alick Yorke (19th Century). Son of the fourth Earl of Hardwick, courtier to Queen Victoria and the provoker of the most famous remark in British regal history. He was attending one of the Queen's dinner parties at Windsor Castle and at one point turned to his German neighbour and told him a slightly risqué story. The German, who was evidently easily pleased, burst into near-hysterical laughter and began to clutch his sides in riotous appreciation. The Queen then asked to hear the story and, after Yorke had reluctantly repeated it, she delivered her historic riposte, 'We are not amused.'

This now seems to be the most widely accepted origin of Victoria's saying, ousting an earlier version which pinned the blame on Admiral Maxse. According to that story, the Queen once asked the admiral to demonstrate his well-known impersonation of her but when he placed a handkerchief on his head and puffed out his cheeks, she turned po-faced and made the famous statement.

However and whenever it was uttered, nothing is now more readily associated with her than the remark. It, and the much-used photographs of her moping over a bust of Albert, have given generations the impression that she was never anything more than a humourless and priggish old biddy who got about as much joy out of life as a blind man in an art gallery. Yet although her knees-ups were virtually non-existent after her consort's death, before then she was certainly more of a fun-lover and less of a prude than most people imagine.

She played cards for money, angered teetotallers by her fondness for more than merely the odd nip and once got in such a lather over the close finish of a race at Ascot that she broke a window of the royal box. Nor was she entirely a strait-lace when it came to sexual matters. Her wedding present to Albert consisted, in part, of a nude painting of the goddess Artemis; she apparently wrote so freely of the joys of the marriage bed that part of her journals were ordered to be destroyed on her death and, when advised to stop having children after the birth of her ninth, she was said to have replied, 'Oh, Sir James, am I to have no more fun in bed?' It was definitely not a prim queen who wrote in her diary when her carriage overturned, 'Dear Frankie Clark lifted me out of the carriage, and would you believe it, all my petticoats came undone?'

Victoria may not have been one of the great hell-raisers of history but, except for the years of her deepest mourning, she was very often decidedly amused.

'Let us strangle the last king with the guts of the last priest.'

DENIS DIDEROT, 1750.

Bibliography

This book's field of research was not far short of the entire history of the world and obviously this meant a vast number of sources had to be consulted. To list them all here would be absurd and so this bibliography contains only those volumes which provided information actually used. To help anyone who wishes to do some further quarrying of their own, the sources have been divided geographically rather than given in one great long catalogue.

Newspapers
All of these papers were consulted for the entry on Bokassa: *Sunday Telegraph, Mirror, Daily Mail, The Times, Guardian, Observer, Sunday Times Magazine, International Herald Tribune, Mail on Sunday* and the *Observer* Foreign News Service.

General History
Baring Gould, S *Historical Oddities and Strange Events* Methuen 1889.
Beatty-Kingston, W *Monarchs I Have Met* Volume 1 Chapman and Hall 1887.
Bloch, Marc *The Royal Touch* Routledge and Kegan Paul 1973.
Bocca, Geoffrey *The Uneasy Heads. A Report on European Monarchy* Weidenfeld and Nicolson 1959.
Bowler, Peter and Green, Jonathan *What A Way To Go* Pan 1983.

Canning, John (ed.) *100 Great Kings, Queens and Rulers of the World*
Souvenir Press 1973.

Carpenter, Clive *The Guinness Book of Kings, Rulers and Statesmen*
Guinness Superlatives 1978.

Doran, Dr John *Monarchs Retired From Business* Volumes 1 & 2
Richard Bentley 1859.

Fadiman, Clifton (ed.) *The Faber Book of Anecdotes* Faber and Faber
1985.

Frazer, J G *The Golden Bough* Volumes 1 & 2 Macmillan 1911.

Gibson, Peter *The Concise Guide To Kings and Queens* Webb and
Bower 1985.

Gurney, Gene *Kingdoms of Europe* Crown 1982.

Harrison, Michael *They Would Be King* Somers 1947.

Howard, Martin *Victorian Grotesque* Jupiter Books 1977.

Kroll, Maria and Lindsey, Jason *The Country Life Book of Europe's
Royal Families* Country Life Books 1979.

Luke, Sir Harry *In The Margin of History* Lovat Dickson 1933.

Mannix, Daniel P *The History of Torture* New English Library 1970.

Marshall, Frederic *International Vanities* William Blackwood 1875.

Molloy, Fitzgerald *The Romance of Royalty* Volumes 1 & 2
Hutchinson 1904.

Nicolson, Harold *Monarchy* Weidenfeld and Nicolson 1962.

Robertson, Patrick *The Shell Book of Firsts* Ebury Press 1971.

Shakespeare, Nicholas *The Men Who Would Be King* Sidgwick and
Jackson 1984.

Shriner, Charles A *Wit, Wisdom and Foibles of The Great* Funk and
Wagnalls 1918.

Walker, Peter N *Punishment: An Illustrated History* David and Charles
1972.

Wilson, Colin *A Criminal History of Mankind* Granada 1984.

Wood, F A *The Influence of Monarchs* Macmillan 1913.

Wraxall, Lascelles *Remarkable Adventurers and Unrevealed Mysteries*
Richard Bentley 1863.

Inventions That Changed The World Reader's Digest 1982.

The Reader's Digest Book of Strange Stories and Amazing Facts 1975.

Social History

Barrow, Andrew *Gossip 1920–1970* Hamish Hamilton 1978.

Camplin, James *The Rise of The Plutocrats* Constable 1978.

Collier, Richard *The Rainbow People* Weidenfeld and Nicolson 1984.

Doran, Dr John *Table Traits* Richard Bentley 1854.

——*Habits and Man* Richard Bentley 1854.

——*The History of Court Fools* Richard Bentley 1858.
Fryer, Peter *Studies in English Prudery* Corgi 1963.
Garrett, Richard *Royal Travel* Blandford Press 1982.
Hackwood, Frederick W *Good Cheer. The Romance of Food and Feasting* T Fisher Unwin 1911.
Haight, Anne Lyn *Banned Books* George Allen and Unwin 1955.
Hartnell, Norman *Royal Courts of Fashion* Cassell 1971.
Hill, Robert A *Tales of The Jesters* William Blackwood 1934.
Jackson, Stanley *The Savoy. The Romance of A Great Hotel* Frederick Muller 1964.
Jenkins, Alan *The Rich, Rich. The Story of The Big Spenders* Weidenfeld and Nicolson 1977.
Mackay, Charles *Extraordinary Popular Delusions and The Madness of Crowds* Richard Bentley 1841.
Pearsall, Ronald *The Worm In The Bud.*
von Boehn, Max *Modes and Manners* Volumes 1–8 George C Harrap 1935.
Wallace, Irving, Amy and Sylvia and Wallechinsky, David *The Intimate Sex Lives of Famous People* Hutchinson 1981.
Wilson, G H *The Eccentric Mirror* Volumes 1–4 James Cundee 1807.

Africa
Ritter, E A *Shaka Zulu* Longman 1955.
Roberts, Brian *The Zulu Kings* Hamish Hamilton 1974.

Austria
Crankshaw, Edward *The Fall of The House of Hapsburg* Longmans, Green & Co 1965.
Haslip, Joan *The Lonely Express. A Biography of Elizabeth of Austria* Weidenfeld and Nicolson 1965.
Langtry, Lillie *The Days I Knew. The Autobiography of Lillie Langtry* George H Doran 1925.

Belgium
Bauer, Ludwig *Leopold The Unloved* Cassell 1934.

Britain
Alexander, Marc *Royal Murder* Frederick Muller 1978.
Alice, HRH Princess *For My Grandchildren* Evans Brothers 1966.

Anon *Kings, Courts and Society* Jarrolds 1909.

Anon *George III, His Court and Family* Henry Colburn 1824.

Aronson, Theo *Kings Over The Water* Cassell 1979.

Ashton, John *Gossip In The First Decade of Victoria's Reign* Hurst and Blacket 1903.

Brooke, John *King George III* Constable 1972.

Brown, Craig and Cunliffe, Lesley *The Book of Royal Lists* Routledge and Kegan Paul 1982.

Bryan III, J and Murphy, Charles J V *The Windsor Story* Granada 1979.

Churchill, Randolph *Lord Derby, King of Lancashire* Heinemann 1959.

Darby, Elizabeth and Smith, Nicola *The Cult of The Prince Consort* Yale University Press 1983.

Duff, David *Edward of Kent. The Life Story of Queen Victoria's Father* Stanley Paul 1938.

——*Alexandra, Princess and Queen* Collins 1982.

——*Queen Mary* Collins 1985.

Edwards, Anne *Matriarch. Queen Mary and The House of Windsor* Hodder and Stoughton 1984.

Fisher, Graham and Heather *Monarchy and The Royal Family. A Guide For Everyman* Robert Hale 1979.

Fitzgerald, Percy *The Royal Dukes and Princesses of The Family of George III*. Volumes 1 & 2 Tinsley Brothers 1882.

Fraser, Antonia (ed.) *The Lives of The Kings and Queens of England* Weidenfeld and Nicolson 1975.

Fulford, Roger *Royal Dukes. The Father and Uncles of Queen Victoria* Duckworth 1933.

Golding, Claud *The Throne of Britain* Marshall and Snelgrove 1937.

Graeme, Bruce *A Century of Buckingham Palace* Hutchinson 1937.

Gregg, Edward *Queen Anne* Routledge and Kegan Paul 1980.

Hardy, Alan *Queen Victoria Was Amused* John Murray 1976.

——*The Kings' Mistresses* Evans Brothers 1980.

Harrison, Michael *Clarence* W H Allen 1972.

Hibbert, Christopher *George IV, Regent and King 1811–1830* Allen Lane 1973.

——*Edward VII* Allen Lane 1976.

——*The Court At Windsor. A Domestic History* Longman 1964.

Holme, Thea *Caroline* Hamish Hamilton 1979.

Humble, Richard *The Saxon Kings* Weidenfeld and Nicolson 1980.

Jackman, S W *The People's Princess. A Portrait of HRH Princess Mary Adelaide, Duchess of Teck* The Kensal Press 1984.

Jones, William *Crowns and Coronations* Chatto and Windus 1898.

Leslie, Anita *The Marlborough House Set* Doubleday & Co 1973.
Lucas, Reginald *Prince Francis of Teck, A Memoir* A L Humphreys 1910.
MacAlpine, Ida and Hunter, Richard *George III and The Mad Business* Allen Lane 1969.
Mackenzie, Compton *The Windsor Tapestry* 1939.
Magnus, Philip *King Edward The Seventh* John Murray 1964.
Martin, Kingsley *The Crown and The Establishment* Hutchinson 1962.
Mathew, Gervase *The Court of Richard II* John Murray 1968.
Moncrieff of That Ilk, Sir Iain *Royal Highness. The Ancestry of The Royal Child* Hamish Hamilton 1982.
Murray-Brown, Jeremy (ed.) *The Monarchy and Its Future* George Allen and Unwin 1969.
Robertson, Jillian *The Royal Race For The British Crown* Blond and Briggs 1977.
Rose, Kenneth *King George V* Weidenfeld and Nicolson 1983.
——*Kings, Queens and Courtiers* Weidenfeld and Nicolson 1985.
Seaman, L C B *Victorian England* Methuen 1973.
Sinclair-Stevenson, Christopher *Blood Royal. The Illustrious House of Hanover* Jonathan Cape 1969.
Strachey, Lytton *Queen Victoria* Chatto and Windus 1921.
Timbs, John *Curiosities of London* John Camden Hotten 1867.
Timbs, John *Historical Ninepins*.
Tisdale, E E P *Queen Victoria's John Brown* Stanley Paul 1939.
Van der Kiste, John and Jordaan, Bee *Dearest Affie . . . Alfred, Duke of Edinburgh, Queen Victoria's Second Son* Alan Sutton 1984.
Wilkins, Vaughan *Endless Prelude* George Routledge 1937.
Windsor, Duke of *A King's Story* Cassell 1951.
Ziegler, Philip *King William IV* Collins 1971.
——*Crown and People* Collins 1978.

Bulgaria
Constant, Stephen *Foxy Ferdinand, Tsar of Bulgaria* Sidgwick and Jackson 1979.

Denmark
Gade, John *Christian IV* George Allen and Unwin 1928.
Nors, P *The Court of Christian VII* Hurst and Blackett 1928.

Far East
Brent, Peter *The Mongul Empire* Weidenfeld and Nicolson 1976.

Chakrabongse, HRH Prince Chula *Lords of Life. The Paternal Monarchy of Bangkok 1782–1932* Alvin Redman 1960.

Chou, Eric *The Dragon and The Phoenix. Love, Sex and The Chinese* Michael Joseph 1971.

Smith, Malcolm *A Physician At The Court of Siam* Country Life Ltd 1947.

Waugh, Alec *Bangkok – The Story of A City* W H Allen 1970.

France

de Gramont, Sanche *Epitaph For Kings. The Long Decline of The French Monarchy and The Coming of The Revolution* Hamish Hamilton 1968.

Hatton, Ragnhild *Louis XIV and His World* Thames and Hudson 1972.

Hearsey, John *Marie Antoinette* Constable 1972.

Hibbert, Christopher *Versailles* Reader's Digest Associates 1972.

Mitford, Nancy *Madame de Pompadour* Hamish Hamilton 1954.

Norton, Lucy *The Sun King and His Loves* Hamish Hamilton 1983.

Germany

Bennet, Daphne *King Without A Crown* Heinemann 1977.

Blunt, Wilfred *The Dream King. King Ludwig II of Bavaria* Hamish Hamilton 1970.

Hardy, Alan *Frederick The Great* Weidenfeld and Nicolson.

India

Allen, Charles and Dwivedi, Sharada *Lives of The Indian Princes* Century 1984.

Butler, Iris (ed.) *The Viceroy's Wife. Letters of Alice, Countess of Reading 1921–1925* Hodder and Stoughton 1969.

Davies, Philip *Splendours of The Raj* John Murray 1985.

Gascoigne, Bamber *The Great Moghuls* Jonathan Cape 1971.

Hansen, Waldemar *The Peacock Throne* Weidenfeld and Nicolson 1973.

Ivory, James *Autobiography of A Princess* John Murray 1975.

Karaka, D F *Fabulous Mogul. Nizam VII of Hyderabad* Derek Verschoyle 1955.

Lord, John *The Maharajahs* Hutchinson 1972.

Middle East

Forbis, William *Fall of The Peacock Throne* Harper and Row 1980.

McLeave, Hugh *The Last Pharaoh. The Ten Faces of Farouk* Michael Joseph 1969.

Ottoman/Byzantine Empire
Barber, Noel *Lords of The Golden Horn. The Sultans, Their Harems and The Fall of the Ottoman Empire* Macmillan 1973.
Diehl, Charles *Byzantine Portraits* Alfred A. Knopf 1927.
Lane, John *Abdul Hamid: Shadow of God* The Bodley Head 1940.

Romania
Elsberry, Terence *Marie of Romania* Cassell 1973.
Marie, HRH Queen *The Story of My Life* Cassell 1934.

Russia
Almedingen, P *So Dark A Stream. A Study of The Emperor Paul of Russia* Hutchinson 1959.
Coughlan, Robert *Elizabeth and Catherine, Empresses of All The Russias* Macdonald and Janes 1975.
Koslow, Jules *Ivan The Terrible* W H Allen 1961.
Lincoln, W Bruce *The Romanovs* Weidenfeld and Nicolson 1981.
Massie, Robert K *Peter The Great, His Life and World* Victor Gollancz 1981.

Spain
George, Anita *Memoirs of The Queens of Spain* Richard Bentley 1850.
Nada, John *Carlos The Bewitched* Jonathan Cape 1962.
Petrie, Sir Charles *The Spanish Royal House* Geoffrey Bles 1958.
Tighe, Harry *A Queen of Unrest* Swan Sonnerschein 1905.

General Reference
Chambers Encyclopaedia Volumes 1–10 Chambers 1908.
Dictionary of National Biography Oxford University Press.
Who Did What Mitchell Beazley 1979.
Asimov, Isaac *The Book of Facts* Volumes 1 & 2 Hodder and Stoughton 1980.
Attwater, Donald *The Penguin Dictionary of Saints* Penguin Books 1965.
Brewer, E Cobham *The Dictionary of Phrase and Fable* Cassell 1890.

Farmer, David Hugh *The Oxford Dictionary of Saints* Penguin Books
    1965.
Guinness, Martin *The Shocking Book of Records* Sphere Books 1983.
Hellicar, Eileen *But Who On Earth Was?* David and Charles 1981.
Issacs, Alan (ed.) *Macmillan Encyclopaedia* 1981.
McWhirter, Norris *The Guinness Book of Records* (various volumes)
    Guinness Superlatives.
Rees, Nigel *Sayings of The Century* George Allen and Unwin 1984.